The Story of St. Teresa of Avila and Her Reform

by

Joachim Smet, O. Carm.

CARMELITE MEDIA

This book is an extract from The Carmelites: *A History of the Brothers of Our Lady of Mount Carmel*, volume 2, by Joachim Smet, O. Carm., published in 1976.

Edited by William J. Harry, O. Carm.

© 2015 by Carmelite Media
Printed in the United States of America
All rights reserved

No part of this book may be reproduced, stored in a retrieval system, or transmitted in any form, or by any means, electronic, mechanical, photocopying, or otherwise, without the prior written permission of the publisher, except by a reviewer, who may quote brief passages in a review.

Carmelite Media
8501 Bailey Road
Darien, Illinois 60561

Phone: 1-630-971-0724
Email: publications@carmelnet.org
Website: carmelites.info/publications

Printed Book: ISBN: 978-1-936742-13-4
eBook: ISBN: 978-1-936742-14-1

The Story of St. Teresa of Avila and Her Reform

by

Joachim Smet, O. Carm.

Contents

Chapter 1: John Baptist Rossi and Teresa of Jesus 1

John Baptist Rossi | The General Chapter of 1564 | Philip II and the General Chapter of 1564 | The Incorporation of Mount Oliveto | Rossi's Manner of Visitating | The Visitation of Andalusia | The Chapter of Andalusia, 1566 | The Vistiation of Portugal | The Visitation of Castile | The Incarnation at Avila | "Some Affairs of the Order at the Court" | The Chapter of Castile, 1567 | Doña Teresa de Ahumada y Cepeda | A Convent Called St. Joseph's | Teresa's Ideal of the Carmelite Life | Launching the Reform | The Teresian Friars

Chapter 2: The Discalced Reform 39

The Visitation of Aragon and Catalonia | The King's Reform | The Visitation by Dominicans | The Book of Foundations | The Discalced Friars: Duruelo | Pastrana | Peter Fernández in Castile | Fernández and Teresa | Vargas in Andalusia | Nicholas Ormaneto, Reformer of Carmel | Teresa in Andalusia

Chapter 3: "An Intolerable Kind of Feud" 67

The General Chapter of Piacenza and the Discalced | Gracián's Visitation of Andalusia | "Tostado Will See to It" | The Abortive Discalced Province | Ormaneto Under Fire | Gracián versus Tostado | Trouble in Avila | Sega Takes the Initiative | The Discalced Reunited to the Provinces

Chapter 4: A Separate Province 91

The Discalced Appeal to Rome | The Chapter of Alcalá, 1581

Chapter 5: Carmel After Teresa: The Division of the Order 101

Nicholas of Jesus and Mary Doria | Jerome Gracián, Provincial, 1581-1585 | Nicholas Doria, Provincial, 1585-1588 | Gracián Under a Cloud | The Discalced Congregation | Gracián in Portugal | The Revolt of the Nuns | Doria Wins His Case | Gracián in Disgrace | St. John of the Cross | The Order of Discalced Carmelites

Notes 131

Abbreviations 149

List of Authorities Cited 151

Index 155

Recommended Carmelite Websites 169

Chapter I

JOHN BAPTIST ROSSI AND TERESA OF JESUS

Not the least significant feature of the great restoration of Catholic life that followed the council of Trent was the revival of the religious orders. New orders fitting the spirit and needs of the time were founded, old orders were renewed. None of these manifestations was more vital and brilliant than that of the Carmelites; unfortunately, pouring the wine of the new spirit into the old bottle of Carmel had the effect predicted by the scriptures in such cases. The new shoot of St. Teresa's reform, transplanted from the ancient trunk of Carmel– to mix a metaphor– sprang to luxuriant growth; it was not until the 17th century that the old Carmel experienced a similar rebirth.

After the long and fruitful rule of Nicholas Audet who led the Order during the difficult times of the rise of Protestantism, the Carmelites were blessed with another outstanding leader to guide and inspire them in the task of renewal imposed by Trent. At the death of Audet, Pope Pius IV on December 16, 1562, named John Baptist Rossi vicar general of the Order until a general chapter could be convened.[1]

John Baptist Rossi, Vicar General

The choice was a happy one, for as St. Teresa later put it, Rossi was "a most outstanding person in the order, and very rightly so."[2] A descendant of the Rossi of Parma, Counts of San Secondo, Rossi was born in 1507 at Ravenna and entered the Order there. The general chapter of 1524 destined him, age seventeen, for three years of study at Siena.[3] There he studied the arts under the distinguished mathematician and astrologer, Julian Ristori.[4] Rossi made his theological studies at Padua, where John Stephen Facini was regent; by 1540 he had his doctorate. Subsequently he was regent at Naples and Siena.

Before being appointed Vicar General, Rossi had had a distinguished career. In 1543 he represented Audet at Venice in a case involving the nomination of the prior against the community which had appealed to the civil authority. In the Senate he faced the eloquent Sperone Speroni, but succeeded in safeguarding the liberty of the Order. The brethren at Venice got their revenge by accusing Rossi of errors against justification in a sermon preached in St. Mark's during Lent of 1544. Venice, as a matter of fact, was a center of Protestantism in Italy, and Rossi had been recently preceded in the pulpit of St. Mark's by Bernardine Occhino. Recommended by Cardinal Nicholas Ridolfi, inquisitor of Venice and protector of the Order, and by Audet, Rossi had no difficulty in clearing himself before Cardinal Cervini in

Rome.

In 1546 Rossi was named procurator general of the Order and began lecturing at the Sapienza, commenting on the gospel of St. Mark. Paul III admitted him to the group of theologians who disputed theological questions at his table; he also participated in the consultations on the council of Trent held before the same pontiff. He preached in the papal chapel and in various churches of Rome. As prior of San Martino, beginning in 1548, he became the friend of Cardinal Diomedes Carafa, nephew of Paul IV, a frequent visitor at the Carmelite convent, whom Rossi assisted in the hour of death; also a friend of Cardinal Vitelozzo Vitelli and Cardinal James du Puy, protector of the Order, who employed Rossi as his theological consultor. Paul IV enlisted Rossi in the Roman Inquisition.[5]

The new vicar general, like his predecessor, lost no time in getting down to business. On January 21, 1563, he obtained from the Holy See faculties to visit, reform and correct the houses of the Order.[6] From February to April he was at the Carmine in Naples, where he issued certain "Statutes and Ordinances."

"We want it known," Rossi remarks, "that in this visitation our wish has been to proceed with mercy in the matter of penalties, but if in the future any presume to conduct themselves in such a temerarious manner, they may be sure that their forgiven sins will return with greater weight. If such persons are guilty of misdemeanors with regard to divine cult, proper conduct in the convent and the cloister, we are determined to and irrevocably will observe in their regard what is laid down in the constitutions of the order."[7]

While at Naples, Rossi granted permission on February 28, 1563, to Graziano Marcellino, of Palermo, to betake himself with some companions to the monastery of St. John outside the town of the same name and lead "a stricter life."[8] From Naples too, on April 3, he authorized John de Piedad, of the province of Portugal, to remain outside his convent for three years to found a hermitage either in the province of Portugal or of Castile.[9]

In the second half of the year 1563 Rossi is in the north of Italy, where on June 21 he convened the provincial chapter of Tuscany at Florence; on July 10 that of Romagna at Forlí.[10] Probably he visited other provinces at this time.

At the chapters he published extensive ordinances designed to renew prayer, cloister, common life and the economic administration of the houses. "The Most Reverend Father Vicar General ordained," the Romagna chapter states, "that the Reverend Master Provincial be vigilant with regard to the reformation and regular life of our brethren in matters pertaining to reformation and that he remove obstacles to the said reformation lest he held unworthy of his office."[11]

The General Chapter of 1564

When the general chapter opened on Pentecost Sunday, May 21, 1564, five hundred Carmelites gathered in Rome for the occasion. Fifteen provincials and their *socii* brought the total of definitors to forty-two. Besides these there were doctors of theology and preachers to partake in the public disputations presented on the occasion of the chapter and to preach the indulgence granted by the pope for the same reason. Sermons were delivered not only in the churches of the Order– San Martino, Traspontina, San Giuliano– but in the vernacular in the national churches of the city.[12]

The election was held the first day by secret ballot according to the new prescriptions of Trent, Balthasar Nieto, provincial of Andalusia, announcing the votes in a loud voice. John Baptist Rossi emerged the choice of the chapter, *nemine penitus discrepante*. The following day the Carmelites went in procession from San Martino to the Vatican to present their new general to Pope Pius IV. As the procession crossed the bridge of Sant'Angelo, the cannons of the castle on orders from the pope sent out a salvo in honor of the Carmelite general. In St. Peter's Basilica the cardinal protector, Charles Borromeo, had the Holy Shroud of Veronica exposed for veneration by the Carmelites. During dinner at Traspontina the *schola* of Castel Sant'Angelo provided music.[13]

It was a royal send-off for the Counter-Reformation in the Carmelite Order. Behind the festivities lay the serious business of implementing the decrees of the council of Trent. Under the presidency of John Baptist Rossi the chapter in the spirit of Trent issued a number of decrees concerning divine cult, the government and administration of the convents, and reform.[14]

The chapter recalls, first of all, the importance of a pure mind and fervent devotion in divine cult. It imposes on the individual frequent confession in a public place, "so that the other brethren may see him to have a good conscience and to be Catholic and a faithful son of the Holy Catholic Church." Apart from the time of liturgical prayer, the chapter ordains: "After our religious have finished the day and night office, let them not succumb to idleness and sluggishness, but let them devote themselves to some interest such as letters, meditation or prayer or manual labor, provided it be not done for gain, and let them not do anything unworthy; idleness and the Carmelite profession are completely and mutually irreconcilable." The chapter states "the purpose and intention of the Carmelite order with regard to graduate and exempt members," namely that these are excused from attendance in choir for purposes of study, illness or other legitimate (*honesta*) reasons. Those who are exempt from choir should not wander about idly gossiping during office, but should remain in their cells, engaged in reading, meditation and prayer.

Priests should not completely abstain from celebrating Mass; they should do so on Sundays and feast days.

In keeping with the decrees of the council of Trent the chapter ordains that confessors should not presume to hear confessions or preachers to preach, even in Carmelite houses, without authorization from the ordinary.

Carmelites should be uniform in offering Mass; if anyone feels moved to unusual prayers, he should recite them some other time. Two reformers should be appointed in each convent to insure uniformity. The breviary should be reduced to order, "to remove from our order all confusion." All should be ready to accept the prior general's precepts in this matter. There should also be uniformity in the chants, "for it is not reasonable that the members of one order, having the same title, Rule and superior general, should be different in chant and ritual." A calendar of Carmelite saints is to be drawn up.

Other decrees concern the novitiate which must be established in houses located in cities and must be reformed. Where there is no novitiate, candidates may not be received before attaining their sixteenth year. Novices should not be hindered from studying and are not to be admitted to profession unless they can read, sing and speak Latin properly.

In the future only a doctor or *praesentatus* in theology may be elected provincial. A doctor or *praesentatus* is defined as one who has at least preached a Lenten course or preached in the presence of nobles. Provincials may not be re-elected after a three-year term, unless contrary custom prevails or the prior general dispenses. No one may hold the office of provincial or prior in perpetuity, except the general dispense for some special reason, as in the case of the founders or restorers of convents. (The chapter made John Anthony Dario prior for life of the convent of Posilippo, Naples, "or his deserts and services to the said convent.") Provincial chapters should present a list of candidates for the office of provincial to the prior general so that he may select the most suitable for election; conventual chapters should do the same for the provincial. Priors who by custom are elected by the conventual chapter should not be elected in the provincial chapter: "Let the convent enjoy its religious liberty."

Masters in theology who have legitimately acquired their degrees have place and voice in provincial chapters.

The chapter also renewed the ancient ordinances against recourse to secular or ecclesiastical authority in seeking office or settling disputes. In the age of absolute monarchs that was about to be ushered in these strictures were to have less chance than ever of success, but they are worth noting in view of the heated legal battles into which the order in Spain was about to be plunged.

With regard to the important matter of poverty and the common life, the chapter forbids ownership by individuals of immobile goods (lands, pastures, vineyards, houses, etc.). Such goods are to be incorporated into the community, pertinent documents in the name of individuals being transferred to community title.

Superiors may grant the use of mobile goods, not in superfluity but in a measure sufficient for needs: "Our religious should understand that the things they are given to use are not their own but belong to the community." The permission of the superior is required before any goods may be used, as ordained by the council of Trent. The money the brethren acquire is to be kept in a common box. Subsequent events show that although the friars deposited their money in this box, they retained exclusive use of it.

No friar or nun may leave a cell to another in a will, no matter how much effort was spent in furnishing and decorating it. "Primary" graduates and ex-provincials should be given the best rooms, "because in every family and even more in every republic there is order and a diversity of degree."

The chapter abandons Audet's distinction between "completely reformed" and "less reformed" houses. It rejects the division of the order into observants and conventuals and declares all houses to be observant: "Let the brethren of our Order know that the said Order never labored under the name of conventuality: it was ever in flourishing observance, though sometimes some of its members or convents failed to achieve this ideal. The order always lived under obedience to one head, partook of a common refectory, shared all things in common (meager as they might be). Therefore our brethren should in no way declare themselves to be conventuals, but 'of the observance of the provinces,' as is most clearly apparent from the indults of many popes, especially Clement VII."

Rossi's reforming effort was aimed at bringing about a sincere dedication to religious life within the framework of existing obligations. He did not try to raise the ideal or propose a "primitive" way of life. The perhaps deliberately vague directives of Trent regarding poverty were benignly interpreted. The perfect common life, that is the unconditional sharing of all goods in common, was nowhere imposed. The old system of privilege remained basically intact. Rossi unstintingly devoted his not unconsiderable talents and ability to urging upon the brethren in season and out of season a life in keeping with their commitments. But in the post-Tridentine church this sort of "observance" failed to impress. In the popular mind and in official circles the Carmelites were not classed as observant or reformed. Even within the order there were those who would soon be calling for a "stricter observance." In fact, in Spain the first stirrings were being felt of a reform that far outstripped the observance proposed by the order.

Philip II and the General Chapter of 1564[15]

Even before its convocation the Spanish crown had plans for the Carmelite general chapter. After the death of Audet Queen Isabelle in a letter to the pope of November 20, 1563, recommended John Stephen Facini, provincial of Lombardy, for the office of prior general. At Trent the cardinal legates also approached Charles Borromeo, cardinal protector of the Order, with the same suggestion.[16] The motive for this preference is not known, but the Spanish ambassador to the Holy See, Don Louis de Requeséns, never presented the queen's letter to Pius IV. The chapter paid homage to the Spanish court by renewing the three-year term of office as provincial of Facini, "since most wise princes have made no secret of the fact that they judge him worthy to be dignified with a higher office."[17]

From the beginning of his reign (1556) the Most Catholic King Philip II of Spain had at heart the reform of the religious orders in his realms. Trent had entrusted the reform of religious orders to their superiors, but Philip had little faith in a solution that had brought so little result in the past. He continued to take a personal interest in the matter.

His plans for the reform of the orders included the Carmelites. At the court in Barcelona he questioned Michael de Carranza, provincial of Aragon, on conditions.[18] It was from him that the king probably learned of "certain matters unworthy of religious persons which have occurred and still occur in some provinces and convents of Spain." Philip saw in him the man to carry his proposals for the reform of the order in Spain to the coming general chapter. Carranza, as a matter of fact, accommodatingly entered into the plan, providing Philip with information and suggestions in the form of a *memorial* for the implementation of the reform. The king supplied the Aragonese provincial with letters of recommendation, dated February 23, 1564, to the pope, the prior general and his ambassador in Rome. The "main point" the king wished to obtain was the appointment by the prior general of a permanent office of vicar general for Spain with the title and plenipotential powers of reformer. The vicar should be a Spaniard, elected every six years by the general and confirmed with apostolic powers by the pope. His office would not cease with the death of the general. His faculties would include the right to visitate, preside over the election of provincials, confirm them when elected, depose them when negligent of reform, amalgamate and divide provinces, incorporate houses of one province into another, punish delinquent religious.

To urge his plea, Carranza provided the king with precedents for such vicars in the order: the Mantuan Congregation in Italy and the Congregation of Albi in France. The parallel was only too close and designed to disenchant a prior general with the scheme. The institution of a vicar in Spain which such sweeping prerogatives would, as in the case of Mantua and Albi, effectually cut off the prior general from any real influence in Philip's realm.

As he explained in his dispatch to the king on June 16, 1564, Requeséns was not able to interview the prior general on the day of his election, but he had made known his majesty's wishes by letter, later confirming the same by a visit in person. Philip's suggestion was not welcome to the members of the general chapter preoccupied with the implementation of the decrees of Trent in the order. Even the Spaniards – all four provinces were represented at the chapter – did not like the idea, "some" Requeséns reported, "because they do not want reform, others because they suspect Carranza's part in the matter is not disinterested and that he thinks he will be the vicar general."

Rossi managed to refuse the king without alienating him. Spain would have its vicar general, elected by the five provinces (including Portugal), if the prior general did not personally visit the peninsula within two years. The vicar would have the powers of provincials and power over them; he would not be able to divide and unite provinces and transfer houses from one province to another, as the king had requested, neither would he be confirmed by the Holy See. To facilitate communication between Rome and Madrid with regard to the affairs of the Order, the chapter appointed a procurator general to the Spanish court – Desiderio Mazzapica – the same, Requeséns reminded Philip, who had been king's theologian at Trent. Mazzapica was also specially commissioned to reform Andalusia.

Rossi won the good will of the Spanish ambassador, who sent favorable reports concerning him to Madrid. "He is a man," Requeséns wrote to Philip, "held in good esteem here for virtue and letters, and when he arrives there (Spain), I believe he will do all your Majesty commands." When little more than a month later Requeséns was removed from his post in Rome, he left a memorandum for his successor, Cardinal Peter Pacheco, relating events to date in the matter of the Order with a reminder to see that the general got to Spain as agreed. Rossi needed no prodding. This time Spain held priority on the itinerary of the prior general. Whatever else is to be said of King Philip's interference in Carmelite affairs, it brought action deferred for centuries.

Nevertheless affairs kept Rossi in Italy until April 1566.

The question of the re-location of Traspontina at this time reached a crisis. Church and convent were in the way of the completion of the octagonal outworks of Castel Sant'Angelo. The Carmelites thought the question of a new site was still pending, when to their amazement on July 14, 1564, workers began demolishing their church. Rossi managed to have operations suspended. On August 23, 1565, Pope Pius IV granted the Carmelites a site nearer the Vatican in the Borgo Pio, the new suburb he was constructing between the Leonine city and the castle.[19] Pius V, on February 18, 1566 authorized the construction of a new church.[20] In March the general assisted at the laying of the first stone, but construction did not begin until 1569.[21]

San Martino ai Monti, the other Roman house under the generals' jurisdiction, was also in trouble. Cardinal Philbert de la Bourdaisière, titular of the church, with the aid of 100 armed men took possession of the rooms in the convent to which he felt entitled. Rossi, as former prior, was well informed in the matter and was able to settle the dispute in favor of the Order.[22]

From late June until the end of October 1565 Rossi is again in Naples. The record of his activities there during this second visit is no longer at hand, but no doubt he carried forward the measures he had decreed in 1563 and also implemented the decrees of the general chapter.[23]

Back in Rome, on November 12, 1565, the prior general names James Montañaés prior of the convent of Our Lady of Hope at Onda to live there "according to the first Rule taken from that of St. Basil and prescribed for all Carmelites by Albert patriarch of Jerusalem." Montañaés was also allowed to choose a sub-prior from the province of Portugal. But "lest any controversy and disturbance arise," the previous consent of the provincial of Aragon was required.[24]

Rossi's faculties for the visitation and reform of the provinces, obtained from Pius IV, lapsed at the latter's death, December 9, 1565. The *motu proprio* of Pius V, February 24, 1566, created Rossi apostolic commissary with full powers to visitate and reform the whole order, including the congregations.[25] In view of the jurisdictional conflict to follow, his quality as apostolic commissary which even cardinals and legates *a latere* are called upon to respect, is worth special attention.

The Visitation of Spain and Portugal[26]

Sometime after April 18 the prior general finally set out from Rome for the visitation of Spain and Portugal. His method remained more or less the same throughout life. He travelled by mule, sometimes on horseback, accompanied by his secretary, Nicholas Rouhier (*Rotarius*), Valerius Montoni, bursar of the curia, and a *socius* – during the years 1566 to 1568 the Sicilian Bartholomew Ragusio; from 1572 to 1576 the Portuguese Jerome Tostado. Approaching a city or town, he would be solemnly met by a committee of lay and ecclesiastic notables and conducted to the Carmelite convent. At the door of the church he would be met by the community in procession according to the ceremonial of the Order.

In the choir all would approach to kiss his hand in token of filial obedience. After resting a while in the quarters reserved for him, Rossi summoned the community to the chapter room to hear a spiritual conference, sometimes of considerable length. (The chapter at Genoa in 1568 lasted from 2:00

until 7:00 p.m.) He usually ended with an explanation of his plan of reform, insisting particularly on dress and footwear as a sign of the reform. At times he would then and there call in a barber to shave off beards.

After all had been made to promise formally to tell the whole truth, each friar was interviewed concerning private ownership, choir, divine cult, silence, recollection, peace and brotherly love, care of the sick, administration of the goods of the convent, observance of fasts and abstinence, conduct of superiors and officials, the education of novices and students, etc. Meanwhile his associates examined the accounts of the convent and went through the cells, confiscating objects contrary to the religious spirit; musical instruments like the lyre, barbiton and lute, and every sort of arms. Collars and cuffs not of wool were cut from shirts, ornaments from birettas. Those found possessed of incomes or benefices were called upon to renounce them publicly before a notary summoned for this purpose. When he had fully ascertained conditions in the convent, Rossi drew up decrees which he had read in the refectory by the secretary. If legal action had to be taken against any religious, Rossi himself acted as judge and executioner, himself wielding the scourge when this form of punishment was prescribed by law. He did not hesitate to apply the severest sanctions: expulsion from the order and condemnation to the galleys. The times called for decisive measures, and he punished misdemeanor when proved. But he was just, merciful before repentance, quick to acknowledge merit and goodness. He did not supersede his powers nor overrule the authority of his inferiors.

For the most part, Rossi preferred to remain aloof. He ate in his rooms, except at the beginning and end of the visitation and on feast days. On the principal feast days he offered community Mass, distributed Communion and preached before and after Mass. He would remain several weeks in the houses of study, showing special concern for the progress of the students. He tried particularly to win these future superiors, lecturers and masters to the idea of reform. In the general *studia* he would gather the students in his room after dinner or supper and preside at disputations on philosophical and theological questions.

The Incorporation of Monte Oliveto[27]

While in the area of Genoa, Rossi journeyed to nearby Multedo to visit the convent of Monte Oliveto. For fifty years, since its foundation, this community had lived on the fringe of the Carmelite family without contact either with the Mantuan Congregation or the Order. Now Trent required hermits to adopt an approved rule and submit to the superior of an established order. On November 24, 1564, the newly elected Rossi had written to the hermits of Monte Oliveto, inviting them to make their profession in his hands and place themselves under his immediate jurisdiction. This the hermits agreed to do, and on March 30, 1565, Rossi received them under his obedience and protection. On April 9 they renewed their profession to the prior general and his successors, sealing the procedure by notarial act. Appearing now in person, the prior general began his visitation on April 29, 1566, but for some reason, possibly favorable sailing conditions, interrupted it to resume it on his return. There were about twenty hermits in the community.

Rossi and his party travelled by sea from Genoa to Savona, thence by land, passing the Spanish frontier at Salces near Perpignan. He proceeded directly to Madrid, arriving, on June 10, 1566, just within the date agreed on. The purpose of the visit was not purely social; Rossi needed His Catholic Majesty's *placet* to be able to use his apostolic faculties in Spain. The encounter passed without incident. "I have been to kiss the hand of His Majesty," Rossi wrote to St. Charles Borromeo, "and he heard me most courteously."[28]

The Visitation of Andalusia[29]

On the eve of Rossi's visit the four provinces of Spain (Castile, Aragon, Catalonia, Andalusia) together numbered forty eight convents with about 550 religious. Under Audet Castile had been reformed, some progress had been made in Aragon and Catalonia, but Andalusia, torn by rival factions, had effectively resisted all efforts at renewal. Now the nine convents of Castile had little more than 100 members. Provincial since 1560 was Angel de Salazar. Aragon had ten houses with 112 members; Catalonia thirteen houses with 85 members. The largest province was Andalusia with sixteen convents and 250 friars.[30]

At the time there were twelve monasteries or *beaterios* in Spain. In the province of Andalusia there were Ecija, Granada, Seville, Antequera, Aracena, Paterna del Campo, Osuna. The province of Aragon had a monastery in Valencia. Castile had *beaterios* at Avila, Fontiveros and Piedrahita. After her consultation with St. Teresa, Mary of Jesus (Yepes) had founded the monastery of La Imagen at Alcalá de Henares under the jurisdiction of the bishop (1563).

Rossi's account of the Spanish visit, the *Visitatio hispanica*, today survives in the archive of the Order in Rome. The statements of nuns and friars are mostly recorded in Latin by the general's secretary, Rouhier; others are written by Rossi himself in a sort of Italianized Castilian. Most of the account concerns Andalusia; of Castile of a few fragments remain, of Aragon and Catalonia hardly anything at all.[31]

Rossi began his visitation of Andalusia with the convent of Jaen on July 28, 1566. He visited ten of the most important houses of friars. The three monasteries visited by the prior general – Ecija, Seville and Antequera – by this time had adopted the cloister according to the decrees of Trent, and so too perhaps had the other monasteries in the province. In three months more than 150 friars and an equal number of nuns passed before the visitator.

Surprisingly, Rossi did not visit the college at Osuna which the general chapter had ordered improved.[32] He may have sent one of his companions.

The procurator of the order at the court, Desiderio Mazzapica, who had been commissioned to reform Andalusia, had been made bishop of Ugento in the Kingdom of Naples, at the request of the king, August 1, 1565. Whether he was still in Spain at the time of Rossi's visit is not known. All that remains of Mazzapica's visit is the notorious attack on him in the convent of Ecija, August 24, 1565, by Melchior Nieto.[33]

Most of Andalusia's troubles were due to the three Nieto brothers, Caspar, Balthasar and Melchior, whose only resemblance to the holy Magi was their names.[34] "When we came to Andalusia," Rossi later declared, "we strongly rebuked these three brothers for their petulant and libidinous conduct by which they had each befouled themselves."[35] Caspar, apparently the ablest, was provincial and favored his brothers. Balthasar, aged 42 at the time, had been a Franciscan, but was admitted to the Carmelite Order by his brother the provincial, who in 1565 made him his vicar. While stationed in Utrera, Balthasar assaulted the prior, Michael de Ulloa; corrected by Rossi, he replied with an insolent letter. He gave occasion to many rumors about his moral life. The most unsavory of the three was Melchior. One witness, Fray Cristobal de Vargas, a partisan of the Nietos, describes him as "without morals *(un hombre perdido)*, a destroyer of convents." According to Fray Diego de Leon, *pasquinos* appeared on walls in Ecija about his relations with a certain woman. The prioress of Ecija, Dona Maria Ponce de Leon, characterizes him as *loco*. He was prior in various houses before becoming prior of Ecija, from which office also he had to be removed.

On August 25, 1565, in the convent of Ecija, Melchior attacked the visitator Mazzapica, struck him in the face, leaving a mark, seized and tore his capuce and threw him to the ground. Caspar threw himself on his brother, crying that he had committed an injury to the Order, had him put in irons and dispatched him to Seville. En route, in the convent of Carmona, Balthasar got into the cell where his brother was being detained, provided him with a sword and himself with another cleric and layman, all armed, helped him to escape. The priors of a number of houses, partisans of the Nietos, provided him with asylum. He also received support from influential laymen, including Don Gómez Suarez de Figueroa, Lord of Zafara, native place of the Nietos.

Ecija, which was the headquarters of the provincial, had a dubious reputation, and as a matter of fact the visitation revealed that religious observance was far from satisfactory. There were ugly rumors about the friars and nuns, but no misconduct was reported in the interviews. Only later did Rossi come to know that "some serious misdeeds committed by some particular nuns and the former provincial and one of his brothers were not revealed because they (the nuns) had been threatened." The incident, however, had occurred in the past, before the general chapter of 1564.[36]

Caspar Nieto kept himself in power with the help of supporters, principal among them John de Mora, prior of Seville. If frequently repeated complaints are to be believed, the ruling caste treated their subjects despotically and tyranically, "like captives and black slaves," lived comfortably themselves, while communities wanted the necessities. Little wonder that common life suffered. In Utrera each friar bought his own wine for meals. The students were neglected spiritually and materially. More than once priors are accused of punishing students physically. In Granada the students were afraid to buy brooms, because the prior, Gabriel de la Peñuela, would use them on them. The sick were neglected.

Visitations tend to bring out the negative aspects of religious life. The province, Rossi recorded, also had "masters of theology and fathers well deserving of the order, most attached to obedience, whose minds are not a little disturbed by these disputes."[37] It was not easy for Rossi to arrive at the truth from the conflicting testimonies – laudatory of Nieto's partisans, fiercely resentful of those he had alienated. The situation was complicated by the fiery Andalusian temperament, prone to exaggerations – *andaluzadas* – and to violence. Nevertheless the general picture emerged clearly enough.

The Chapter of Andalusia, 1566 [38]

On September 22, 1566, the provincial chapter opened in the Casa Grande of Seville with a great affluence of friars and the usual pomp, processions, sermons and public disputations. Rossi excluded John de Mora, "a tyrant and a person of ill fame," and other Nieto supporters from candidature for provincial, presenting instead a slate of six names of his choice. John de la Quadra, a neutral in the warring factions, was elected and immediately confirmed by the prior general. Michael de Ulloa, a protagonist of reform, became prior of the important convent of Seville; John de Mora moved to Utrera. Caspar Nieto was made prior of Castro del Rio, an insignificant house. Rossi was indulgent to these two; he even provided Nieto with a patent praising his services to the province, "so that he might live in peace and to the honor of the divine majesty."

All defamatory papers relating to the past were burned, "to preserve the public honor of that province." Balthasar, for aiding and abetting his brother Melchior, got three years' exile in Castile or Portugal with privation of place, voice and grades. Before leaving he spent eighteen days in irons and was administered the discipline on naked shoulders by the prior general himself. Later his exile was commuted to confinement in the convent and town of Utrera and again, at the intervention of illustrious persons, to Jaén or Gibraleón. Melchior, still at large, was declared apostate, rebellious, contumacious and excommunicated and condemned to three years in his majesty's galleys. Superiors of the provinces are ordered to have him captured by the secular arm. Influential friends interceded on behalf of the Nieto brothers – the *provisor* of Cordova, the nobles of Ecija, the marquis of Priego, the lord inquisitors of Seville, the marquis of Valderas, and other nobles of the court – but Rossi would not relent.

Diego de Castro, who had provided Melchior with a white cloak, was deprived of his grade and exiled to Aracena, "a mountain place." He also received discipline at the chapter. Gabriel de la Peñuela received a number of penances for offenses proved against him. Many malefactors were punished. A certain John de la Magdalena, convicted of living with a prostitute for more than six years, was condemned to the galleys. All in all, Rossi considered that he had acted with restraint; while seeking to remove the causes of dissent, he did not wish to give anyone reason to complain of excessive punishment.

The *Institutiones et Ordinationes*[39]

At the end of the chapter Rossi published *Institutiones et ordinationes*, printed before he left Seville (Sevilla, Juan Gutierrez, 1566). A blue-print for the reform of the province, it is practically a complete body of constitutions with directives listed under the headings of divine cult, studies and students, the observance of the regular life, the care of the sick, the preservation of peace, the rule and administration of convents, the office of provincial, novices and professed, nuns. These are all areas of particular concern in the province; besides, there are frequent references to prevailing abuses.

Thus, priors and subpriors should faithfully attend choir – their failure to do so had been the subject of frequent complaint during the visitation. Priests should not go gadding about saying Mass in other churches. All taint of simony should be removed from hearing confessions, sale of religious objects, collection of alms. Seville and Ecija are to maintain regents of studies; every convent should have a grammarian to teach the young. The decrees of Trent and of the general chapter regarding poverty had not been implemented in the province. Each friar is to deposit his money in the community chest, after having counted it and placed it in a purse with his name. It would then be dispensed to him according to his needs. He should also deposit in the community chest a list of the moveable goods conceded to his use. He may not own horses or mules in his own name.

Neglect of silence is to be remedied; severe penances are prescribed against swearing. Rules are laid down for the care of the sick. "The sick who suffer from French disease should be separated from the rest; they should be served their meals with charity, but no great expense should be undertaken for their cure, so that after all they may deplore the testimony of their iniquity." Ample treatment is accorded the most important problem of the province, the lack of peace and harmony. No one should make accusations without being able to prove them; misdeeds of the past, repented and atoned, should not be revived. In unusually severe terms, echoing complaints of the visitation, priors are told to "remember they are shepherds, not lions, tigers, rapacious wolves or tyrants. We admonish and exhort them, moved by the love of God, that they should not use injurious, insolent and contumelious language against the brethren, nor mistreat them, using violence... In the Carmelite order there are no masters and slaves, no tyrants and captives, but superiors and subjects, fathers and spiritual sons."

Novices, professed or lay brothers are not to be struck. Correction is not to be administered by sticks, bows or punches, but by the penances prescribed by the constitutions. Weapons are absolutely forbidden. All quarrels, denunciations and accusations are to be considered at an end in this chapter; documents, processes and censures of the past are annulled and cassated. The decrees against apostates were no mere formality; at the news of the coming of an apostolic visitator a number of the brethren had taken to their heels with the intention of returning when the coast was clear. The gate of the monastery is to be closed at sunset, and the key entrusted to the prior. The porter of Seville and other porters are not to allow the friars to talk to young women at the door. Unless they themselves request it, religious are not to be changed within a year from the house to which the chapter assigns them – this to put an end to the despotic maneuvers of superiors.

The provincial should not credit the prior's word only against a subject; he should break up cliques and gangs. A series of decrees are designed to prevent priors from wasting the goods of the convent, using them for selfish comfort and neglecting the community. Priors should attend the common refectory and be served the same food as the community; a set sum must be set aside for the food of the community and may not be used for other purposes. Ways of dress in the province are to be standardized within a month. Goods of little value left by the deceased are to be given to the young and the poor religious, the rest to the convent. Goods are not to be left in wills. Rossi continually returns to the matter of friars leaving the convent; as a rule they should not go out more than twice a week.

The decree concerning the office of provincial read like a catalog of the sins of Nieto. The provincial should not be suspect of favoritism, least he offend his conscience as judge. He should not change the taxes of the province, burden the houses financially with his visits, live continually in one house. After three years a provincial may be re-elected only after two terms – a special regulation for Andalusia. In their differences religious should not have recourse to the court ("recourse to force"). The prior general reserves to himself to grant permission to go to the Indies of His Catholic Majesty. Novitiates are instituted in Seville, Ecija and Granada. Rules for the careful selection and admission of candidates are laid down; in the past there had been considerable neglect in this matter. Every Saturday novices are permitted to go home to their mothers to have their laundry renewed, "for hygiene is not contrary to the regular life." Professed clerics are to live in a separate part of the convent under the sub-prior. Those destined to serve a master or other father must be eighteen years old. Although all nuns are immediately subject to the prior general, their care is entrusted to the provincials because of the distance. The latter should see that the nuns observe the constitutions, especially the cloister. The provincial should not revive faults of the past, friars should not visit the churches or parlors of nuns.

In conclusion, an appendix contains directives on a miscellany of subjects. Religious may not pass from one province to another without the consent of the respective provincials and the knowledge of the prior general. The publication of defamatory pamphlets is severely condemned. Religious are forbidden to have recourse to lay authority against their superiors. Religious should not resent the presence in the convent of members from other convents or provinces. Gaming with cards is forbidden. Friars are not to go from one convent to another without permission in writing.

Rossi's *Institutiones* in printed form provided each member of the Andalusian province with a handy code of laws, detailed and adapted to the particular needs of the province. Rossi's visitation had been thorough, his action prudent. Andalusia had finally received the sort of spiritual attention and leadership it had long lacked. There is no doubt that under other circumstances the visitation would have borne good and lasting fruit.

The Visitation of Portugal

On November 2, 1566, the prior general set out from Seville to visit Portugal. Portugal now numbered nine friaries. In 1541 a *beaterio* in Beja had been aggregated to the Order. Two Carmelite sisters were transferred from Castile to inaugurate the foundation. Beja gave rise to foundations in Lagos (1558) and Tentugal (1565).[40]

Before the general chapter an incident involving Portugal had occurred. On September 20, 1560, the king of Portugal had obtained apostolic faculties for the Cardinal Infante Henry to visit and reform the religious orders of the realm. By virtue of these faculties the cardinal without consulting the general had appointed visitators of the Carmelite Order Manuel de Goes and Louis da Luz, who deposed the provincial, John Limpo, and appointed Gabriel de Santiago in his stead. Rossi refused to confirm the new provincial and in April 1563, sent Angel de Salazar, provincial of Castile, and Antique Romeu, visitator of Catalonia, to investigate the matter. Limpo, then in Salamanca, was to continue in office. The Cardinal Infante refused to recognize the representatives sent by the vicar general in Rome.[41]

If the prior general had any misgivings about his reception in Portugal, he was soon reassured. The thirteen-year old King Sebastian, the cardinal Infante Don Henry, Queen Catalina sent courtiers to the Carmelite convent to welcome the prior general from Rome. "Not only was I not hindered," he wrote to Charles Borromeo, protector of the Order, "but I was shown favor and could do what I desired, reforming and reducing all to the regular life; although," he adds, "this province is very exemplary as regards the common life and of great observance." In 1551 the convent at Lisbon counted seventy members; at the time of Rossi's visit there were probably more. The general found nothing to censure, much to praise. "When I was there," he later recalled, "I experienced great joy at your service of God, honorable ways inside and outside the convent, perfect silence in the designated places, merciful correction of the erring, cleanliness in the sacristy, modesty in everything and at much else worthy of no little praise."

On December 13, Rossi opened the provincial chapter. Louis da Luz, one of those presented by the general and favored by Don Henry, was elected provincial. He was thought to be a natural son of King John I and had been appointed visitor of the province by Don Henry in 1563. Some time previously all masters of theology in the province had been deprived of their grade because of misuse of privileges. Rossi restored the masters not guilty of the abuses alleged in the general condemnation, but restricted their privileges, because there was need of priests for the ministry and the masters were not actually lecturing. He also passed judgement on malefactors; Jerome of Castile, long in prison on strong suspicion of scandal and theft, was given three "very severe" scourgings, three days on bread and water and sent back to Castile under threat of three years in the galleys if he did not present himself at his destination. At the end of the chapter the decrees of reform were printed (Lisbon, Manuel João, 1567). No copy is known.

Esteem for the learned Carmelite general was not lessened by the sermons he preached on two separate occasions before the king, queen and nobles of the realm. "Because the king did not well understand our language," he wrote to Borromeo, "I used a mixture of Spanish and Italian, so that they understood me and were satisfied."

The Visitation of Castile

On January 23, 1567 Rossi left Lisbon to begin the visitation of the province of Castile. His first stop, Salamanca, had been designated by the general chapter of 1548 as the interprovincial house of studies for Spain.[42] The general chapter of 1564 had ordered the house "enlarged for the fame of the order," and made available to students from all of Spain and Portugal.[43] Rossi found there only four students of theology and seven of the arts. Small though their number was, they were all to distinguish themselves in their later careers. One of them, John of St. Matthias, of Fontiveros, a third year student of the arts, with permission of his superiors was following the primitive Rule and was considering becoming a Carthusian. "There is no friar who does not speak well of him," St. Teresa testified about him at this time. He was of course St. John of the Cross. Unfortunately the account of the visitation of Salamanca is wanting, but one early biographer of St. John, Alonzo of the Mother of God, states that the holy young friar made the impression of the prior general who in later years remembered the encounter at Salamanca.[44]

Rossi entrusted the visitation of Toledo, the principal house of the province, to Mariano di Leone, successor as procurator of the Order at the court of Desiderio Mazzapica and like him a Sicilian. On February 12 Rossi began the visitation of the *beaterio* in Piedrahita. The sisters wore the white veil and took the three vows of religion, but were not cloistered. Like many sisters in Spain they felt they should not be bound by Trent to a cloister they did not profess, nor did Rossi press the point. The sisters did not go outside the convent except with permission and for just reasons, among them to beg, for the convent was desperately poor. "Certainly these nuns have embraced the three vows of religion with fervor," Rossi concludes, "excellent morals prevail among them, they dedicate themselves to divine cult with great diligence and integrally keep the cloister." At this time Rossi apparently was unaware of Pius V's legislation of the previous May 29, which put an end to all discussion. Back in Italy, in May or June, 1568, Rossi revoked all dispensations from cloister granted in Spain.[45]

The Incarnation at Avila[46]

Rossi arrived in Avila on February 16 or 17. The Carmelite friary lay along the north wall of the city. Almost opposite it was the monastery of the Incarnation. According to his custom, facilitated by the proximity of the two houses, Rossi alternated interviews with the friars and nuns; only the visitation of the nuns remains, and this includes the interviews of only about half of the 180 members of the monastery. Yet these amply suffice to provide an insight into life in the monastery in which St. Teresa passed 27 years of her life.

The prioress was Dona Frances de Briceno. From the visitation account it is immediately apparent that the monastery was in serious economic straits. The income was inadequate to meet the needs of the community, property had to be sold and debts incurred. Very little could be provided in the common refectory and the sick lacked adequate care. To make matters worse the monastery had to provide for a certain number of hangers-on – relatives and friends of the nuns as well as a few children. This state of affairs had its effect on observance. About twenty nuns asked the prior general for permission to have rents and to retain alms and money, as in fact they had been doing hitherto. Cells were bought and sold, goods left to relatives by testament. On the other hand a certain amount of luxury and frivolity of dress were not wanting.

The Incarnation had also become a haven for the daughters of nobility, the *señoras donas*, whose dowries permitted them more spacious quarters with a small hallway, kitchen and sitting room with alcove, in which to entertain relatives and friends. There was a noticeable tension between the "ladies" and the sisters who slept in the common dormitory. Even in the choir the ladies insisted on the first places instead of observing the order of profession. A number of ladies ask permission to retain their maids. Dona Aldonza de Valderrabano requested "to be allowed to keep her black slave girl." The comings and goings of the maid servants caused no little distraction in the monastery.

The nuns took advantage of the presence of the apostolic visitor to obtain permission to visit relatives; the motive of such visits was mostly economic: to obtain financial help from theft families. (Here, as in Piedrahita, the nuns did not consider themselves bound to cloister.) The same motive in part lay behind the frequent visiting in the parlors of the Incarnation. Such visits were the occasion for offering and receiving much-needed alms. Not all the visiting took place in the parlors; some of the nuns complained of talking going on at the windows at the door of the sacristy. The many confessors who served the monastery added to the busy scene. Besides the two Carmelites from the nearby friary, about ten priests, secular and religious of other orders, appear in the partial account of the visitation. They include clerics of the highest caliber such as Julian of Avila. It is not surprising that in this complex society the common life would be affected. Rossi was asked for dispensations from the common refectory, from the fasts, or simply from all common acts. Of the ninety nuns interviewed forty asked to be dispensed from office in choir.

The populous Incarnation, the largest Carmelite nunnery in Spain, its innocent and bustling existence, dedicated to the grim business of survival, seems ill suited to a life of prayer and reflection. Yet the monastery numbered many dedicated religious, some of whom were to form the nucleus of the reform of St. Teresa. From numerous testimonies it is evident that peace, harmony, good morals, fervent devotion reigned in the Incarnation. The sisters themselves were aware of and deplored their shortcomings, many of them beyond their control.

Rossi's provisions for the reform of the Incarnation have not survived. It is known that he tried to alleviate the problem of poverty by forbidding the acceptance of more nuns. In time this remedy, plus the exodus to the reform of St. Teresa, had its effect. In the next 25 years the number of nuns of the black veil was reduced to half.

"Some Affairs of the Order" at the Court [47]

For a reason not entirely clear Rossi interrupted his visitation of the Castilian province to return to Madrid, where we find him on March 17, 1567. In a letter to Borromeo of the 22nd he simply states that he had come "to treat of some affairs of the order." He had audiences with King Philip, Queen Isabelle, Prince Charles, Fray Bernard de Fresneda and other notables at the court. The prior general's purpose may have been to obtain a foundation for the order in Madrid, "because of the affairs which every day occur to our entire brotherhood, and lest our religious run about as vagabonds to the great scandal of the faithful." [48]

It may also be that the situation in Andalusia brought Rossi to the court. The peace he hoped he had established in Andalusia proved illusory; the Nieto party had not waited for him to cross the Portuguese border to counterattack. The ousted group claimed the chapter had not been free, accused the prior general of venality and called for a visitation by the king. Focus of the trouble was Utrera, where John de Mora was prior, and Christopher de Vargas, another Nieto partisan, was sub-prior. Balthasar did not bother to perform the penance imposed on him, sat at the prior's table as though he still had precedence and left the convent at will. At Castro del Rio, Caspar Nieto fomented opposition to the prior general and his visitation. The provincial, John de la Quadra, presented Rossi with a formal complaint against Mora and other rebellious subjects. The prior general, on March 21, 1567, "in our hospice at Madrid," cited Caspar Nieto and Mora, "the stronger ones in controversy," to appear before him at Avila by mid-April.

Shortly afterwards, on April 5, Rossi got rid of Melchior Nieto, changing his sentence to the triremes to expulsion from the Order with the obligation of entering another. Melchior subsequently became a Third Order Franciscan.[49]

The whole while that Rossi was at court Philip II, serenely indifferent to the Carmelite apostolic visitator and reformer, was pursuing his own plans for the reform of the religious orders in Spain, Carmelites among them. He had finally found a sympathetic if now wholly pliant collaborator in Pius V, who on December 2, 1566, issued the *Maxime cuperemus*, entrusting the reform of religious orders to the bishops. These with the aid of an observant provincial and religious were to reduce all conventuals to observance.[50] On December 12 followed *Cum gravissimis de causis*, applying the same measures to nuns.

Next Philip turned his attention to the reform of orders that had no observance, among which he classed the Carmelites. On March 17, 1567 – at the very time Rossi was at the court – Requeséns wrote to the king from Rome that things looked good for the royal plan. As a matter of fact, on April 16 appeared the brief, *Superioribus mensibus*, instructing the bishops personally or through delegates to reform the Carmelites, Trinitarians and Mercedarians. For this work they were to avail themselves of the assistance of two observant Dominicans.[51]

The king's action set aside religious exemption and the decree of the council of Trent entrusting reform to religious superiors. The Carmelite general chapter of 1564 had laid claim to the title of observant and had denounced conventuality.[52] It was in the interest of observance that the prior general by apostolic delegation and with the leave of the king was visiting the Spanish Carmelite houses.

Mercifully *Superioribus mensibus* still lay in the womb of the future during Rossi's visit to Madrid. Later he was to blame the Andalusian insurgents for bringing the visitation of the bishops on the Order, but this arrangement was only a part of Philip's large design. The Carmelites' clamor against the Italian visitator may only have helped convince the king, if that were necessary, of the correctness of his course of action.

From Madrid Rossi continued his visitation of the Castilian province, March 24, visiting San Pablo de La Moraleja, Medina del Campo and Valladolid. At Fontiveros he visited the *beaterio* of the Mother of God. The community numbered forty-five sisters, but only five interviews remain. The cloister here resembled that of Piedrahita and Avila: women and girls lived in the monastery with the same inconvenience to regular life, which however was found to be satisfactory.[53]

The Chapter of Castile[54]

On April 12, 1567, the provincial chapter of Castile began. Voters at the chapter numbered about twenty. Only the nominations to office are known.[55] The new provincial turned out to be the sixty-eight-year old Alonso González, in the past active for the reform of the province. The foundation of a college at Alcalá de Henares was approved. Toledo, Avila and San Pablo de la Moraleja were named novitiates.

As in Andalusia and Portugal, Rossi no doubt published decrees of reform in Castile, but no copy is known to exist. After his visitation of the province in 1571, the Dominican Peter Fernández claimed only to summarize and to translate into Castilian Rossi's decrees of reform. Authorities disagree concerning the degree to which Fernández may have departed from his model.

"The province on the whole is in good state," Rossi concluded, "though there are some disorders." He may have been referring to shortcomings in administration on the part of priors who did not keep proper records or share responsibility with the designated officials. Castile had accepted the reform of Audet and as a consequence had suffered a drastic reduction in membership; the fewness in numbers in turn must have effected observance. The province had no *studia* of its own; it managed to muster only two masters of theology and four candidates for the doctorate (*presentati*) for the chapter. In short the province was small, but to present the level of religious fervor as unsatisfactory or downright decadent, as has been done, is inaccurate.

It was probably during the chapter that the bishop of Avila, Don Alvaro de Mendoza, told the prior general of a monastery of nuns under his jurisdiction which followed the primitive Rule of Carmel. Strangely, during the visitation the sisters of the Incarnation had hardly mentioned the new house which had been founded four years previously by one of their members and which had roused such opposition at the time. Rossi no doubt knew about the foundation of San José, but he waited for the bishop to broach the subject. Foundress of San José was Dona Teresa de Ahumada.

Dona Teresa de Ahumada

The life of St. Teresa, one of the most remarkable women of all time, has been told by herself and has been the subject of innumerable biographies.[56]

Teresa de Ahumada y Cepeda was born March 28, 1515, at Avila, probably at the family's country estate in the neighboring village of Gotarrendura.[57] She was the third child of the second marriage of Don Alonso Sánchez de Cepeda with Dona Beatrix de Ahumada. A well-kept secret of hagiographers until recently is the fact that Teresa lacked *limpia sangre*: Juan Sánchez, her grandfather on her father's side was a converted and lapsed Jew of Toledo.[58] This part of her personality may account for her open and unabashed manner, her shrewdness and practicality. On All Souls' Day, 1535, she secretly left home to enter the monastery of the Incarnation. "When I left my father's house," she writes, voicing the collective heartbreak of all young people who have left cherished homes, "my distress was so great that I do not think it will be greater when I die. It seemed to me as if every bone in my body were being wrenched asunder." But when she was clothed in the Carmelite habit, she knew her decision had been the right one: "At the time my entrance into this new life gave me a joy so great that it has never failed me even to this day."[59]

Dona Teresa's life at the Incarnation was similar to that of the other wealthy ladies there. She had her rooms where she could converse with her friends. She was permitted to leave the monastery for her health and for other sufficient reasons. Her health almost immediately gave cause for concern. Even before entering the monastery Teresa had suffered "serious fainting fits, together with fever."[60] Now her fainting spells increased in number, she suffered from "heart trouble" and "many other ailments."[61] In desperation her father put her under the care of a popular healer in Becedas who had a great reputation for cures. The drastic remedies and purges nearly killed the young nun. At the nadir of her illness she fell into a comatose state and was given up for dead. Her grave was dug, and in one Carmelite monastery the prayers prescribed for the dead were recited. When she finally regained consciousness, Teresa found wax on her eyelids, placed there in preparation for her burial. "My tongue was bitten to pieces; nothing had passed my lips; and because of this and my great weakness my throat was choking me so that I could not even take water. All my bones seemed to be out of joint and there was a terrible confusion in my head. As a result of the torments I had suffered during these days, I was all doubled up, like a ball, and no more able to move arm, foot, hand or head than if I had been dead, unless others moved them for me... They used to move me in a sheet, one taking one end and another the other." She was finally delivered to the monastery "nothing but bones." Over a period of three years, her paralysis gradually improved. "When I began to get about on my hands and knees, I praised God."[62] All her life Teresa suffered ill health.

Teresa found the Incarnation "a secure state" and a "house in which there were ... many servants of God from whom I might take example."[63] Earlier in her sickness she had made the acquaintance of Francisco de Osuna's *Third Spiritual Alphabet* (Toledo 1527) and began to practice mental prayer, sometimes attaining the prayer of quiet and even the prayer of union.[64] After her recovery she did not return to these practices; she had in fact compromised, though in outward appearances she continued to lead a devout and exemplary life. "On account of this they (the sisters) gave me as much liberty as is given to the oldest nuns, and even more, and they had great confidence in me. For I did no such things as taking liberties for myself or doing anything without leave – such as talking to people through crevices or over walls or by night."[65]

Besides herself, she blamed the lack of enclosure in the monastery for her lapse from prayer: "I think it was a very bad thing for me not to be in a convent that was enclosed. The freedom which the sisters, who were good, might enjoy without becoming less so (for they were not obliged to live more strictly than they did as they had not taken a vow of enclosure) would certainly have led me, who am wicked, down to hell, had not the Lord, through very special favors, using means and remedies which are all His own, delivered me from this peril. It seems to me, then, that it is a very great danger for women in a convent to have such freedom; for those who want to be wicked it is not so much a remedy for their weaknesses as a step on the way to hell. But this is not to be applied to my convent, where there are so many who serve the Lord in very truth and with great perfection, so that His Majesty, in His goodness, cannot fail to help them. Nor is it one of those which are completely open, for all religious observances are kept in it: I am comparing it now with others which I know and have seen."[66]

Don Alonso died on Christmas eve, 1543. His confessor, the Dominican Vincent Barrón, who was also Teresa's, persuaded her to take up prayer once more. At the same time she could not bring herself to make the absolute renunciation of worldly interests and friendships. "I spent nearly 20 years on that stormy sea, often falling in this way and each time rising again, but to little purpose, as I would only fall once more ... I can testify that this is one of the most grievous kinds of life which I think can be imagined, for I had neither any joy in God nor any pleasure in the world. When I was in the midst of worldly pleasures, I was distressed by the remembrance of what I owed to God; when I was with God, I grew restless because of worldly affections. This is so grievous a conflict that I do not know how I managed to endure it for a month, much less for so many years." [67] "Very often, over a period of years, I was more occupied in wishing my hour of prayer were over, and in listening whenever the clock struck, than in thinking of things that were good. Again and again I would rather have done any severe penance that might have been given me than practice recollection as a preliminary to prayer." [68]

The "Conversion" of St. Teresa

St. Teresa's "conversion" began with a memorable experience which apparently took place during Lent of 1554.[69] "It happened that, entering the oratory one day, I saw an image which had been procured for a certain festival that was observed in the house and had been taken there to be kept for that purpose. It represented Christ sorely wounded; and so conducive was it to devotion that when I looked at it I was deeply moved to see Him thus, so well did it picture what he suffered for us. So great was my distress when I thought how ill I had repaid Him for those wounds that I felt as if my heart were breaking, and I threw myself down beside Him, shedding floods of tears and begging Him to give me strength once for all so that I might not offend Him ... I believe I told Him then that I would not rise from that spot until He had granted me what I was beseeching of Him. And I feel sure that this did me good, for from that time onward I began to improve." [70]

Her resolve was strengthened by the newly translated *Confessions* of St. Augustine (Salamanca, 1554) which came into her hands at this time. "When I got as far as his conversion and read how he heard that voice in the garden, [8, ch. 12] it seemed exactly as if the Lord were speaking in that way to me, or so my heart felt. I remained for a long time dissolved in tears, in great distress and affliction ... I believe my soul gained great strength from the Divine Majesty: He must have heard my cries and had compassion on my tears. I began to long to spend more time with Him, and to drive away occasions of sin, for, once they had gone, I would feel a new love for His Majesty."[71]

Teresa did not know how to cope with the mystical experiences which now began to flood her being. The devout friends in whom she confided, especially Francis de Salcedo, the "Holy Cavalier," and the priest, Gaspar Daza, caused her no little confusion and distress by announcing that it was their considered opinion that she was being deluded by the devil. From this state she was rescued by a series of Jesuit confessors whom she now began to consult.[72] The priest who probably in June of 1554 arrived at the Incarnation to hear the confession of the visionary nun was Diego de Cetina, a newly ordained Jesuit of twenty-three. His talents were not above the ordinary, but he practiced mental prayer and recognized the Spirit of God in the soul of his penitent. He was content to let the Spirit do his work and confined himself to encouraging and approving. "He left me comforted and strengthened ... I began to make many changes in my habits, although my confessor did not press me to do so and in fact seemed to trouble about it all very little. But this moved me the more, for he led me by the way of love for God which brought me, not oppression, as it would if I had not done it out of love, but freedom."[73] Cetina took advantage of a visit to Avila of St. Francis Borgia, probably in the summer of 1555,[74] to arrange an interview with his penitent. The "Holy Duke" assured her that she was being led by the spirit of God.[75]

Cetina left Avila probably early in August, 1555.[76] At the same time Teresa's health took a turn for the worse and she went to live with Dona Guiomar de Ulloa, a friend who plays a large role in her life. A widow at twenty-five, famous for her beauty and frivolity, Dona Guiomar now devoted her life to piety. She probably got to know Teresa at the Incarnation where she had a sister and two daughters. Her enthusiastic nature tended to lead her to extreme courses, and contemporary opinion on her was divided. Teresa thought highly of her; the two women became as sisters over the years. On this occasion, Teresa remained in Dona Guiomar's house for three years, 1555-1558.[77]

It was Dona Guiomar who introduced Teresa to her own confessor, John de Prádanos, the brilliant twenty-six year old rector of the Jesuit college in Avila. "This Father began to lead me to greater perfection."[78] He guided her to a solution of a problem that continued to haunt her: what to do about human relationships which did not offend God and even appeared obligatory, yet seemed to form an obstacle to her perfect freedom. "He told me to commend the matter to God for a few days, and to recite the hymn *Veni, Creator*, and I should be enlightened as to which was the better and then, beseeching the Lord that He would help me to please Him in everything, I began the hymn. While I was reciting it, there came to me a transport so sudden that it almost carried me away: I could make no mistake about this, so clear was it. This was the first time that the Lord had granted me the favor of any kind of rapture. I heard these words: 'I will have thee converse now, not with men, but with angels.' This simply amazed me, for my soul was greatly moved and the words were spoken to me in the depths of the spirit. For this reason they made me afraid, though on the other hand they brought me a great deal of comfort, which remained with me after the fear caused by the strangeness of the experience had vanished."

"The words have come true: never since then have I been able to maintain firm friendship save with people who I believe love God and try to serve Him, nor have I derived comfort from any others or cherished any private affection for them. It has not been in my power to do so; and it has made no difference if the people have been relatives or friends. Unless I know that a person loves God or practices prayer, it is a real cross to me to have to do with him. I really believe this is the absolute truth."

"Since that day I have been courageous enough to give up everything for the sake of God, Who in that moment – for I think it happened in no more than a moment – was pleased to make His servant another person ... Blessed forever be God, who in one moment gave the freedom which, despite all the efforts I had been making for so many years, I had never been able to attain, though sometimes I had done such violence to myself that it badly affected my health."[79] This experience of Teresa, which probably took place during Pentecost, 1556, has been identified as the grace of the spiritual espousals.[80]

On June 29, 1559, St. Teresa experienced her first vision. Her soul now began to be flooded with a stream of mystical experiences: visions, ecstasies and the experience immortalized in the celebrated statue of Bernini, the "grace of the dart," or the transverberation of the heart. Such phenomena, in part perceptible to observers, brought Teresa much unwelcome notoriety, and her solicitous friends were more obstinately than ever convinced that she was being deluded by the devil. They caused the saint no little anguish. Her confessor now was the Jesuit Balthasar Alvarez. He was young, intelligent, but at this time still inexperienced, and his direction was vacillating.[81]

The legendary Franciscan penitent, St. Peter of Alcantara, who seemed to Teresa "to be made of nothing but roots of trees,"[82] during a visit to Avila in mid-August, 1560, calmed her spirit and spoke to Alvarez and in particular to the "Holy Cavalier" who of five or six friends caused her the greatest difficulty. St. Peter was a good friend of Dona Guiomar de Ulloa and actually was in Avila to complete arrangements for the foundation of a reformed convent of his order on property in Aldea del Palo provided by Dona Guiomar. Pope Paul IV had named him commissary general for reform, and he had established the reformed province of St. Joseph. Recently he had taken part in the founding of the royal monastery of Discalced Franciscan nuns in Madrid. Teresa kept him informed and consulted him until his death in 1562. Considerable importance must be accorded to this relationship of St. Teresa with the Franciscan reformer at a time when she was launching her own reform.[83]

The Growth of an Idea

Shortly after St. Peter's visit Teresa experienced a fearsome vision of hell which profoundly affected her. "I was terrified by all this, and, though it happened nearly six years ago, I still am as I write: even as I sit here, fear seems to be depriving my body of its natural warmth."[84] Thereafter she lost all fear of the sufferings and disappointments of life; they seemed slight in comparison with those of hell. She increased the rigor of the penances she practiced and made a vow to do always the more perfect thing the first case, according to her biographer Francis de Ribera, of such a vow ever being made.[85]

"This vision, too, was the cause of the very deep distress which I experience because of the great number of souls who are bringing damnation upon themselves – especially of those Lutherans, for they were made members of the Church through baptism."[86] This was a time of great concern over the infiltration of Protestantism from France into Spain. The previous year, 1559, the first *auto de fe* had been held, and the very archbishop of Toledo, Fray Bartholomew de Carranza, had been deleted on suspicion of heresy. This very year Philip II had addressed circular letters to all religious of his realms requesting prayers and processions for the unity of the faith. It was the king's wish that religious live up to their calling, for the laxity of religious orders had given the heretics an excuse for destroying them.[87]

The desire for a more committed life was also enkindled in Teresa by her vision of hell. "I desired, therefore, to flee from others and to end by withdrawing myself completely from the world. My spirit was restless, yet the restlessness was not disturbing but pleasant: I knew quite well that it was of God and that his Majesty had given my soul this ardour to enable me to digest other and stronger meat than I had been in the habit of eating."

"I would wonder what I could do for God, and it occurred to me that the first thing was to follow the vocation for a religious life which His Majesty had given me by keeping my Rule with the greatest possible perfection. And although in the house where I was living there were many servants of God, and He was well served in it, yet, as it was very needy, we nuns would often leave it for other places where we could live honorably and keep our vows. Furthermore, the Rule was not observed in its primitive rigor but, as throughout the Order, according to the Bull of Mitigation. There were also other disadvantages, such as the excessive comfort which I thought we had, for the house was a large and pleasant one. But this habit of frequently going away (and I was one who did it a great deal) was a serious drawback to me, for there were certain persons, to whom my superiors could refuse nothing, who liked to have me with them, and so, when importuned by these persons, they would order me to go and visit them. So things went on until I was able to be in the convent very little."[88]

The unwelcome notoriety which her mystical experiences brought on her in the open world of the Incarnation had also turned her thoughts to a place of greater solitude. "When these raptures or these periods of deep recollection began, and I could not resist them, even in public, I would become so ashamed after they were over as to want not to appear where anyone would see me ... The temptation reached such a point that I wanted to leave this place and go and take my dowry to another convent, much more strictly enclosed than the one I was then in, which I had heard remarkably well spoken of. It belonged to my own Order and was a long way away; it is the distance that would have given me the greatest relief, for I should have been where nobody knew me. But my confessor never allowed me to go."[89]

One day early in the Fall of 1560 a group of friends and relatives were gathered as usual in the cell of St. Teresa, and the conversation turned to the way of life in the monastery. The topic may have come up in connection with the austere life led by the Discalced Franciscan nuns St. Peter of Alcantara had just founded. "Half in jest," writes Teresa's niece, Maria de Ocampo, they began to plan "how to reform the Rule observed in that monastery ... and found monasteries after the manner of hermitages, like the original one kept at the beginning of this Rule, which our holy fathers of old founded." (Teresa and the other sisters would have been fully informed of the life of the "holy fathers of old" from the *Institution of the First Monks*, of which the Incarnation possessed a Spanish translation, extant today.)[90] Maria offered to contribute 1000 ducats to the project. Some objected that they could not go to a hermitage, but that they should found a small monastery with a few nuns where they might all go to do penance. To Dona Guiomar who arrived late Teresa laughingly explained: "These young ladies were saying a short while ago that we should found a small monastery after the manner of the Discalced Nuns of St. Francis." Dona Guiomar volunteered to help as much as she could with so holy a work.[91]

A Convent Called St. Joseph's

At the time nothing definite was decided: "We agreed to commend the matter very earnestly to God." Nevertheless the business was not suffered to remain unfinished. "One day, after Communion, the Lord gave me the most explicit commands to work for this aim with all my might and made me wonderful promises – that the convent would not fail to be established; that great service would be done to Him in it; that it should be called Saint Joseph's; that he would watch over us at one door and Our Lady at the other; that Christ would go with us; that the convent would be a star giving out the most brilliant light; and that, although the Rules of the religious orders were mitigated, I was not to think He was very little served in them, for what would become of the world if it were not for religious? I was to tell my confessor this and to say that it was He Who was giving me this command

and that He asked him not to oppose it nor to hinder me in carrying it out."⁹²

Subsequently the Lord appeared to Teresa repeatedly and proposed many arguments and motives. Her confessor, Father Alvarez, did not dare to tell her to give up the idea. He told her to talk the matter over with her superior and do what he advised. St. Peter of Alcantara advised her to go ahead with her plan. Eventually it was Dona Guiomar who approached the provincial of Castile, Angel de Salazar, proposing the idea as her own. "The Provincial, who is well-disposed to the religious orders, took the idea very well, gave her all necessary help and told her he would give the house his sanction. They discussed the revenue which the convent would need, and we decided that, for many reasons, the number of nuns in the convent ought never to exceed thirteen."⁹³

When Teresa's project became known, a storm of opposition arose. "People talked about us, laughed at us and declared that the idea was ridiculous. Of me, they said that I was all right in the convent where I was living, while my companion was subjected to such persecution that it quite exhausted her." Teresa and Dona Guiomar then turned to the Dominicans and sought the advice of Peter Ibáñez, "the most learned man in the place," who after a week of reflection encouraged them in their plan and told them ways to accomplish it. Not only Ibáñez but a number of other Dominicans were to offer Teresa significant assistance by their spiritual counsel and practical advice.⁹⁴

At this point, on the eve of signing the deeds for the purchase of a house, the provincial withdrew his consent for the new foundation, because of the opposition it aroused in the town, and Teresa's confessor forbade her to have anything to do with it. "For five or six months I remained silent, taking no further steps with regard to the plan and never even speaking about it."⁹⁵ "I was now very unpopular throughout my convent for having wanted to found a convent more strictly enclosed. The nuns said that I was insulting them; that there were others there who were better than myself, and so I could serve God quite well where I was; that I had no love for my own convent; and that I should have done better to get money for that than for founding another. Some said I ought to he thrown into the prison-cell; others came out on my side, though of these there were very few."⁹⁶

This was also a time when her mystical experiences were at their peak and added a complication to her situation. "People came to me in great concern to say that these were bad times and that it might be that something would be alleged against me and I should have to go before the Inquisitors."⁹⁷ Teresa revealed her interior state to her new-found Dominican director, Peter Ibáñez, who in his detailed *Dictamen* thoroughly approved her spirit.⁹⁸

In April 1561, Gaspar de Salazar took over as rector of the Jesuit college of St. Giles in Avila. He had less reservations about the visionary nun of the Incarnation, and consequently Father Alvarez felt freer in his direction. He now lifted his ban on Teresa's efforts to found a reformed monastery. It was agreed to proceed in secret without the permission of the provincial. Dona Guiomar and Father Ibáñez wrote to Rome for apostolic faculties to found a Carmelite monastery. St. Peter of Alcantara apparently also had a hand in the arrangements. The new foundation was to be placed under the jurisdiction of the bishop. St. Teresa writes that the Lord "told me to send to Rome, and to follow a certain procedure, which he also described to me."[99] A small house was purchased in the name of Teresa's brother-in-law, Don John de Ovalle, the husband of her sister Joanne.[100]

On Christmas night of 1561 Teresa received an order from the provincial to go and comfort Dona Louisa de la Cerda in Toledo, widow since January 13 of Don Arias Pardo de Saavedra. Dona Louisa was a very great lady, the daughter of the Duke of Medinaceli, descendant of King Alfonso X. During her stay of six months in the Medinaceli Palace Teresa met Mary of Jesus (Yepes), a Carmelite *beata* of Granada, who about the same time as Teresa had conceived the idea of founding a reformed convent of nuns and had "walked barefoot to Rome to obtain the necessary patent ... During the fortnight she was with me we made our plans as to how these convents were to be founded."

From Mary, Teresa learned "that our Rule, before its severity became mitigated, had ordered us to possess nothing." From Mary, too, Teresa may have obtained her Spanish translation of the Rule; at least the two foundresses possessed a common version.[101] Teresa determined to found her house without income. This time she did not heed the learned advice of Ibáñez, "two sheets long, full of refutations and theology;" instead she welcomed the approval of her idea by Peter of Alcantara who came to visit her on her request.[102]

In the house of Dona Louisa de la Cerda another important event took place. At the suggestion apparently of the Dominican Fray Diego García de Toledo, Teresa wrote the first version of her autobiography.[103]

The very evening of her return to Avila in early July 1562, after an absence of six months, Teresa received the rescript from the Apostolic Penitentiary authorizing the foundation of a Carmelite monastery under the jurisdiction of the bishop of Avila. Dated February 7, 1562, it was addressed to Dona Guiomar de Ulloa and her mother, Dona Aldonza de Guzmán.[104] Since it had been requested before Teresa decided to renounce incomes in connection with the monastery, the rescript did not specify that it should be founded in absolute poverty. Another with this provision was acquired under the date December 5, 1562.[105] Teresa was also delighted to find at hand in Avila her old friend Fray Peter of Alcantara. It was he who overcame the misgivings of the bishop, Don Alvaro de Mendoza, about founding the house in poverty, and who persuaded him to accept it under his jurisdiction.[106]

A sickness of her brother-in-law, John de Ovalle, who was living alone in the house destined for the monastery, provided Teresa with an excuse for staying there to attend him; at the same time she could oversee last-minute preparations for the opening of the monastery. On August 24, 1562, four women took the habit: Antonia de Henao (of the Holy Spirit), a penitent of St. Peter of Alcantara; Maria de la Paz (of the Cross), a serving girl of Dona Guiomar de Ulloa; Ursula de Revilla (of the Saints), a protege of Gaspar Daza; Maria de Avila (of St. Joseph), sister of Julian de Avila. With Teresa were two nuns of the Incarnation, her cousins Inés and Anna de Tapia. Also at hand were her brother-in-law, John de Ovalle, and her sister Joanna; her steadfast friends, Francis de Salcedo, Julian de Avila and Gonzalo de Aranda. Gaspar Daza, as representative of the bishop received the vows of the candidates, offered Mass and reserved the Sacrament. "So with the full weight of authority this convent of our most glorious father Saint Joseph was founded in the year 1562 ... I was so happy," St. Teresa writes, "that I was quite carried away by the intensity of my prayer."[107]

Yet shortly afterwards this state of euphoria gave place to a violent attack of misgivings. Her conscience rebuked her for having acted without the provincial's permission. She wondered whether the sisters would be able to stand the austere life, whether she herself would be happy away from the Incarnation and her many friends there. "I certainly think this was one of the worst times that I have ever spent in my life ... I made a great effort, and in the presence of the Most Holy Sacrament promised to do all I could to get permission to enter this new house, and, if I could do so with a good conscience, to make a vow of enclosure. The instant I had done this, the devil fled, leaving me quiet and happy and I remained so and have been so ever since."[108]

A Great Deal of Commotion

"Now what we had done became known in my convent and in the city, and for the reasons I have given there was a great deal of commotion – not, it seemed, without some cause."[109] The prioress of the Incarnation, Dona Maria Cimbrón, ordered her to return. Teresa placed Sister Ursula in charge and chose Gaspar Daza as chaplain and intermediary between her and the sisters.[110] Teresa went, fully expecting to be consigned to the monastery prison, but the prioress on hearing Teresa's version of the affair was mollified. The provincial, Angel de Salazar, on being summoned, rebuked the foundress severely. Later she had to face the conventual chapter. She spoke calmly without attempting to excuse herself; in the end no one found fault with her. "Afterwards, when I was alone with him (the provincial), I spoke to him more plainly, and he was quite satisfied, and promised me, if my foundation succeeded, to give me permission to go there as soon as the city was quiet – for there had been a very great commotion in the city."[111]

So there had been indeed. The house had been founded not only without permission of the superiors of the Order but also without authorization of civil authorities. In an extraordinary session, August 26, the municipal council of Avila decided that the new monastery of St. Joseph had been founded in prejudice to the interests of the city. It was decided to appeal to the crown and to the bishop. On August 30, the magistrates met with representatives of the bishop, cathedral chapter and the religious houses of Avila. Bishop Mendoza's representative, the Licentiate Brizuela, presented the Roman rescript for the foundation of St. Joseph's. The city officials were not slow in pointing out that the document could not be executed with the royal *placet*. After much debate it was decided that the new monastery should be suppressed. The Dominican lector at the College of St. Thomas, Dominic Báñez, spoke out in its favor.[112]

Another meeting of the same group was held, probably the following day, to persuade the bishop to suppress the foundation and so save the trouble and expense of an appeal to the crown. Don Mendoza, represented by Teresa's friend, Gaspar Daza, refused to comply, so the case went to Madrid early in September. Teresa had no funds to wage a legal battle, but her friend, Gonzalo de Aranda, generously agreed to represent her. It soon became evident to "those of the city" that the royal council was not about to suppress a reformed convent; prudent men of the world that they were, they decided on a compromise. They insisted only that the monastery agree to accept rents. Teresa was on the point of submitting, when a vision of St. Peter of Alcantara, deceased since October 12, changed her mind. The case dragged on and finally died of apathy.[113]

Particularly helpful to the cause of St. Joseph in its latter phase was Peter Ibáñez who returned to Avila around mid-December. He persuaded Bishop Mendoza to obtain permission (apparently oral) for Teresa and some companions to live at St. Joseph's, to initiate the divine office, and to instruct the novices. Four nuns from the Incarnation, Anne Dávila, Anne Gómez, Mary Ordóñez and the novice Isabel de la Peña, accompanied her. Teresa made Anne Dávila prioress and Anne Gómez subprioress. Early in 1563 the bishop made Teresa prioress. The sisters dropped their family names, and Teresa de Ahumada became Teresa of Jesus. On August 22, 1563, Salazar gave permission to Teresa and three companions from the Incarnation to remain in St. Joseph's for one year. (Anne Dávila had returned to the Incarnation.) At the end of this period Teresa asked the papal nuncio, Alexander Crivelli, permission to be confirmed by the provincial, to transfer definitively from the Incarnation to St. Joseph's.[114]

Teresa's Ideal of the Carmelite Life

In founding St. Joseph's Teresa purposed to restore Carmelite life to its pristine purity. She professed to observe the "first" or "primitive" Rule, in contrast to the Rule "according to the Bull of Mitigation."[115] "I have tried to ensure that this Rule of Our Lady shall be kept as it began."[116] Teresa's "first Rule" was in reality the mitigated Rule of 1247: "We observe the Rule of Our Lady of Carmel, and we keep it without mitigation, in the form drawn up by Fray Hugo, Cardinal of Santa Sabina, and given in the year 1248 [*sic*], in the fifth year of the pontificate of Pope Innocent IV."[117] The Rule mitigated by Innocent IV in 1247 was textually that already observed through the Order, together with the bull of mitigation of Eugene IV of 1432.

The confusion was by no means limited to the mind of St. Teresa; ignorance of the genesis and development of early Carmelite legislation was general at the time. Still there was a special reason why St. Teresa persisted in calling the mitigated Rule of 1247 "without mitigation." The Spanish translation of the Rule actually used by St. Teresa as the basis of her reform, as well as by Mary de Yepes at her monastery of La Imagen in Alcalá, is a free translation of the bull of mitigation of Innocent IV (1247) which contains the test of the Rule as mitigated. The translation is carelessly made by one not very familiar with Latin. Most serious of all, the Rule as mitigated by Innocent is declared to be "without such a mitigation." This untrust worthy text is the source of Teresa's mistaken conviction that in fact she was following the original Rule of the Order. Teresa is not to be blamed for accepting it uncritically; not so the many historians since her time.[118]

In any case Teresa's concern was to restore the life of prayer in solitude which was the essence of the life on Mount Carmel. "This will always be the aim of our nuns – to be alone with Him only." Thus does she sum up the story of the foundation of St. Joseph's.[119] She taught the sisters at St. Joseph's: "The whole style of life which we profess to live is not only to be nuns but to be solitaries."[120] Again in the *Interior Castle* she tells them: "All of us who wear this sacred habit of Carmel are called to prayer and contemplation – because that was the first principle of our Order and because we are descended from the line of those holy Fathers of ours from Mount Carmel who sought this treasure, this precious pearl of which we speak (contemplation), in such great solitude and with such contempt for the world."[121]

Teresa's new foundation was meant to present "a picture, however imperfect, of our Order as it had been in its early days."[122] Yet the tiny monastery of St. Joseph's in Avila – in reality a re-converted private house – was no hermitage. The sisters lived in a close relationship from which all distinctions of class and rank were eliminated. (Teresa devotes a sprightly chapter of the *Way of Perfection* to "the importance for those who are daughters of God of not making much of their linage.")[123] In St. Joseph's there were no lay sisters, though Teresa admitted them in her later foundations. All sisters, including the prioress, shared in the housework. If Teresa limited her communities to thirteen sisters to avoid financial difficulties and consequent relaxation of poverty and the common life resulting from large numbers, this limitation also had the effect of creating an intimate family atmosphere. A happy innovation that contributed effectively to a close community spirit was the recreation period.

Into this closely-knit community Teresa paradoxically infused the spirit of prayer in solitude proper to the eremitical life. Strict enclosure was imposed. Visitors to St. Joseph's should have a good reason for coming, not just to waste time. During visits the sisters kept their faces veiled. A high wall enclosed the environs, and cells or hermitages were constructed in the garden. The sisters kept to their rooms as much as possible. Prayer other than liturgical, spiritual reading and work was carried out in solitude. If Teresa's ideal of absolute poverty, in common as well as individually, had a Franciscan inspiration, she was delighted to discover through Mary of Jesus the eremitical and Carmelite aspect of this condition. Another characteristic of Teresa's foundation fitted the eremitical pattern: austerity. The sisters wore woolen habits and sandals, their rooms contained only the poorest and barest necessities. Total abstinence from meat, an ancient monastic tradition, was observed.[124]

In her work of founding reformed Carmelite monasteries Teresa did not lay claim to originality: "I am not asking anything new of you, my daughters – only that we should hold to our profession."[125] She may be said to have realized her goal of restoring the observance of the Rule of 1247 – the eremitico-cenobitical life. (If necessary, she was even ready to forego her requirements of community poverty and abstinence – in short, in the latter case to accept the "Bull of mitigation.")[126] Her originality lies in the formula she devised for making this way of life viable in the post-medieval world.

The Teresian way of life gradually took shape during the first years in St. Joseph's. Authorization to make statutes and ordinances was included in the rescript of February 7, 1562, though only in view of one monastery. At the time of Rossi's visit in 1567, Teresa was able to present him with constitutions for his approval. These first constitutions no longer exist; those known today as hers date from a later period when several foundations had been made.[127] They comprise fifteen short chapters (also divided into sixteen) concerning things spiritual, things temporal, fasts, cloister, reception of novices, common life, care of the sick, remembrance of the dead, community officials. The last six chapters, concerning the chapter of faults and punishment of misconduct, are taken from the constitutions of the Incarnation.

To promote her work Teresa wrote her classic books. Without pretension she lavished the treasures of her mystical experience and religious genius on the handful of "poor orphans" she had collected in her little monastery. Hardly had she completed her "big book," her autobiography which is really an account of her spiritual state and contains much material on the mystical life, than at the insistence of Dominic Bañez she began her "little book," the *Way of Perfection*, in which she undertakes to set down for her sisters "certain things about prayer" (ca. 1565).[128] *The Interior Castle* (1577), the product of her mature years, completes St. Teresa's incomparable trilogy.

Teresa's gaze lifted beyond the horizon of the Carmelite Order; her reform had an apostolic and ecclesial dimension. She who liked to call herself "a daughter of the church" understood the power of the witness of religious in the church. She realized that the answer to the challenge of Protestantism, more than the maneuverings of diplomats or recourse to arms, lay in renewed Catholic life and, as far as she was concerned, in conscientious adherence to the ideal of the Order. Her vision of hell quickened her zeal for souls, her concern for heretics. The growth of Protestantism in turn influenced her efforts to renew Carmel.

"About this time," she writes in the *Way of Perfection* concerning the foundation of St. Joseph's, "there came to my notice the harm and havoc that were being wrought in France by these Lutherans and the way in which their unhappy sect was increasing. This troubled me very much, and, as though I could do anything, or be of any help in the matter, I wept before the Lord and entreated Him to remedy this great evil. I felt that I would have laid down a thousand lives to save a single one of all the souls that were being lost there. And, seeing that I was a woman, and a sinner, and incapable of doing all I should like in the Lord's service, and as my whole yearning was, and still is, that, as He has so many enemies and so few friends, these last should be trusty ones, I determined to do the little that was in me – namely to follow the evangelical counsels as perfectly as I could, and to see that these few nuns who are here should do the same."[129] "No human strength," she goes on to say, "will suffice to quench the fire kindled by these heretics (though attempts have been made to organize opposition to them, as though such a great and rapidly spreading evil could be remedied by force of arms.)"[130]

The apostolic dimension of Carmel caused no problem to cloistered nuns, but Teresa's friars would eventually be faced with the question of the compatibility of prayer and activity. Teresa had restored the pristine spirit of Carmel, but the world to which she restored it was not the same. The 16th century which in the Jesuits saw the rise of religious orders with an active purpose had lost the medieval sense of religious life as a contemplative state that was at ease with the service and salvation of the neighbor. In the new age a dichtomy arose between contemplation and action. Orders came to be divided into "contemplative" and "active," and for those that purported to be contemplative pastoral work presented a problem of conscience.

Launching the Reform

When the prior general of the Order appeared in Avila, Teresa was understandably uneasy. "I was afraid of two things," she candidly admits, "first that the General might be angry with me... secondly, that he might make me go back to the Convent of the Incarnation."[131] Nevertheless it was she who took the first step toward an understanding. "I arranged for him to come to Saint Joseph's and the Bishop was pleased that he should be shown all the respect which was paid to his own person. I told him my story quite truthfully and simply, for, whatever the consequences, I am always inclined to deal in that way with prelates, as they are in the place of God, and also with confessors, for otherwise I should not think my soul was safe. And so I told him about my soul, and about almost the whole of my life, wicked as it has been."[132]

Teresa's fears proved to be groundless. "The General is such a servant of His (the Lord's), and so discreet and learned, that he regarded the work as good, and, for the rest, showed me not the least displeasure ... He comforted me greatly and assured me that he would not order me to leave."[133] The juridical gist of Rossi's conversations with Teresa is not clear. According to Julian de Avila, Rossi challenged the bishop's jurisdiction over St. Joseph's on the grounds that he, Rossi, had not been consulted.[134] However, there is no record of such a challenge, and St. Joseph's remained under the bishop until August 2, 1577.[135]

Apparently all the prior general did was to point out to Teresa that although St. Joseph's was subject to the bishop of Avila, she did not on this account cease to be a Carmelite. First of all, he straightened out the matter of the nuns' profession; after his visit they began to make profession in his name, not that of the bishop.[136] Secondly, he immediately grasped the significance for the Order of what was going on at St. Joseph's. He took Teresa's work under his immediate jurisdiction and made plans for its propagation. In other words, as a result of Rossi's initiative what might be called the "observance of Avila" became the Teresian Reform.

Teresa writes: "Being willing, as he was, that we should continue what we had begun, he gave me complete patents for the foundation of more houses, and also added censures, so that no Provincial should be able to stop me. I did not ask for these, but he realized from my manner of prayer that I had fervent desires to help souls come nearer to God."[137] The saint is referring to Rossi's letters patent of April 27, 1567, by which he authorized her to found an unspecified number of monasteries of the Order in Castile. The nuns, whose number in each monastery is not to exceed twenty-five, are to follow the "first Rule" and wear habits of grey *xerga*. The monasteries are to be under the immediate jurisdiction of the prior general and immune from interference by provincials. For each monastery to be founded two nuns from the Incarnation might volunteer.[138] Later Rossi wrote, urging her to found as many monasteries as she had hairs on her head.[139]

New motivation for extending her reform had been given Teresa only a few months before, by the visit, late in 1566, of Fray Alonso Maldonado, Franciscan missionary from Peru. His eloquent account "about the many millions of souls perishing there for lack of teaching" deeply moved Teresa. "I went to one of the hermitages, weeping sorely, and called on Our Lord, beseeching him to find me a means of gaining some soul for his service when so many were being carried away by the devil." Later Christ said to her, "Wait a little, daughter, and thou shalt see great things."[140] These words which puzzled her at the time became clear at the general's visit. "When I found how desirous our most reverend General was that more religious houses should be founded, I thought I saw them already built. Remembering the words which Our Lord had addressed to me, I now began to foresee a start being made with things I had not previously been able to envisage at all."[141] Without the prior general's patronage and leadership Teresa's dream of reviving the Order's primitive way of life might have remained confined within the crenellated walls of the city of the cavaliers.

The Teresian Friars

If Teresa was to extend her reform, she would need friars to direct her nuns. The friars of the province might not understand her ideals and be too free with dispensations. Even Julian de Avila, confessor of St. Joseph's, to whom "the Lord had given ... the same desires as He had given me," let her down. In 1581 she wrote to Jerome Gracián: "The things the nuns at St. Joseph's, Avila, say they would like done are of such a kind that they would do away with any difference between them and the nuns of the Incarnation. I am shocked at what the devil is doing, and nearly all the blame lies with the confessor, good though he is: he has always been wanting them all to eat meat and that was one of the things they asked for. Just think what a time they would have!"[142]

According to St. Teresa the bishop of Avila, Don Alonso de Mendoza, first approached the general for "a license for the foundation in his diocese of a few monasteries for Discalced friars of the primitive Rule." Rossi would willingly have obliged him, "but he found that there was opposition in the Order," and rather than "set the province at variance, he refrained for the time being."[143] But Teresa's request pursued the prior general after he had departed from Avila. "After some days, I began to think how necessary it was, if convents of women were to be founded, that there should be friars following the same Rule, and, seeing how few there were in this province – it seemed to me that they were dying out – I commended the matter earnestly to Our Lord, and wrote a letter to our Father General, begging him as well as I could to grant this permission." Not the least cogent reason adduced by Teresa was the great "service it would be to Our Lady to whom he was most devoted. It must have been she who brought it about."[144] Rossi could not refuse his daughter when she appealed to his love of the Virgin.

Rossi's patent is dated from Barcelona, August 10, 1567. Desirous that all friars and nuns of the Order be as "mirrors, lamps, burning torches, and shining stars to light and guide wayfarers in this world and should speak with God in prayer and unite themselves to him in meditation," the prior general acceded to the request to found "some houses of friars of our Order in which Mass will be said, divine office recited and chanted, prayers, meditations and other spiritual exercises engaged in, so that they be called and actually be houses or monasteries of contemplative Carmelites; the latter should also help their neighbor when occasion arises." They are to observe "the old constitutions" (Soreth's, revised by Audet and Rossi himself) and be subject to the provincial, and Fray Angel de Salazar, prior of Avila, and are to receive two houses "of our profession, our obedience and our habit, in the form which will be specified and declared in our acts." The letters reflect a solemn appeal for unity, "for it is not our intention to give occasion to hellish quarrels, but to promote the perfection of Carmelite religious life." The contemplative Carmelites are "to live perpetually united to the obedience of the province of Castile, and if at any time any friar under pretext of living in greater perfection should seek to separate himself from the province by the favor of princes and with briefs and other concessions of Rome, we pronounce and declare them men moved and tempted by the evil spirit, authors of seditions, quarrels, contentions and ambitions to the deceit and loss of their souls."

At a time when Rome was not overly particular in granting dispensations, religious superiors vainly sought to discourage appeal to the curia by such fulminations. It has been observed that this prohibition of Rossi was invalid, since subjects cannot be forbidden higher appeal. On the other hand, it should be remembered that Rossi at the time was an apostolic commissary and as such employed a formula used by the Holy See in its own documents. The early Discalced historian, Francis of St. Mary, omitted the clause forbidding separation from the order, thereby occasioning considerable confusion in later historical accounts, not to mention serious doubts about his scientific integrity.[145]

Plainly Rossi was captivated by his vivacious daughter and did everything in his power to smooth her way. Teresa on her part conceived for him a deep regard and warm affection that survived the storms of later misunderstandings. "He showed me very real and genuine kindness: whenever he could be free he would come here to talk of spiritual things, and, as he was one to whom the Lord must have granted great favors, it made us very happy to hear him on this subject." It was with a sense of loss that St. Teresa bade him goodbye on his last visit. "I was very sorry when I saw our Father General returning to Rome; I had conceived a great love for him and felt very much deserted when he left."¹⁴⁶

Chapter II

THE DISCALCED REFORM

Caspar Nieto and John de Mora, the chief trouble-makers in the Andalusian province, failed to appear in Avila by mid-April 1567 to account for their rebelliousness, as ordered by the prior general. Instead, the latter found himself early in May called on the carpet at Madrid. Nieto and Mora had gone to the court to lodge a complaint against him and his visitation of the province and had been received by the king. It was the "recourse to force," the appeal to the royal council against ecclesiastical authorities. The charges are not known today, but they can easily be imagined from the complaints the malcontents had been voicing since the chapter of Seville: there had been no freedom of election at the chapter, the prior general had limited the choice for provincial, he had been bribed, etc.

The Andalusian friars were supported by the Duke of Feria, Don Gomez Suarez de Figueroa, likewise Lord of Zafra, birthplace of the Nieto brothers. Rossi found himself in the humiliating position of having to account for his visitation to the royal council, presided over by Cardinal Diego de Espinosa. Dr. Morilla, auditor of the royal council who examined the acts of the Seville chapter, could find nothing not worthy of praise, with the exception of certain decrees concerning the novitiate. When these were explained, he was satisfied.[1]

Next the royal council wanted to examine Rossi's credentials as visitator. Once the ministers got possession of the *motu proprio*, which the general needed to continue his visitation, they delayed returning it – the usual gambit in these cases. The general had to appeal to the nuncio, John Baptist Castagna, before he could regain the document. In spite of the fact that the accusations of Nieto and Mora had proved groundless, the council ordered Rossi to absolve them from their censures and provide them with commendatory letters by which they might return to their convents rehabilitated. The Italian general courageously replied that the two friars had not been excommunicated for appealing to the king, but for other reasons, and refused to give them patents or rehabilitate them. The royal council then on its own authority sent the friars back to their province; their censures remained. When the news got back to Andalusia, ninety friars under Vincent de la Trinidad, vicar provincial (John de la Quadra did not return to the province until mid-May), wrote to Rossi, deploring the action of Nieto and Mora and asking that they be banned from the province. Rossi was not disposed to let the matter drop. By letter of May 21, 1567, he ordered an official investigation into the accusations brought against Nieto and Mora, to be sent to the procurator of the Order at the court, Mariano di Leone, no doubt with a view to prosecuting the case after his departure.[2]

On the other hand, about this time, on May 18, when Balthasar appeared in Madrid and manifested signs of penitence, Rossi absolved him from his penance of confinement and agreed to restore his active and passive voice, if he would leave the province and live in Valderas in the province of Castile.[3]

The brief, *Superioribus mensibus*, of April 16, 1567, which entrusted the visitation and reform of the Carmelites to the bishops, had not yet reached Madrid, but its imminent arrival was awaited. Rossi, convinced that this step too was the result of the machinations of the rebel Andalusian friars, requested an audience with the king to register his protest. The Prudent King denied all knowledge of the affair. He declared himself satisfied with the general's efforts and urged him to continue in the same way in the province of Aragon. In token of his pleasure Philip ordered for the Carmelite general a banquet fit for a king, served by his own staff under his majordomo, Bartholomew Santoya.

All Rossi could do is continue his visitation and prepare as best he could for the "reform of the king."[4]

The Visitation of Aragon and Catalonia

Rossi visited few houses in these provinces.

On June 7, 1567, the Aragonese chapter opened at Valencia. Four reformers of the province were elected: Master Michael Carranza; Fray Michael Guarda, prior of Zaragoza; Fray Jerome Jordán, prior of Valencia; Master Nicholas Escrivá. The provincial, John Nadal, had his term prolonged to consolidate the reform. The chapter members promised to extirpate from the province not only the name but all customs and practices of conventuality, "especially after having heard from the Most Reverend Father of the Order that the Carmelite Order has never admitted conventuality, as he demonstrated in effect from the Rule and constitutions, although occasionally, due to evil times and negligence and lack of care on the part of superiors, the ways of some became lax."[5]

Of the observance of "the first Rule" which Rossi had authorized James Montañés to inaugurate at Onda no word is spoken, so it had failed to materialize. On the other hand Montañés submitted to the prior general a report "on that which in this house and province remained to be remedied," but its vague and rhetorical style was of little help to the visitator or us in forming an idea of the state of the province. "Every day there is obstinacy, contention, presumption, little obedience, no perseverance and chastity by

Chapter Two: The Discalced Reform

which God is appeased, little silence, much murmuring, lying, perjury, cursing, envy, anger, little humility, little patience and prudence, little punishment and much dissimulation, friends of money and contempt of poverty, little prayer and reading, much curiosity and pride and much care both in dress and conceit as well as in many other things it would take too long to recount... What is this great blindness of us poor friars when we neither realize nor try to consider that we do not properly lead either the active or contemplative life?. . . What about the delightful contemplative life which is ours in the Carmelite Order after having left the laborious, dangerous and restless life of the world? What about the holy and spiritual life that is ours by our profession and cloister after having left the liberty and carnality of the world?"[6]

Montañés' tortured cries demonstrate the desire for the perfect life that was abroad among the Spanish Carmelites, if also the lack on Montañés part of the practical ability to realize his dreams. Perhaps it was well that the holy Aragonese friar failed to introduce the "first Rule" into Onda, for this would have separated the house from the province. Onda continued to enjoy a reputation for observance and produced such members as Jerónimo Casset and Juan Sanz (1557-1608).

The chapter of Valencia also published *Instituta* (Valencia, Juan May, 1567), for the most part identical with the decrees of Seville. The booklet opens with chapter twenty two of the 25th session of the Council of Trent concerning the reform of religious, an obvious reminder of the fact that the council entrusts the reform of religious to their own superiors. Not yet aware of the contents of the brief *Superioribus mensibus*, Rossi could only point out that he had visited and reformed his Spanish provinces, removing all forms of conventuality and reducing all to observance, and that consequently his religious could not be visitated again by another, unless the pope decreed otherwise. In such a case the faculties the pope conferred were not to be presumed contrary to the council and should be examined carefully. Thus, though he must have been aware of the inadequacy of these preparations, Rossi expressed his disapproval of the interference of the bishops in the reform of the Order. Such dual authority could only bring confusion and enable disobedient religious a chance to play off one superior against another.[7]

The chapter of the Catalonian province opened on August 3. John Montaner was elected provincial. Together with the provincial, Jerome Tostado, prior of Barcelona, was named reformer general of the province. Here too decrees of reform were published, though no copy has survived, and conventuality was renounced.[8]

On September 8 Rossi left Barcelona to return to Italy. His departing footsteps were dogged by his nemeses in Andalusia. The provincial, John de la Quadra, had discovered that Caspar Nieto and John de Mora were hatching a new plot against the general: "by their lies and misdeeds to bring it about that the king would command that your Most Reverend Paternity would not be obeyed in anything you write." The provincial imprisoned Balthasar and John de Mora in Utrera. Melchior, now a Third Order Franciscan, made another dramatic appearance on the scene and stabbed one of two friars charged with the task of transferring the two prisoners to Seville. De la Quadra could not lay hands on Caspar who was staying with the Count of Comares, the son of the Duke of Feria. On August 20, following the provincial's suggestion, Rossi expelled Caspar and Balthasar Nieto and John de Mora from the Order, "as incorrigible and putrid members," and obliged them to enter another order. Caspar did not delay in appealing to the king's council with the support of influential friends. Not only was the general's decree of expulsion not implemented, but the king ordered the provincial to release the two prisoners. The visitators of Seville, those created in virtue of *Superioribus mensibus*, absolved the three rebels from excommunication and even made John de Mora vicar provincial.[9]

This happened when Rossi was already back in Italy. His feelings on leaving Spain must have been mixed. His efforts at pacifying Andalusia had failed completely; moreover the recalcitrant Andalusians had discredited him in Madrid and given the king's council an excuse to interfere in the affairs of the Order. Over the Spanish provinces hung the threat of the king's reform under the jurisdiction of the bishops. On the other hand, Rossi had everywhere inspired the brethren to renewed dedication to their vocation and in his person had re-established lines of communication between Spain and Rome. Most consoling of all was the renascence of Carmelite life in the little house of St. Joseph under Mother Teresa of Jesus. "I give infinite thanks to the divine Majesty," Rossi later wrote, "for the great favor bestowed on this Order by the diligence and goodness of our Reverend Mother Teresa of Jesus. She profits the Order more than all the Carmelite friars in Spain."[10] He had at once properly evaluated the significance of Teresa's vision and had made sure, or so he thought, that this vital force would from the very outset be injected into the body of the Order and renew its members.

The King's Reform

Meanwhile preparations for the king's reform went forward with utmost secrecy. A memorandum dated August 30, 1567, outlined the procedure to be followed by the bishops who received their faculties early in September. They were not to change the habit, Rule or constitutions of the three orders concerned, but only eliminate abuses. To each Carmelite, Trinitarian and Mercedarian convent in his diocese the local bishop was to assign his vicar or other suitable ecclesiastic. Likewise for each house the Dominican provincial was to supply two of his friars. The visitators were to be accompanied by the secular arm to which they could appeal in case of resistance. The friars and nuns could not allege that they had already been reformed: this was a new reform decreed by the pope. On October fifth the visitation was to begin simultaneously in all convents and monasteries of the realm. Since property was the worst abuse, the visitators were to pounce on the guilty ones before they could hide or otherwise dispose of their ill-gotten goods.[11]

Philip was to learn that all the king's horses and all the king's men couldn't put religious life together again. His reform, which lasted from 1567 to 1569, brought no measurable improvement to the orders concerned. Visitators unfamiliar with the ideals, customs and obligations of a religious order were unsuitable for reforming it. The situation was worsened by the fact that Philip decided to dispense with the services of the Dominicans, so that the visitation was carried out exclusively by diocesan clergy and laymen.[12]

In a report to the Holy See Rossi gives an account of his visitation of Spain and that of the king, and asks that the latter be revoked. He lists some of the complaints that reached his ears. In Toledo the secular arm broke down the doors of the cells. In other places the friars who protested and appealed to the Holy See were imprisoned. In Antequera the nuns were withdrawn from the jurisdiction of the Order, and the friars who spoke out were put in prison. "The bishop there," Rossi observes, "has long been feuding with the friars and now he has the chance to satisfy his soul." In Lérida the bishop made the friars sell the mules they needed to cultivate their fields. Some Catalonian bishops charged the convents twenty or twenty-five *scudi* for the visitation. Superiors were made subjects, subjects were protected from superiors. "In great and abominable" legal proceedings the friars were driven to say "most horrible things" about each other.[13]

The protocol of the visitation of Valderas (Castile), on September 30, 1567, by the Licentiate Guerra, vicar general of the bishop of Leon, has been preserved. The observance in this convent, founded only a year and a half ago, is found to be "perfect."[14]

In Andalusia, the visitation of Ecija and Carmona was carried out by Don Hernan Ramírez, dean of Seville, assisted by Don Lope Ponce de León. The provincial, John de la Quadra, was turned out of doors and ordered to appear before the authorities. Lawrence de Ripera, removed from office by the provincial chapter of 1566, was reinstated as prior of Carmona. John de la Mora, expelled from the order by the prior general, was made vicar provincial. Obviously the Nieto party was again in the driver's seat. According to the provincial, Ripera and Caspar Nieto had the ear of the visitators and through them were ruling the province.[15] The visitators of Seville had absolved from excommunication Caspar and Balthasar Nieto and John de Mora; Rossi claimed this excommunication, imposed for hindering superiors from correcting and for opposing reform, was reserved by Callixtus III to the Holy See.[16]

Rossi moved to counteract these measures of the king's reformers. In a letter of June 2, 1569, he forbade the celebration of a chapter in Andalusia; after his triennium John de la Quadra was to continue as provincial without a new election. The prior general took the occasion to review his action in the province and to renew the sanctions against offenders. No less than king and pope he desired that all lead a reformed life according to the constitutions. If he had condoned deeds that deserved punishment at the Seville chapter of 1566, it was so that offenders might be encouraged to repent. Instead, "prevaricators" in the province had made themselves guilty of offenses to which the constitutions assigned well-defined punishments: they had rendered themselves liable to the excommunication imposed by Callixtus III on those who hinder superiors from correcting the insolent and who obstruct reform; they had become liable to exclusion from all legitimate acts in the order and privation of the use of theft goods by appealing from correction; by conspiring to defend each other, they had incurred another excommunication *ipso facto*, to which censure perpetual imprisonment accrued, if divisions or parties resulted. Rossi went on to deprive of office and grades any officials of the province guilty of the above offenses; if they remained pertinacious after receipt of his patents, they would fall again under excommunication.[17]

The Visitation by Dominicans

On July 14, 1569, the nuncio, John Baptist Castagna, reported to the pope's nephew and secretary, Michael Bonelli, cardinal "Alessandrino," that he had in hand the reports of the visitations of the Carmelites, Trinitarians and Mercedarians, though some were not original.[18] At this point however Pius decided to remove the visitation from the hands of the bishops and entrust it to the Observant Dominicans. Perhaps the laments of the superiors general finally had their effect, or the Dominican pope resolved to terminate an arrangement he never really liked. On January 31, 1570, he formally revoked the brief *Superioribus mensibus*.[19]

Meanwhile Dominican visitators were assigned to the Carmelites: Peter Fernández for Castile, Francis Vargas for Andalusia and Michael Hebrera for Aragon and Catalonia. Fernández' faculties, dated August 20, 1569, and valid for four years, enable him to take charge of the reports of the episcopal visitation and implement their directives. The Dominican may re-visitate houses if necessary. Further he has the power to punish superiors (vicars general, provincials, and priors) and any other religious found guilty of misdemeanors. He is to reduce the term of office of superiors to three years, may appoint superiors even outside the chapters, convene and preside at provincial chapters, depose superiors without process, make statutes, regulations, and ordinances and change existing ones. He should increase the size of communities and suppress houses unable to support twelve members and unite such houses and their perquisites to other houses. Further, he may move religious from house to house and province to province, assist superiors in their offices or depute others from the Dominican and Carmelite Orders for this task. Such deputies may live in Carmelite convents. Fernández may visit, correct and reform Carmelite convents and command, correct and punish superiors and their subjects. He may perform all acts necessary for the visitation, correction and reform of head and members of all houses of friars and nuns; if such acts require greater faculties than are herein expressly stated, these are granted. Finally he may take other Dominicans or Carmelites as his associates or subdelegate his powers to them.[20]

The same faculties were extended to Vargas and Hebrera.[21]

On November 1, 1569, "since much may happen beyond the commission of the pope," Rossi appointed 20 commissaries to defend the rights of the Order in Spain, instructing them how to conduct themselves in the new visitation. The prior general bows to the supreme authority of the Holy See and praises the zeal of the king whom Carmelites profess to obey and pray for. At the same time Rossi ventures the opinion that the king's purposes would have been better served by reformers chosen from the Order itself. He instructs his commissaries first to ask for a copy of the apostolic brief of the visitators. If the visitators wish to make constitutions already found in the legislation of the Order, they are to be shown these laws, "lest it appear to anyone that our Carmelite Order has so far existed without institutions and a Rule." The commissaries should allow no directives contrary to the Order's legislation for reform or permit the privileges granted to the Order by the Holy See to be infringed. Those under censure of the prior general are not to be absolved. The Order is to be judged according to the mitigated Rule and the old constitutions (Soreth's, revised by Audet and Rossi himself). If the apostolic letters of the visitators contain very wide powers to make changes beyond the matter of reform, the commissaries are to accept them in respectful silence.[22]

Obviously Rossi does not consider that their faculties for reform give the visitators a *carte blanche* to do as they please, or that his own faculties as apostolic visitator and the rights of the Order bestowed by the Holy See have ceased to exist. Much of the controversy to follow was due to the interpretation the authorities in question put on the powers conceded them by the Holy See.

The *Book of Foundations*

Rossi was still in Spain when Teresa bestirred herself to carry out his wish that she found more houses in the pattern of St. Joseph's in Avila. In the spring of 1567 she was 52 years old and in poor health. She had written the story of her life; nothing seemed to remain for her but to spend the remainder of her days in the happy seclusion of the contemplative monastery she had founded with such pains. Yet she was about to begin a new book, the book of her foundations, the book of the *"monja andariega*— the wandering nun," as the papal nuncio Philip Sega was to call her. The rest of her life was spent in ceaseless journeying up and down Spain, spreading and confirming her reform.

"Here was a poor Discalced nun, without help from anywhere, except from the Lord, loaded down with patents and good wishes but devoid of all possibility of making them effective."[23] In these straits Teresa turned to her old friends, the Jesuits, specifically to her former confessor, Balthasar Alvarez, now rector in Medina del Campo, a prosperous trade center some 50 miles northwest of Avila. Alvarez helped to obtain consent for a foundation in poverty from the town magistrates and the bishop. Fray Antonio de Heredia, prior of the Carmelite convent of St. Anne at Medina, acquired a house that could eventually be bought. Teresa took with her for the new foundation two nuns from St. Joseph's, her niece, Mary Baptist, and Anna of the Angels, and four from the Incarnation, all cousins: Agnes of Jesus, Anne of the Incarnation, Isabelle of the Cross, and Teresa del Pilar. The house on arrival proved to be in a very dilapidated condition, but the next morning, the feast of the Assumption, 1567, after a few makeshift arrangements Mass was offered for the first time, the nuns assisting through the chinks in the door opposite the altar.[24]

Teresa kept the prior general informed of everything. "The Reverend Mother Teresa of Jesus has written us about the whole affair," Rossi wrote to the sisters at Medina on January 8, 1569, "the great honor in which you are held in that city and its great satisfaction at your presence. I give infinite thanks to the divine Majesty for the great favor bestowed on this order by the diligence and goodness of our Reverend Mother Teresa of Jesus. She profits the order more than all the Carmelite friars of Spain. God grant her many years of life. I admonish all to obey the above mentioned Teresa as a true superior and a jewel to be much valued as precious and a friend of God."[25]

The prior general showed the same interest and satisfaction with regard to Teresa's later foundations. "He wrote to me about every house that we founded, saying it gave him the keenest pleasure that the foundations in question were being made. Really the greatest relief I had in all my trials was to see what joy this gave him, for I felt that in affording it to him I was serving Our Lord, as he was my superior, and, quite apart from this, I have a great love for him."[26]

On May 15, 1569, Rossi appointed the provincial of Castile, Fray Alonso Gonzalez, his commissary for the nuns professing the first Rule.[27] Gonzalez was given this commission independently of his office as provincial and he was to exercise it "not according to your own will, nor according to the mitigated Rule, but, as stated, according to the injunctions of the first Rule and our constitutions insofar as they are not contrary to the aforesaid Rule."

On April 6, 1571, the prior general renewed his faculties to Teresa of April 27, 1567, this time without any limit of place in which she might found houses.[28]

Rossi called Teresa "our vicegerent for founding monasteries of nuns."[29] Teresa testifies: "I have all possible freedom, from both the General and the Provincial, to receive postulants, to move nuns from one house to another, and to help any one house from the funds of others."[30] She insists that "these foundations were made, not only with a license from our most reverend Father General but under an express command subsequently given."[31] In 1575 she laments, "Again and again, I have reflected how much better it would be if I stayed quietly where I am and had no command from the general."[32]

Teresa, laboring up to the end of her life, founded Discalced nunneries in Avila (1562), Medina del Campo (1567), Malagón (1568), Valladolid (1568), Toledo (1569), Pastrana (1569), Salamanca (1570), Alba de Tormes (1571), Segovia (1574), Beas (1575), Seville (1575), Caravaca (1576), Villanueva de la Jara (1580), Palencia (1580), Soria (1581), Granada (1582), Burgos (1582).[33]

Among the novelties of Teresa's foundations were their homogeneity, coherence and drive to multiply. With the clearly defined ideals formulated by their saintly and dynamic foundress and their close spirit of cooperation, spiritual and material, they contrasted with the monasteries of the old Order, each of which grew out of local circumstances, possessed its own customs and ordinances and showed little inclination to expand. The closest administrative parallel to the Teresian nunneries were those of the Mantuan Congregation.

The Discalced Friars: Duruelo

In his letter of January 8, 1569, to the sisters of Medina del Campo Rossi wrote, "I would like to hear that the two convents of contemplative Carmelites to serve your houses and our sisters in spiritual matters have been founded."[34] As a matter of fact one was already in existence.

With her second foundation a reality, Teresa began to give serious thought to acquiring some contemplative friars. She mentioned her problem to the prior of Medina, Fray Anthony de Heredia, who offered to be the first to join her reform. She thought he was joking, but he told her that he had made up his mind to become a Carthusian. Teresa did not think he had "sufficient spirituality." They agreed that he should undergo a year of trial.

Shortly afterwards St. Teresa was introduced to a young Carmelite studying at Salamanca, Fray John of St. Matthias. About him Teresa had no doubts:

"I liked him very much; he told me that he too was preparing to go to the Carthusians. I described to him what I had in view and begged him earnestly to wait until the Lord gave us a monastery, pointing out what a great blessing it would be, if he were destined for a higher life, that he should lead it within his own Order, and how much better service he would thus render to the Lord. He gave me his word to do this provided there were no long delay." Teresa concludes, "When I saw that I had two friars to make a beginning with, the thing seemed to me settled, although I was still not quite satisfied with the Prior."[35]

John de Yepes was born at Fontiveros, June 24, 1542.[36] His father, Gonzalo de Yepes, came of a noble family, but he had been disowned when he married a girl beneath his rank, Catalina Alvarez. Gonzalo took up his wife's trade of weaving, but died soon after John's birth, after which Catalina was obliged to support her three sons by her own labor. In 1551 Catalina moved to Medina del Campo, a large town with better chances for finding work. There in 1563 John entered the Carmelite convent of St. Anne, taking the name John of St. Matthias. The following year he was sent to the Carmelite *studium* at Salamanca and from 1564 to 1568 attended the famous university, then experiencing a period of flourishing activity. After Rossi's visit to the college in 1567 John was ordained a priest.[37]

In June of 1568, when St. Teresa was back at St. Joseph's in Avila, a gentleman of that town, Don Rafael Mejia, offered her a small house he owned in Duruelo, a hamlet on the road to Medina del Campo. His bailiff used it to store the grain he collected as rent. In June she stopped to look at it on her way to make a foundation in Valladolid. "It had a fair-sized porch, a room divided into two, with a loft above it, and a little kitchen: that is all there was of the building which was to be our monastery." Proceeding to Medina, she sought the opinion of Fray Anthony who said that "he would be willing to live, not only there, but in a pigsty." Fray John also approved of accepting the house. Fray Anthony was given the job of collecting furnishings, while Teresa took John with her to Valladolid, to tell him "all about our way of life, so that he might have an exact knowledge of everything, both of the mortification we practise and of the sisterly way in which we live and the recreation we take in common. All this is characterized by such a moderation that it serves to bring out the sisters' faults, and gives us a little relief from the austerity of the Rule." The provincial, Alonso Gonzalez, "an old man, very well disposed and quite devoid of guile," also happened to be in Valladolid at this time. From him and from Fray Angel de Salazar Teresa obtained permission for a foundation at Duruelo.[38]

On November 28, 1568, the first convent of contemplative friars was formally opened. The provincial offered Mass and received the profession according to the Rule of 1247 of Anthony of Jesus (Heredia), John of the Cross, and Joseph of Christ, a deacon and member of the convent of Medina. From the provincial too the friars received the Discalced habit of rough undyed wool and discarded their shoes.[39] Thus Teresa, in spite of her misgivings about the province of Castile, ended by finding there the friars to initiate her ideal of Carmelite life.

St. Teresa, passing through in March, 1569, has left an unforgettable description of life in the "little Bethlehem" of Duruelo. "I arrived in the morning: Fray Antonio de Jesus was sweeping out the church porch with that happy expression which never leaves him. 'How is this, Father?' I said to him. 'Whatever has become of your dignity?' And he answered. . . 'I curse the time when I had any.' Then I went into the little church and was amazed to see what spirituality the Lord had inspired there. . . There were so many crosses about and so many skulls. . . The choir was in the loft, the centre of which was quite high, so that they could say the Hours, but they had to stoop very low in order to enter far enough to hear Mass. They had turned the two corners next to the church into two little hermitages; as the place was very cold these were filled with hay, and they could only sit or lie in them, for the roof almost came down on their heads. The hermitages had two little windows overlooking the altar, and two stones for pillows, and above these their crosses and skulls. I gather that, after finishing Matins, they did not go back to their cells until Prime, but remained here in prayer, and they would pray so earnestly that sometimes, when the hour for Prime came, their habits would be covered with snow without their having noticed it ... They used to go out and preach in many places in the district which were without instruction. . . They went out to preach, as I say, as far as a league and a half or two leagues, bare-footed (for at that time they had not the hemp sandals which they were ordered to wear later) and through all the cold and snow. When they had preached and heard confessions and had returned to their monastery for a meal it would be very late. But it was very little trouble to them, so happy were they."[40]

During a visit about this time González appointed Fray Anthony prior, Fray John sub-prior. When the first candidates presented themselves in the fall, Fray John took over as novice master.[41] In a letter of June 21, 1574, on the occasion of the founding of Almodóvar del Campo, the prior general refers to Fray Anthony of Jesus, "who was and is the director and rector of those Discalced."[42]

At Duruelo constitutions were already observed which in revised form (1576) eventually became the constitutions of the Discalced Carmelites. Adapted from the legislation already observed by the nuns, they were drawn up at Medina del Campo by Teresa, John of the Cross, and Anthony of Jesus. Anthony sent a copy of the part concerning "the division of time" to the prior general for his approval.[43]

In 1570 the community of Duruelo moved to Mancera de Abajo, a village about three miles away. The provincial and other friars of the province accompanied their barefooted brethren in solemn procession to Mancera on the feast of St. Barbara, June 11.[44]

Pastrana

Meanwhile a second convent of contemplative friars had been founded at Pastrana. Teresa was about to found a nunnery there, sponsored by the princess of Eboli, wife of Ruy Gómez de Silva, one of the most powerful men in Spain, when she was introduced to a hermit named Mariano Azaro. Azaro was born in 1510 at Bitonto in the kingdom of Naples. A fellow student of the future Gregory XIII, he was proficient in theology, canon law, mathematics and engineering. He attended the council of Trent from which he was sent on a mission to the court of Poland, serving for a while Catherine of Austria, consort of King Sigismund of Poland. He became a Knight Hospitaller of St. John and fought under Philip II against the French at the battle of Saint Quentin (1557). Philip employed him on a project to make the Guadalquivir navigable between Cordova and Seville. He decided to leave the world and entered the hermitage of El Tardón in the Sierra Morena. Prior of the hermitage was Matthew de la Fuente, a disciple of John of Avila. When the hermits were obliged to adopt an existing approved Rule, Matthew chose the Rule of St. Basil and became the reformer of the Order of St. Basil in Spain. When Teresa met him, Mariano was engaged by Philip on a canal to bring the waters of the Tagus to Aranjuez.[45]

Azaro was accompanied by John Narducci (d. 1616), a Neapolitan whom he had known in Italy and had met again at El Tardón. Narducci had studied painting under Claude Coello and under his later name in the reform, John de la Miseria is remembered for his portrait of St. Teresa who on first viewing it is said to have exclaimed, "May God forgive you, Fray John! To think that after all I have suffered at your hands, you should paint me so bleary-eyed and ugly!" But the noted Discalced writer, Bruno of Jesus, remarks, "The portrait at Seville is so maternal, with such a tenderness of supernatural love, that we should be deeply grateful to Giovanni Narducci for what is almost a masterpiece."[46]

Mariano described life at the hermitage of El Tardón: "Each hermit had his own cell and they lived separately, not saying the Divine Office, but meeting in an oratory for Mass. They had no money, nor would they receive alms; each maintained himself by the labour of his hands and each took his meals alone in conditions of extreme poverty."

"When I heard of this," Teresa continues, "it seemed to me a picture of the life of our holy fathers," and she immediately set about, as she had with John of the Cross, to win him for the order. "I showed him our Primitive

Rule and told him that in our Order he could keep all his observances with less trouble, for they were the same as our own." Ruy Gómez had offered Mariano a hermitage at Pastrana; Mariano now presented this to Teresa, and he and Narducci agreed to enter the Order there. Teresa obtained authorization for her second house of friars from Fray Alonso Gonzalez and Angel de Salazar, provincial. On July 13, 1569, Anthony of Jesus officially opened the hermitage of St. Peter.[47]

Fray Mariano was to become one of the leaders of the Discalced reform, also one of the most active agents for secession from the Order. Within the reform he favored the contemplative life and de-emphasis of the ministry. His lack of experience of Carmelite life inhibited his grasp of the problems involved.

Pastrana became the novitiate for the friars of the first Rule. The candidates who presented themselves included members of the Order. Among the latter was Balthasar Nieto, at the time a member of the community of Valderas. He took the name Balthasar of Jesus and was prior of Pastrana from 1570 to 1575, though he did not renounce the mitigation until the latter year.[48]

The admission of members of the provinces into the ranks of the contemplatives brought a reaction from the prior general. "We have heard that things have been happening which can give rise to dissent and quarrels," he states in his letter of August 8, 1570. To remedy the situation he requires the members of the provinces of Spain and Portugal to have his written permission before seeking admission to "our contemplative Carmelites, or Discalced as they are popularly called, who profess the first Rule." Members of the Portuguese and Castilian provinces (the two observant provinces of the Iberian peninsula) may join with their provincials' written consent, though the provincial of Castile should take care not to reduce his already meager personnel to the extent of jeopardizing divine cult and the obligation of Mass foundations. "Most of all we forbid to be received those members of the Andalusian province punished by us and rebellious and contumacious to our obedience, such as Master Ambrose de Castro, formerly prior of Valladolid, Friars Caspar Nieto, Melchior Nieto, John de Mora, and their accomplices, lest the whole flock of contemplatives be corrupted by them, for they have always been intent on differences and quarrels." If any of these mentioned above have already been accepted among the contemplatives, they are to be expelled at once.

In all things that do not concern the stricter life, Rossi continues, the contemplatives are to be subject to the provincial who may visitate and correct them in their own houses. He may not transfer them to houses of the province. Priors of contemplative houses and their *socii* have the right to participate in provincial chapters. Each community is not to have more than twenty members. No more contemplative houses are to be founded.[49]

In spite of this ban on further expansion a house of studies for the Discalced at the university town of Alcalá de Henares was almost immediately opened. According to one witness, Mary of St. Joseph, Rossi himself authorized the foundation at the request of the prince of Eboli, Ruy Gómez.[50] At the same time the Castilian province was engaged in founding a college at Alcalá. The project had been approved by the chapter of Avila of 1567 and by Rossi the following May 9. Francis Espinel, a Catalan from Perpignan, was its founder and rector. Certain allegations "against his life" were brought against him by Diego de Cardenas. From Barcelona on August 14, Rossi ordered a trial, the outcome of which is not known.[51] Perhaps against this troubled background is to be seen Espinel's entry among the Discalced at Pastrana, and he may have been one of the reasons for Rossi's prohibition of August 6, 1570. As Francis of the Conception, Espinel now turned over to the Discalced the house he had obtained for the province. The college was inaugurated November 1, 1570, with Balthasar of Jesus as superior.[52]

The college at Alcalá became an important center of study for the Discalced; the *Complutenses* became the philosophical counterpart of the *Salmanticenses*, the prestigious theological *summa* produced by their college at Salamanca.

Before he lost control of the movement Rossi issued six more patents for Discalced foundations, of which three were realized: Altomira (1571), La Roda (1571), Almodóvar del Campo (1574).[53]

Fernández in Castile

In the province of Castile the apostolic visitation by the Dominicans went forward without a hitch. Fernández tactfully carried out his responsibilities within the normal legislative channels of the Order.[54]

On September 23, 1571, Fernández, having completed his visitation of the province, summoned a chapter at San Pablo de la Moraleja and published "acts and ordinances. . . with the counsel and consent of the Very Reverend Father Provincial and definitors of the provincial chapter." His purpose, the apostolic commissary declares, is "not to make new laws but to call to mind and emphasize some of those which the Most Reverend General made and to put them in a form which all can read and understand, since not all know Latin." As a matter of fact Fernández' decrees only seek to reinforce existing legislation, though there are some exceptions. Fernández' decrees concern the divine office, poverty, obedience, proper conduct, novices, study, sacred orders, religious observance, silence, elections, entering nunneries, fasting. In urging compliance, the Dominican visitator opportunely recalls the origin of the order and refers to its Rule.

Fernández does not alter existing requirements regarding poverty. Superiors are not to grant general permission to have money. All moneys are to be kept in the common deposit box. Permission must be had for each expenditure.

It is fitting that the poverty of religious should be manifest in their dress, especially the brothers of Our Lady of Mount Carmel who were founded as hermits. Habits should be of rough cloth (burial), and each friar should have only one. However, since the black habit was worn in Andalusia and Aragon, Fernández does not impose the rough habit until he has conferred with the visitators of those provinces. Similarly he postponed prohibiting the use of the black instead of the white mantle until he can seek the advice of the prior general.

All general permissions for leaving the convent are revoked. "Because it is repugnant to the Rule which requires special recollection in the cell in this sacred order," the visitator recommends and commands all friars–superiors as well as subjects–to remain in their cells as much as possible. Leaving the convent should not only be limited to once a week but to many weeks, unless there is "a just and very grave cause and necessity." This restriction is more severe than the Constitutions, but reflects a good grasp of the spirit of the Rule.

So do his observations about prayer. "Because communication with God is the cause of all good," he writes, "the religious should not be content with the prayer of the divine office, but should also make mental prayer and as much as possible meditate constantly on the law of God, as the Rule enjoins: in this matter there has been no mitigation." But since there is not always leisure for this, in order to supply what may be wanting, the visitator directs that at least a fifteen minute meditation be made in common twice a day. This practice, again, is not found in the legislation of the time.

The Dominican's remark that the Rule was not mitigated in the matter of constant reflection on the law of God is worthy of note. This may be the first time this fact was officially pointed out.

Reflecting perhaps a particular condition in the province, one decree forbids two friars to live in the same room. Superiors are given six months to provide that convents have as many cells as there are friars. No one is to enter the cell of another without permission, except the cells of superiors and masters of theology. At night visits are absolutely forbidden.

Special emphasis is given to the selection and formation of novices and to studies and proper education for the ministry. Rossi had already provided for the lack of vocations in the province by establishing novitiates in the larger houses in Toledo, Avila and San Pablo. Fernández now added Salamanca and Pastrana. The need for a reform of studies is already evident in the fact that the visitator had to publish his directives in Castilian.

Priors are to be elected by conventual chapters, as Rossi decreed, and may not be immediately re-elected. In both friaries and nunneries priors and prioresses may be elected from the membership outside a particular house.

The provincial or his delegate presiding at elections should not confirm one who is unworthy of office. He need not give his reasons for nullifying an election.[55]

At the close of the general chapter at Piacenza in 1575 Rossi ordered Fernández' decrees to be put into practice, even after he had obtained the termination of the Dominican visitation.[56] Interestingly, the chapter of 1571 was not included in the *liber provinciae*.[57]

Fernández sponsored Anthony of Jesus for the office of provincial, but Angel de Salazar was elected.[58] The visitator might have used his powers to impose his candidate, but that was not his way.

Fernández and St. Teresa

It is not clear when the Dominican visitor first met St. Teresa. In the course of the transactions for the foundation at Medina del Campo (1567), he felt obliged to come to her defense against a certain religious who compared her to the spurious mystic of Cordova, Magdalena de la Cruz.[59]

Though he used his apostolic powers sparingly, the Dominican did not hesitate to apply them in strategic situations involving the progress of the reform.

Thus he interposed his authority in a situation which arose in the nunnery at Medina del Campo, 1569-1570. A novice, Isabelle of the Angels, wished to leave her not inconsiderable fortune to the monastery; her family wanted to endow a chapel. The community favored the novice, while the family was seconded by Alonso González, provincial and delegate of the prior general for the Discalced nuns. González also favored for the office of prioress due to fall vacant Teresa de Quesada, formerly of the Incarnation. Teresa, accompanied by Agnes of Jesus, also a former Incarnation nun and prioress of Medina, hastened from Salamanca, which she had just founded, to smooth the waters at Medina. González who was also displeased that Agnes had left Medina without his permission ordered Teresa back to Avila and installed Teresa de Quesada as prioress. During a subsequent visitation of Medina Fernández was made aware of the troubled state of the community. Dona Teresa had no objection to terminating her experiment in Discalced living and returned to the Incarnation. Fernández held an election which chose St. Teresa.[60]

On July 13, 1571, before witnesses, Teresa and Agnes renounced the mitigation. On October 6 Fernández accepted the renunciations and assigned Teresa conventuality at Salamanca.[61] This does not mean that she was required to live there.

The reason for this ceremony becomes apparent from the "acts or constitutions" which Fernández issued for the Discalced nuns. Only fragments remain of the text which is dated Medina, September 2, 1571.⁶² The Dominican confirms Rossi's decision that the nuns should remain under the jurisdiction of the prior general. The visitator of the nuns should be a friar of the primitive Rule. He should visit the monasteries once a year, may make directives but may not change the Constitutions. (The Constitutions of the nuns will be considered later.) Nuns may join the Discalced without renouncing the mitigation, but they may not be superiors unless they do. Communities without possessions are to be limited to thirteen or fourteen nuns; those with incomes may have twenty. Since the reform is new and has few persons experienced in government, prioresses may be re-elected. To spare the friars distraction and continual coming and going, the ordinary chaplain of the monastery should be a diocesan priest. The chaplain may also be confessor, but the prioress may call in suitable religious to confess the nuns, even outside the three times allowed by the council of Trent.

In these constitutions, the result no doubt of close collaboration between the apostolic visitator and the mother foundress, the basic juridical structures of the institution of Discalced nuns, embodying the freedoms Teresa deemed essential, are already present.

Teresa did not long remain in Medina. A visit to the Incarnation convinced Fernández that the leadership of Teresa in material and spiritual matters was required. In agreement with the definitory of the provincial chapter of September, 1571, he appointed Teresa prioress.⁶³ On October 6, the new provincial, Angel de Salazar, introduced her into the monastery in spite of the vehement protests of the nuns. Teresa soon won them over by her unruffled manner, her love, and concern. She excluded lay persons from the monastery and cut down visits from outside. She tried to remedy the hopeless problem of the poverty of the Incarnation. The community could supply only bread to its members; by begging alms from her friends, Teresa was able to provide meals for the poorest nuns. She herself took only bread from the community; for the rest of her food she depended on her friends.⁶⁴ "The Lord has wrought such an abundance of favours to this house that I am not more troubled here by disobedience and lack of recollectedness than I was at St. Joseph's," Teresa wrote to her former Jesuit confessor, Gaspar de Salazar, February 13, 1573. "Such favours does the Lord seem to be granting all these souls that I am amazed at it, as was the Father Visitor when he came to see us about a month ago and found nothing that needed correction."⁶⁵

In fact, at about the same time, January 22, Fernández was reporting to the Duchess of Alba: "At the Convent of the Incarnation, there are one hundred and thirty nuns and there is as much tranquillity and sanctity there as among the ten or twelve Discalced nuns in the Convent at Alba. I was extraordinarily surprised and encouraged to find this. And it all comes from the presence of the Mother."⁶⁶

Well, not all of it; no little credit for the changed atmosphere at the Incarnation must go to St. John of the Cross. Teresa was dissatisfied with the quality of the spiritual guidance of the confessors supplied by the Carmelite convent of Avila and determined to have them replaced by her own friars. She appealed to Fernández, who after some hesitation acquiesced.[67] Teresa was particularly pleased with one of the confessors. On September 27, 1572, she reported to her sister Joan: "This Discalced Father who is confessor is doing a great deal of good: his name is Fray John of the Cross."[68] At first John stayed at the friary of Avila; later he moved to a small house close to the Incarnation. He remained confessor at the Incarnation until his clamorous removal in 1577. During this time, for a nun of the Incarnation, Anne Mary of Jesus, he made his famous drawing of the crucified Christ which inspired the masterpiece of Salvador Dali. These years too constituted the longest period that John and Teresa were together, and the two saints acted as powerful spiritual catalysts on each other. On November 18, 1572, St. Teresa attained the mystical marriage.[69]

Evidently Fernández did not feel that he could—or should—require the general's vicar of the nuns to be a Discalced friar. Teresa did not hit it off as well with González as she had with Father General. On the other hand, between the Dominican and her there grew a deep mutual respect and an easy working relationship. More and more she turned to him for necessary permission. "He is our principal superior now," she wrote to Dona Maria de Mendoza in mid-June of 1571. Referring to a needed permission, she adds, "We can ask for the licence from the Father Provincial. . . Alternatively, we can go to the Father Visitor, who will give his consent at once. I can work with him better than with the Father Provincial, who simply will not answer my letters, however often I write to him."[70] On May 27 she had written to her friend, Diego Ortiz: "After the letter to our Father General had gone, I realized that there had been no need to write. For anything that the Father Visitor does is authoritative: it is as if it had been done by the Pontiff—no General or Chapter-General can undo it. The Father Visitor is very sagacious and learned and you will like talking to him."[71] Notwithstanding this rather simplistic canonical *postilla*, the ordinary superior for the Discalced nuns remained the general's vicar, Fray Alonso González. Rossi renewed his faculties in 1575.[72]

Fernández used the Discalced friars to reform the convents of the province. In view of the Incarnation he was especially solicitous for the convent at Avila. "I stayed here almost a fortnight," he wrote to the Duchess of Alba, January 22, 1573, "to organize the convent of friars, so that it should be a help, and not a hindrance, to the monastery of nuns. I have brought a number of Discalced friars here, not because I want the community to become Discalced, but so that it may be governed according to their laws; if

Chapter Two: The Discalced Reform

they keep these, they will be holy. I am leaving Fray Antonio, prior of Toledo as president (i.e., vicar), and another Father from Mancera as sub-prior: for the encouragement of these Fathers the Mother's presence is necessary." Balthasar of Jesus was also prior here for a time. At Toledo, too, as appears from the letter, Fernández placed Discalced in charge.[73]

To organize the growing number of Discalced houses in Castile, Fernández made Balthasar of Jesus vicar provincial.[74]

The Dominican visitation of Castile may be said to be a success. The reform of the province was peacefully progressing. The Incarnation had been permanently reformed, as Angel de Salazar was to attest many years later.[75] The houses of the Discalced friars and nuns had multiplied– the former, still attached to the province, were harmoniously developing a needed internal structure.

Vargas in Andalusia

On September 9, 1571, the nuncio John Baptist Castagna could report to the secretary of Pope Pius V, Jerome Rusticucci, that the visitors of the Carmelites had finished visiting the houses and were ready to convene chapters in a month.[76] Without the presence of the Discalced the visit by Hebrera of Aragon and Catalonia seems to have come off in routine fashion.[77] From Catalonia Hebrera reported to Castagna his distrust of Jerome Tostado, appointed defender of the Order by Rossi, because he had among other things persuaded the friars to withhold information.[78] Hebrera's opinion need not necessarily be taken as the last word. Tostado may have been advising the Catalonian friars on their rights.

In Andalusia things had not gone so well. Castagna's report quoted above has a familiar ring: "In the province of Andalusia matters are less good, because of the presence among those friars of some of a very bad disposition, who for a long time have nourished emnities and divisions among themselves. To remedy this situation, since the leaders who after a fashion profess to foment and maintain these divisions are four, I am trying to remove them from that province and transfer them to another. This is very difficult because of the following and favor they have."

On October 26, Vargas reported to the prior general on the chapter he had held two days previously. He would have liked to make Master Diego de León prior of Seville, but he was hindered by the opposition of the Ulloa brothers, Michael and Ferdinand. For provincial he chose Master Albert Farias, "a man of learning, conscientious and held in good esteem in this city of Seville." He will punish those who were disobedient to the general. Vargas asks Rossi not to favor the Ulloas, "who, I have heard, are the cause of all the passions and controversies in this province due to their ambitions." Thus Vargas' estimate of the situation differs entirely from that of Rossi during his visitation.[79]

The Dominican visitor contented himself with emphasizing certain reform decrees of the prior general. He continued the use of the deposit box. Permissions to leave the house should be granted only once a week.[80]

At this point Vargas, taking a page from his fellow Dominican's book, decided that the only solution to his problem was the Discalced Carmelites of Castile. Francis of St. Mary declares that it was the Discalced friars themselves, ex-members of the Andalusian province, who urged him to this conclusion. Many Andalusian Carmelites, students at Alcalá or living elsewhere, drawn by the example of virtuous living, had joined the Discalced.[81]

On November 20, 1571, only a month after his report to the prior general, we find the Dominican visitor writing to Mariano Azaro, known by his religious name as Ambrose of St. Benedict. He had already offered Azaro his choice of several houses of the mitigated friars, but had been refused. He now commanded the Castilian friar by virtue of holy obedience to fill with religious a house he owned outside Seville. (Question: how could a Discalced friar own a house?) There he might receive novices, provided they were not members of the Andalusian province. The house (or houses) were to be under the direct jurisdiction of the prior general after Vargas' commission had lapsed.[82]

It is difficult to conclude otherwise than that Vargas here exceeded his powers. Ample as his faculties were, they remained restricted to the Carmelite province of Andalusia. He had no power over the friars of Castile. It may also be questioned whether he had the right to found houses of the Order. His instructions "to do each and every thing (necessary) for the reform of the Order" are not to be taken in an absolute sense, but presume the continuance of the ordinary structures and legislation of the Order.[83] Finally one wonders how he could put under the prior general's jurisdiction houses which the prior general had forbidden to be founded.

The prior general was not one of those whom Vargas' patents entitled him to command. While in Castile the Discalced houses formed part of the province, and their superiors had voice in the chapters, Vargas' creations hung in a jurisdictional void with no other allegiance than to him. Vargas lacked the diplomatic sense of his brother in Castile, the instinct to apply the exact remedy a situation required. He embarked the Discalced enterprise on a collision course with the prior general which, even if legally defensible, was bound to end in disaster for the Order.

Azaro rejected Vargas' proposal, but the commissary had better luck with Diego of St. Mary (formerly of the Andalusian province) and Ambrose of St. Peter, a professed cleric, who visited him at Cordoba. Vargas made over to the Discalced the convent of the Andalusian province at San Juan del Puerto and placed Diego in charge. Five members of the community, including

Diego's brother, John de Heredia, joined the Discalced, which suggests that the initiative for Vargas' action may have come from the community itself. The Discalced took charge in late October, early November, 1572.[84]

On April 28, 1573, Vargas delegated Balthasar of Jesus, of the province of Castile, with his powers over the Discalced houses founded or to be founded in Andalusia. He could name and depose priors and receive novices, provided these were not of the province, in which case permission of the provincial was required. The appointment had in view two convents to be founded in Granada and La Peñuela.[85] Nieto founded Los Mártires in Granada on May 19. The following June 29, La Peñuela was founded by Gabriel of the Conception (de la Peñuela), one of the friars punished by Rossi at the provincial chapter of Seville in 1566.[86] Balthasar did not choose to exercise his prerogatives personally, perhaps because the memory of his past was still green in those parts. He returned to Pastrana, where he was prior, and on August 4, 1573, entrusted with the task of visitator of the Discalced in Andalusia a young friar fresh from the novitiate, Jerome Gracián.[87] Thus enters on the scene one destined to play a leading role in the history of the reform, a sign of contradiction fated for conflict with the Order and the reform.

Jerome Gracián (1545-1614) was born at Valladolid, one of 15 children of Diego Gracián and Juana Dantisco.[88] Don Diego was a secretary to the king, Dona Juana the natural daughter of the Polish ambassador. Two of Jerome's brothers, Anthony and Thomas, followed their father in the king's service as secretaries, a career for which Jerome too was destined, but after obtaining the master's degree in arts at Alcalá he was ordained to the priesthood in 1570. He owed his spiritual formation to the Jesuits and thought of joining them, but he never returned from a visit to the Carmelite novitiate at Pastrana. His novitiate, during which he had the spiritual charge of the nuns at Pastrana and heard confessions in the village and environs, was followed by profession, April 25, 1573.

Gracián now took over the leadership of the Discalced reform. A gentle, charming and courtly person, he approached his task in a wholly charismatic manner. His concept of his office of apostolic commissary and visitator, later conferred on him, was that all things were permitted him in the name of reform. Gracián, Mariano Azaro, John of Jesus Roca and other leading spirits turned the Discalced movement down a separate path. Their protests of following an authority higher than the prior general were shown for what they were when that authority turned against them and they sought refuge in the court of the king.

To leave his province in order to carry out his commission, Gracián had to practise a slight deception on his superior, Fray Angel de Salazar. Mariano received permission to go to Seville with an unspecified companion to see to certain personal affairs. Thereupon in September 1573, he and Gracián travelled to Seville for a meeting with Vargas. When he discovered he had been tricked, Salazar ordered his two subjects to return to Pastrana, but Vargas overrode him, a step he evidently felt justified in taking. On October 17 Gracián restored San Juan del Puerto to the province; the attempt to make of it a Discalced foundation had failed. On January 5, 1574, Gracián opened a new house for the Discalced in Seville (Los Remedios).[89]

The Discalced now had three houses in Andalusia: Granada, La Peñuela, Seville. Gracián once composed a memorandum to show that an apostolic visitator could found houses in Andalusia. With characteristic fondness for numbering the sequence of his thoughts, he musters eleven arguments to prove his point. His approach is logical rather than juridical, though his syllogisms are not always above exception. Some samples: "The 3d (reason): the visitator has higher faculties than the general in all that pertains to the good of the Order. The general can grant permission to found the said houses; therefore so can the visitator. The 4th: the visitator can place primitive friars in mitigated convents for their reform; therefore he can place houses in the province for the good of the whole province. . . The 7th: although the brief does not explicitly grant permission to found houses of primitives, it is enough that general authorization be given to do what is most suitable for the reform and well being of the Order. For, tell me, what is more perfect: to increase the number of primitives or mitigated friars?"[90]

The Dominican visitator took care to enlist the support of the king. "I discovered," he wrote on March 15, 1574, "that the complete remedy for this reform was the Discalced friars of Pastrana whom I summoned and are now in this city of Seville, Father Mariano and Father Master Jerome Gracián, and other fathers who by their lives and doctrine give much edification in this city, although there are not lacking persecutions on the part of the Calced fathers. I wanted to notify Your Majesty, so that you might favor them in all that may occur, and so that so holy a work as they have begun may go forward, and the others may amend their lives which certainly have need of it."[91]

As to the "persecutions," though there were those who cheerfully put any stick in the wheel of reform, others, including the prior general, may be forgiven for objecting to what they considered the flagrant violation of the Order's rights.

In a letter to the prior general that has not survived Gracián described his activities in Seville. Rossi failed to be impressed. "You are scarcely a novice," he wrote, April 26; "without knowledge of the institutions of the Order you may easily be led along ways and paths that are not good. I believe actions take their goodness from circumstances, and that the intention is not enough. Your intention is according to God, but because you act against obedience and your conscience is burdened with sanctions and censures, I think you are not acting in the service of God. I am afraid that beneath the pretext of laudable zeal there lie suspicions and contention. God will provide the remedy for violence. I will do what pertains to my office and I will not do what is improper."[92] With this shot across the bow contact between Gracián and Rossi seems to have ended.

Nicholas Ormaneto, Reformer of Carmel

Meanwhile the new pope, Gregory XIII, was wondering what had happened to the visitation of the Carmelites in Spain.[93] The current nuncio, Nicholas Ormaneto, wrote to the pope's secretary, Ptolemy Galli, on January 5, 1574, that he had heard that the Dominican visitation of the Carmelites had gone off well, especially in Seville and all Andalusia, where the Order was very lax. He would make further inquiries of the archbishop of Seville and in Castile. "These Carmelite Fathers," he concludes, "want to shake off the yoke, and when the matter has been properly settled, they may be given this satisfaction; otherwise it is better to keep the bit in their mouth."[94]

The Veronese Nicholas Ormaneto, of about the same age as St. Teresa, had already played an important role in post-Tridentine reform. He had acted in close collaboration with and enjoyed the highest esteem of some of the most prominent figures in Catholic reform. A disciple of John Matthew Giberti (1495-1543), noted reforming bishop of Verona before the council of Trent, he was carefully selected as his vicar general to initiate reform in his archdiocese of Milan by none other than St. Charles Borromeo, the very incarnation of post-Tridentine reform. St. Pius V conferred on Ormaneto the unprecedented office of "reformer of Rome" with the Herculean task of cleaning out the Augean stable of the eternal city, not excluding the papal court itself. Little wonder that as nuncio in Spain he should have a personal interest and more than usual tenacity in pursuing religious reform.[95]

On February 28, 1574, Ormaneto was able to pass on to Galli a list of Carmelite sins in Seville. The police had picked up a member of the Seville community, Roderick Curiel, who was in the habit of wandering about in secular dress; they would not surrender him to his superiors until these condemned him to the galleys. The sub-prior, Peter Cota, had been caught in the house of a woman of bad repute. When the provincial deprived him of office, he had appealed to Rome, and the prior general had reinstated him in Seville, the scene of his misconduct, to the scandal of all. In November or December of 1563 one friar had struck another in the course of an argument. Another had struck a master of theology and not only was not punished but was allowed to continue his studies. Among most of the friars there are factions such as are not found in the lowest company, not to mention licentiousness and profanity said to exist in this convent.[96]

Curiel had pleaded innocent and had demanded a trial, which Rossi granted him on July 1, 1573, as he was bound to do. Cota too was promised an investigation (July 7). He was a favorite of Rossi: "We cannot forget the kindness with which he accompanied us from Zaragoza to Madrid."[97]

Vargas had left his visitation unfinished, Ormaneto states in his letter quoted above. "He is a good man, but lacks the spirit needed to tame these wild horses." Ormaneto is convinced that the visitation should be continued, especially in Andalusia, and is resolved to find a suitable person to carry it out.

Vargas reported to the nuncio on March 15, 1574, the same day he wrote to the king. He had withdrawn his hand because he was in doubt as to the validity of his patents after four years. Also he wanted to observe the fate of the acts and ordinances he had drawn up. These had been mostly ignored. The friars he had exiled from the province as a source of unrest and factions were all back and offering Mass as though they were not excommunicated. Those he had deprived of voice and office because of public and notorious misdeeds had won absolution from the prior general, claiming that witnesses had testified falsely against them, whereas they had been caught *flagrante delicto* in houses of ill repute by the secular arm.[98]

After this, on April 5, Ormaneto reiterated to Galli his conviction that the reform of the Carmelites was not ripe, and that the visitators should not be removed. On May 4, Galli communicated to Ormaneto the pope's consent to the continuation of the visitation, but it should be dispatched as quickly as possible.[99]

On May 8, "to remove all difficulty and hesitation," Ormaneto renewed Vargas' apostolic commission to visitate and reform the Carmelite province of Andalusia.[100] But the Dominican had no more stomach for reforming Carmelites. On June 13 he made Gracián vicar provincial of both Discalced and Calced Carmelites in Andalusia.[101] It is not clear whether by this act Vargas replaced the provincial, Augustine Suarez, or simply created an office beside that of provincial. Suarez certainly continued to function as provincial and attended the general chapter of 1575. On the other hand Gracián later began to use the title of provincial. This is another jurisdictional muddle that Vargas bequeathed to posterity.

On September 22 Ormaneto appointed Vargas and Gracián *in solidum* apostolic visitators of Andalusia.[102] In practice the work of visitating was to devolve on the youthful shoulders of the Discalced friar.

The Carmelites of Andalusia on their part took steps to present their point of view. On June 25, 1574, the provincial, Augustine Suarez, formally gave notice to Mariano Azaro, "president" of Los Remedios in Seville, of the prior general's prohibition to found houses of the Discalced in Andalusia. Azaro refused to recognize the document on the grounds that he could not believe that "so holy a prelate" would issue a command contrary to the will of the Roman pontiff expressed through his commissioners.[103]

Not long after this, the pontiff whose wishes Azaro was so anxious to fulfill made his will clear. On August 13, 1574, Gregory XIII *motu proprio* declared the Dominican visitation ended and ordained that henceforth the Order should be visitated by the prior general and his delegates.[104] The Carmelites lost no time in presenting the apostolic brief to the nuncio. On October 10 Ormaneto communicated this action to the papal secretary, Ptolemy Galli. He personally, Ormaneto declares, thinks the visitation should be continued, but anything that comes from the hand of His Holiness he considers well done, as guided by the Holy Spirit. The wording of the papal brief, however, makes him wonder whether his own faculties as nuncio to visit and reform religious orders in Spain have been affected. Although he does not believe this is so, as an obedient servant, he has abstained from all activity in this area until he learns the mind of the pope. If the pope wants him to use his faculty, he will do so for the glory of God, the salvation of souls and "the restraint of these people who have need of it"; if not, he will spare himself a lot of trouble.[105] On December 16 Galli assured the nuncio that the recall of the Dominican visitators did not affect his powers to visit and reform religious orders.[106]

Ormaneto now took the reform of the Carmelites personally in hand, as he had the power to do. That reform, however, no longer emanated immediately from Rome, but had local, Spanish origins, even though "apostolic," and depended on the initiative of the nuncio in office.

The Prudent King did not take kindly to having his project of reform so unceremoniously ended without so much as a word to him. He declared the papal brief invalid because it lacked the royal *placet* and ordered a hunt through the Carmelite convents for copies.[107] Nevertheless the papal visitation by Dominicans was over and done with.

Teresa in Andalusia

Teresa was delighted with the progress of her spiritual sons in Andalusia. On May 14, 1574, the saint wrote to Mary Baptist Cepeda y Ocampo, prioress of Valladolid: "Oh, if you could see the to-do that is going on—secretly of course—in favor of the Discalced! It is something one ought to praise the Lord for and it has all been aroused by the Fathers who went to Andalusia, Gracián, and Mariano. My pleasure is greatly tempered by the distress it will cause the Father General, for whom I have such affection; on the other hand, I can see that our position was getting hopeless."[108]

Although Gracián had been in correspondence with St. Teresa even before his entrance into the Order, the two did not meet until April 1575, at the monastery of Beas which Teresa had recently founded. It is an interesting insight into the femininity of St. Teresa that this personable, intelligent but imprudent young man should have so completely captivated her. Their attachment must be ranked among the classic friendships of saints of the opposite sex. Gracián told her the story of his life. "It may seem an improper thing," Teresa later reflected, "that he should have spoken to me in such detail about his soul."[109]

On the other hand Teresa opened her heart to him. "She communicated her spirit to me," Gracián recalled, "without concealing anything, and I declared all my interior to her in the same way; and there we agreed always to work together in all our affairs."[110] To Teresa it seemed that she had finally found the leader her movement among the friars had always lacked. Still under the spell of their first meeting, Teresa wrote to Agnes of Jesus, prioress of Medina, on May 13: "Oh Mother, how much I have wished you were with me during these last few days! I must tell you that, without exaggeration, I think they have been the best days in my life. For over three weeks we have had Father Master Gracián here; and, much as I have had to do with him, I assure you I have not yet fully realized his worth. To me, he is perfect, and better for our needs than anyone else we could have asked God to send us. What your Reverence and all the nuns must do now is to beg His Majesty to give him to us as a superior. If that happens, I can take a rest from governing these houses, for anyone so perfect and yet so gentle, I have never seen. May God have him in His keeping, and preserve him; I would not have missed seeing him and having to do with him for anything in the world."[111] As a result of a vision Teresa made a vow always to obey Gracián.[112]

On May 29, 1575, Teresa made a foundation of nuns in Seville. In a letter of June 18 to the prior general Teresa feels obliged to excuse and explain her presence in Andalusia. As soon as she settled in, the prior of Seville, Michael de Ulloa, one of the defenders of the Order appointed by Rossi in 1570, showed up to ask by what authority she had done so. "Some of the Fathers have been to see me," Teresa related to Rossi. "I like them; the Prior especially is particularly nice. He came to ask me to show him the patents authorizing me to make the foundation. He wanted to take a copy of them away with him. I told him they must not start a lawsuit, as he could see that I had the authority to make these foundations."[113] However Ulloa caused her no trouble, even though Seville already had a monastery of the order, the Incarnation.[114]

Rossi himself was trying to reach "his daughter." He penned letters in October 1574, and January 1575, which showed up simultaneously at Seville on June 17. In them the prior general had evidently expressed his displeasure with Gracián and Mariano whom he considered disobedient and with the acceptance among the contemplatives of Gabriel de la Peñuela; the Discalced houses in Andalusia would have to be closed. Teresa's answer on

Chapter Two: The Discalced Reform

the following day is characterized by the Teresian scholar, E. Allison Peers, as "one of the most striking in the entire collection" of her letters.

"Every day," Teresa begins, "a special prayer for your Reverence is said in choir, and, apart from that, all the sisters are careful to pray for you, since they are aware how much I love you. They, too, knowing no other father, have a great love for your Reverence, which is not surprising, for you are all we have in the world. They are all very happy, and so they never cease to be grateful to your Reverence, since it is to you that the Reform owes its beginning." She goes on to protest the loyalty of her Discalced friars. "They are defending their position, and I honestly believe they are your Reverence's loyal sons and desire not to offend you; but still I cannot altogether acquit them of blame. I think they are now gradually coming to realize that they ought to have followed a different course, so as not to offend your Reverence. I have had some heated arguments about it, especially with Mariano, who is very hasty. Gracián, on the other hand, behaves like an angel, and, if he alone had been concerned, the thing would have turned out very differently. He came here because he was sent by Fray Balthasar, who at that time was Prior of Pastrana. If your Reverence knew him, I am sure you would be delighted at having him for a son, and I am quite sure he is your true son, as, for that matter, Mariano is too. This Mariano is a virtuous man, leading a penitential life, and his talent is recognized by all. Your Reverence may be perfectly certain that he has been actuated only by zeal for God and the good of the Order, but, as I say, he has gone too far and been indiscreet ... I have suffered from him again and again, but, knowing what a good man he is, I pass it over ... I beg your Reverence to realize that the whole body of the Discalced Fathers mean nothing to me by comparison with anything that so much as touches your Reverence's garment ... You may be quite sure that, if I found they were disobedient, I would neither see them nor listen to them any more; but I myself cannot be as loyal a subject to your Reverence as they are proving themselves."

According to Mariano "that man Pinuela got the habit by a trick. He went to Pastrana, and said that Vargas, the Visitor here, had given it him, and then it became known that he had given it to himself. They have been thinking for some time of turning him out, and they will certainly do so. [Gabriel died in the Discalced Order, 1593.] The other one is no longer with them ... It was never their wish to admit Fray Gaspar, or to have friendly relations with him, in spite of the persistent requests which he made, of them and of others."

With regard to the juridical status of the Discalced houses in Andalusia, Teresa points out that in Castile the visitor did nothing without the general's leave, "and, if Teresa of Jesus had been there, things might have been still more carefully looked into, for there could never be any question of founding a house save with your Reverence's license–if there ever had been, I should have come out against it most strongly." But in Andalusia "the houses were founded by a mandate from the Visitor Vargas, by virtue of his apostolic authority; for people here consider that the foundation of Discalced houses is the most important reform that can be undertaken ... The Visitor here has given these Fathers so many licenses and faculties and requested them to act upon them, that, if your Reverence sees what they hold, you will realize that they are not so blameworthy."

As to closing the Discalced houses in Andalusia, Teresa in her forthright manner reads the general a lesson in *Realpolitik*. "It may be that the whole Order is reformed already, but people certainly do not think so here; they consider every one of our friars, without exception, as saints. And they do in fact lead good lives, are extremely recollected, and are much given to prayer. They are outstanding people, and more than twenty of them are taking courses, or whatever they are called—some in Canon Law and some in Theology—so they have good brains ... I cannot imagine what will become of all these or what everybody will think about it, bearing in mind the opinion people have of them. It might be that we should all have to pay for it, for they stand very well with the King, and the Archbishop here says they are the only real friars there are. Now if your Reverence drives them out of the Reform—assuming you do not want them there—you must believe me that, even if you have all the right in the world on your side, people will not look at it like that."

Her final suggestion is a saint's and eminently correct, but perhaps not possible, given the state of men's minds: "I beg you to commend the matter to His Majesty, and, like a true father, forget the past, and remember that you are a servant of the Virgin and that she will be offended if you cease to help those who, by the sweat of their brow, seek the increase of the Order."[115] The expansion of the Discalced reform in an atmosphere of unity and harmony did not lie entirely in the general's hands.

Even as Teresa wrote these wise words the general chapter at Piacenza had passed into history.

Chapter III

"AN INTOLERABLE KIND OF FEUD"

The general chapter which convened at Piacenza, May 22, 1575, lost no time addressing itself to the question of the Discalced friars in Andalusia.

The General Chapter of Piacenza and the Discalced

The brief of August 3, 1574, recalling the Dominican visitors, was read, followed by another, dated April 15, 1575, the purpose of which was to invest the acts of the chapter with apostolic authority. This brief specified that those who had been made superiors against the general statutes and obedience due to superiors of the Order, who had accepted or lived in convents or places prohibited by the same superiors, should be removed; to this end all opportune remedies were to be applied in order to restore obedience without the right of appeal. Archbishops, papal nuncios, legates *a latere* were obliged to aid the general in the implementation of his decrees.

At the opening of the chapter, so important for the Order in Spain, of the Spanish definitors only the Catalans were at hand. The provincial of Andalusia, Master Augustine Suarez, and his *socius*, arrived on June 8. The definitor for Castile arrived after the chapter was over, but approved and signed the acts. The Aragonese failed to appear. Since no fresh information on developments in Spain was available, the chapter confined itself to reaffirming the position the prior general had so far taken: those who have opened houses against the will of the general are deposed from office without the right of appeal. The convents at Granada, Seville, and La Peñuela are to be abandoned within three days. The authorities indicated in the papal brief are called on to implement these decisions. Those concerned who do not obey are cited to appear within three months. Mariano Azaro and Balthasar Nieto are to be expelled from the Order if they remain obdurate.[2]

The Castilian definitor, Martin Garcias, brought letters from his province and provincial. Though the chapter was over, the definitors were still at hand and these delegated the prior general to provide for the situation as revealed by the letters from Castile. Rossi's directives, which are the general chapter's, forbid the contemplative fathers to form a province or congregation separate from the province of Castile. Alphonse González is confirmed as delegate for the nuns of the first Rule, and Angel de Salazar, provincial of Castile, is to examine their confessors. The friars and nuns of the primitive Rule are to follow the Order's liturgy with regard to the chants of the office and Mass. They are not to go completely barefoot, "since nowhere in the Rule is such a thing prescribed." They are not to be called "discalced," but "contemplatives" or "primitives." No rift should be created in the Order by calling some "discalced," others "of the cloth." The contemplatives are not to use staffs, except on long journeys or in case of sickness. Only priors and their *socii* of houses founded with due authorization have voice in the chapter of Castile; Anthony de Heredia in any case is to enjoy this right. Each contemplative house elects its own prior, to be confirmed by the provincial, who has the right to visitate. He may not send primitives to houses of the province, or members of the province to contemplative houses, nor may he open new houses. No additions are to be made to the formula of profession.[3]

The general chapter and Rossi, whose actions it confirmed, did not want to suppress the primitives, but tried to confine it within the Order. "We protest before God and men," Rossi declared in the post-chapter decrees, "that we have always had the one desire to grant them every favor, grace and benefit, if only they consulted the interests of peace, tranquillity, concord and friendship, remaining faithful to obedience."[4] Nevertheless the attitude of the chapter was too unyielding and was designed to exacerbate the conflict. The Andalusian convents, as Teresa had suggested, should have been accepted as a *fait accomplit* and the Discalced should have been erected into a separate province with the prospect of forming other provinces as the need arose. Such a measure would not only have met a real need—the mixture of reformed and unreformed was impracticable; it would have exorcised the spectre of Discalced fear, real or imaginary, of being "undone" and perhaps would have created a climate in which the unity of the Order might still be salvaged.

One decision of the chapter was not published but communicated to the person concerned by the provincial, Angel de Salazar: Mother Teresa of Jesus was not to leave her monastery. She accepted the will of her superiors, though not without a sense of hurt. "It has never been realized here," the saint pointed out to Rossi in February 1576, "nor is it realized now, that the Council, or the *motu proprio*, deprives superiors of the right to send nuns to particular houses for the good of the Order, or for any reasons pertaining to it, of which there may be many."[5] The decree of the chapter has not survived; its gist is known only from Teresa's reply to the prior general. It has generally been interpreted as a penance. No doubt it was at least occasioned by the difference with the Discalced. On the other hand the situation in the church with regard to nuns had considerably changed since Rossi's visit to Spain. After Pius V, interpreting the directives of Trent, had imposed cloister on all nuns, the prior general had had to revise his own more benign position. Ormaneto himself, as will be seen, disapproved of Teresa's travels. Later under their own superiors the Discalced monasteries were due for some painful adjustment to the new rigid concepts of cloister. Little wonder that the general chapter seized the occasion to quote Trent to Teresa.

Gracián's Visitation of Seville

As far as Ormaneto was concerned the general chapter of Piacenza might never have occurred, or Gregory's brief of April 15, 1575, written. Gracián was visiting the Discalced houses when Ormaneto called him to Madrid. The friar arrived for Pentecost, May 22, 1575, and remained three months, often conferring with the nuncio concerning the visitation of the province of Andalusia. Gracián wanted nothing to do with the mitigated friars and in fact tried to persuade the nuncio and the king to institute a separate province of Discalced.[6] Teresa added her appeal to the king. "I have lived among them (the mitigated) for forty years, and, taking everything into consideration, I am quite convinced that, unless the Discalced are made into a separate province, and that quickly, much harm will be done, and further progress will, I think, be impossible." She goes on to recommend that the new province be placed in care of "a Discalced Father named Gracián, with whom I have recently become acquainted."[7]

On August 3, 1575, Ormaneto named Gracián commissary and reformer of the Carmelites in Andalusia and of the primitives in Castile, "apostolic letters granted to the Carmelite Order and its superiors, persons and general chapters in general, in particular or otherwise to the contrary notwithstanding.[8]

In his letter the nuncio addresses Gracián as "provincial and reformer in the province of Andalusia." Challenged by the pope's secretary, Ptolemy Galli, Ormaneto later claimed that Vargas had been the one to make Gracián provincial.[9] After the recall of the Dominican visitation the general chapter of Piacenza had confirmed Augustine Suarez as provincial of Andalusia and had decreed that the friars of the first Rule were to remain under the provincial of Castile.[10] Gracián continued to use the title. Little wonder that the Andalusians balked.

Gracián understandably procrastinated, but Teresa encouraged him to begin the visitation. In Seville, on September 26, she was visited by the provincial, Augustine Suarez, the prior of Seville, Vincent de la Trinidad, and two other doctors. The previous day Caspar Nieto had come. (The chapter of Piacenza allowed him and John de Mora to remain in the Order without voice.)[11] "I find they are all determined to obey your Paternity," she writes to Gracián, "and to help you put right anything they do that is wrong, and that they are not extreme in other matters. I am assuring them, from my knowledge of your Paternity, that you will be gentle with them, and there I am saying what I really believe to be true ... I assure your Paternity that, if you go gently at first and avoid making a stir, I believe you will get a great deal of good work done, but you cannot expect to do it in a day. I really think there are reasonable people among them."[12]

Teresa also received assurance in prayer regarding the visitation. "One night I was in great distress because for so long I had had no news of my Father, and also because he had not been well when he last wrote to me ... Suddenly he appeared to me. It could not have been imagination, for I became conscious of an inward light and he himself was coming gaily along the road, with a bright countenance. . . Then I heard these words: 'Tell him to begin at once and not to be afraid, for his is the victory.'"[13]

The victory was not easily won. On November 21, 1575, the feast of the Presentation, Gracián began his visitation of the Casa Grande in Seville. When he presented his credentials, the friars raised a tumult, locked the doors of the convent and at first would not let him leave. Gracián thought they were going to lay violent hands on him.[14] Some one ran to tell Teresa he was dead. She was in such a state she could not pray, when she heard the words: "O woman of little faith, be still; things are going on very well." In thanksgiving for Gracián's escape Teresa thereafter had her nuns celebrate the Presentation with special solemnity.[15] A shudder of excitement thrilled through the Discalced nunneries.

Dramatics aside, the community of Seville refused to acknowledge Ormaneto's authority, holding to the brief of August 13, 1574, which restored the right of visitation to the superiors of the Order. When Gracián produced Galli's assurance to Ormaneto that his powers to reform were intact, they replied they were not bound by secretaries' letters. They also rejected Gracián's patents, claiming they had been obtained *subreptitie* or *obreptitie*, because they referred to him as provincial and stated that he had begun the visitation, both of which allegations they denied. In a letter of December 8, presented by Gracián on December 19, Ormaneto assured the recalcitrant friars that he had indeed appointed Gracián reformer and visitator and ordered them under pain of excommunication to obey him. The nuncio's letter, addressed to the provincial and friars of Andalusia, makes no mention of Gracián's title as provincial. When the friars continued obdurate, Gracián excommunicated them."[16]

"Even if they do not obey," Teresa had written Gracián on November 30, "your Reverence should hesitate before issuing them letters of excommunication: they ought to be given a chance to consider what they are doing. That is how it seems to me. You and your advisers will know better than I, but," Teresa the chess player concludes, "I should not like it to appear that they are being checkmated."[17]

Michael de Ulloa was made prior of the embattled community; he had been favored by Rossi during his visitation, but exiled and excommunicated by

Vargas.[18] Peter de Cota and Louis de Navarrete were dispatched to Rome to protest the visitation by the nuncio.[19] The latter warned the pope's secretary, Galli, who promised that "if the Carmelites of Andalusia appear, they will be treated in such a way that they will be more anxious to return to Spain than they were to come to Rome."[20]

In the end the provincial capitulated, and Gracián was able to begin his visitation on January 15, 1576.[21]

Gracián's plan of reform in itself was excellent, outstripping that of Rossi and foreshadowing the reforms in the Order of the 17th century. Unfortunately Gracián's bloated concept of his prerogatives as visitator caused him to function without reference to the legislation of the Order and the consequent limits to the obligations of its members.[22]

How seriously Gracián went about his reformer's task is a moot question. "I was charged with the visitation and reform of the Calced Carmelites of Andalusia," he wrote in his autobiographical *Pilgrimage of Anastasius*, "in which I was engaged for four or five years, although my principal intention was to carry through the foundations of the Discalced, because the Calced were opposing us and we could better defend ourselves by keeping them subject than by having them rule us."[23]

On January 16, Gracián began the visitation of the Incarnation of Seville with its community of about fifty nuns. He introduced two half hour periods of meditation. On consultation with Ormaneto he removed adult women boarders from the monastery (its constitutions allowed it to keep girls under twelve years of age) and abolished the "escala," a room where the nuns received guests. There one of the lay boarders, Dona Blanca de Guzmán, held dances and masques, "such as is done in the streets." There too a banquet had been held shortly before his arrival in which Dona Blanca, the provincial, the sub-prioress and other nuns had participated. Ormaneto ordained that the nuns should receive visitors only in the monastery parlor, "which should have double grilles so disposed that not even a finger can reach outside; eventually we can consider adding iron plates between the grilles, such as are found here in the monastery of the Discalced."[24]

In Milan Ormaneto under orders from Borromeo and Pius IV had introduced perforated metal sheets into the monastery parlors. Both nuns and their families had protested this device. Ormaneto here obviously approves the idea.[25]

The interviews produced some very serious accusations against the provincial and two priors "in matters concerning the chastity of the holy virgins." Ormaneto instructed his commissary to look into the matter, but to be "very careful of the testimony of friars, because of the passions that exist between them."[26]

According to Ormaneto conditions in the nunneries of all the Orders in Andalusia left much to be desired. On January 31, 1576, he wrote to Ptolemy Galli: "(Immoral) practices of the friars with the sisters are here so common that it is a shame. There seems to be no remedy, because the superiors who should punish their subjects are the worst of all, and after the example of the friars, laymen themselves frequent the monasteries. Thereby arise great sins and scandals for which an opportune remedy should be provided." At least in the case of the Carmelites this remedy would be to put the Discalced friars in charge of the nuns. Ormaneto concludes with the example of an Andalusian Carmelite who recently had been caught wandering about by night in "quite improper" secular clothing. It turned out he had seduced a penitent and possessed false credentials and counterfeit money. He twice attempted suicide in prison.[27]

Gracián forbade the prior of Seville to receive the three vows of *beatas* and ordered them enclosed. If they were too poor, they were to be absolved from the vows of poverty and obedience. In that state they were not to wear the habit, but as a consolation could be given the small scapular and the *bulla de la hermandad* (letters of affiliation).[28]

He abolished the office of vicar of the nuns and placed them under the direct jurisdiction of the provincial.[29]

The visitation of the friary of Seville took place from February 21 to April 1. The visitator laid the axe to the root of private possession in whatever form. Inventory was made of all the belongings and furnishings of the house, including the rooms, and all was declared common property. Similarly all books in the convent (over 1,000) were collected into one room, designated as the library, for the use of all. A common supply room administered by the prior and officials of the house was established, to which the friars were to have recourse for their needs, even the most insignificant. The *depositum* was abolished. Gracián revoked all permission for friars to live outside the convent on their properties and to receive rents. Goods held in surety outside the convent were to be brought in and incorporated into the house. Horses and mules were taken away from individuals and assigned to community use. Possession of money was prohibited, no matter how small the amount; permission to keep money up to three *escudos* was rescinded.

The community should not exceed forty members and ten guests, the number which the income of the house could support, supplying all wants. (In overpopulated houses the budget could manage only the most urgent needs: *vestiarium*, bread, wine, oil; for the rest individuals were expected to forage on their own.) A dozen members of other orders were sent back to their communities; some of these at least are known to have had patents from Rossi.

Permissions to leave the house should be granted only in cases of grave necessity and rarely. General permissions to leave the house a certain number of times a week or a month were revoked. (The legislation of the Order permitted religious to leave the house twice a week.)[30] The lay brothers are no longer to go out to beg; besides being a distraction to them and a disgrace to the Order, "the agreement to give (them) three *reales* a day is a detestable thing."

Apostasy, or vagrancy, was a special problem of the province. No friar was to be received in a convent unless he had written permission from the provincial to leave his own house. Gracián asked the police and the bishops to pick up any footloose brethren found without letters. "I hereby warn all religious," the visitator apostolic writes, "that during my commission I will punish all apostates, even if they have letters from the Most Reverend General in Rome; for the reformation of this Order it is necessary by all means to close the door on vagrancy and apostasy. So if anything contrary to reform should come from his Most Reverend Paternity, as a son of obedience I will place it (reverently) on my head, but as apostolic reformer I will cause to be observed the statutes and constitutions which he himself has made for the good government of this province." Gracián drew up a list of twenty-nine apostates in the province.

Seville was declared the only novitiate in the province. The novices had been living together in one large room, but Gracián had separate cells made according to the Rule. He himself took the personal charge of the novices. In his absence the Discalced friars Gregory Nazianzen and Louis of St. Jerome were to give the novices instructions according to the conferences Gracián had given them at Los Remedios and of which they had written copies. The novices were withdrawn from the jurisdiction of the prior of the Casa Grande and placed under Gracián or the Discalced prior of Los Remedios. The instructions of the novices were to take into consideration the mitigation of the abstinence of Pope Eugene IV; "in all the rest there is no difference between Discalced and Calced." The novitiate was to become the hothouse of the reform, to which Gracián gave the name "Reform of Gregory XIII and King Philip."

It is interesting to note how Gracián, like the Dominican Peter Fernández in Castile, reduces the difference between the primitives and the mitigated to the matter of abstinence. Had Gracián been more interested in salvaging the old Order and conducted himself with greater prudence towards its authorities, the Spanish provinces might have been reduced to "perfect" observance, the Stricter Observance anticipated by a quarter of a century, and the unity of the Order preserved. But against this happy eventuality also stood the strong eremitical tendency of the primitives and the fact that Gracián's concept of the Carmelite life was not shared by many Discalced.

The apostolic visitator appointed one of his few supporters, Juan Evangelista, prior of the Casa Grande. He made Dominic of St. Albert subprior and named new *clavarii*.

Two half hours of meditation were introduced. At the king's request for prayer, Gracián instituted perpetual adoration, all Carmelite houses, Discalced or Calced, in Castile and Andalusia taking turns.[31]

Gracián deposed the provincial from office, as "the head of the band (that caused all) of these disturbances," and kept the reins of government in his own hands.[32]

"Tostado Will See to It"

In early May 1576 Peter de Cota returned from Rome, bearing according to Gracián's later recollection the decrees of the general chapter and the papal brief confirming them.[33] The provincial was also rumored to be on his way to Seville with a *motu proprio* from the pope. Unless this was the brief mentioned by Gracián, it might have been the confirmation of Rossi's faculties issued March 6, 1572, with the added clause commanding obedience by cardinals and legates *a latere*, or the confirmation of his faculties to punish incorrigible subjects even with the triremes, obtained Jan. 28, 1576.[34]

Don Christopher de Rojas, archbishop of Seville, Don Francis Zapata, *asistente* of Seville, and Dr. Francis de Arganda, *fiscal* of the Inquisition, decided that Gracián should absent himself a while in Castile, lest he be served with a summons before the nuncio could advise him. Gracián made the prior of Seville, John Evangelist, vicar provincial in his absence. Zapata was to give him necessary support.[35]

On May 8 Gracián left Seville for Madrid to try to rid himself of the visitation of Andalusia, but both king and nuncio insisted that he continue as before.[36]

On May 12, 1576, Castile held its chapter at San Pablo de la Moraleja. John Gutiérrez de la Magdalena succeeded Salazar as provincial. The acts of the general chapter of Piacenza were published.[37] Francis of St. Mary adds that the Discalced delegates did not arrive until the chapter was over, and that in their absence legislation was passed designed to destroy the reform: the primitives and the observants were to wear uniform habits and were to live together in the same houses.[38] The first provision reflects the decrees of Piacenza, but the second is the opposite of what was ordained there. It was Fernández who had placed Discalced friars in the houses of the province to improve observance.

On July 20 Galli forwarded to Ormaneto a petition presented by the procurator of the Carmelites, John Baptist Suriano, to the pope, "to whom it seems right that their ordinances, constitutions and privileges be preserved.

Since what is explained in the said petition is true, His Holiness wishes that Your Lordship in the best manner possible remove all occasions for complaint."[39] The petition probably did not differ much from an undated request of Rossi to Galli, asking that the pope forbid Ormaneto to interfere in the visitation of the Carmelite houses in Spain or allow the Discalced to visitate, but admit the ordinary visitator who had gone there for that purpose.[40]

The visitator to whom the prior general alludes is Jerome Tostado (1523-1582). He was born in Lisbon where he made his vows in 1545. He is said to have acquired his doctorate at Paris and was afterwards invited to lecture in the province of Catalonia. When Rossi visited Barcelona in 1567, he was prior there. The general added the office of reformer general of Catalonia. Tostado was among the defenders of the Order appointed by Rossi in 1569. He accompanied the prior general on his visitations in Italy, 1572-1575, and was his *socius* at the general chapter of Piacenza. On December 10, 1575, Rossi appointed him visitator, reformer and commissary general of the Spanish provinces. In May, 1576, Tostado was elected provincial of Catalonia. On November 18, 1581 Gregory XIII confirmed him as visitator and reformer of Spain,[41] but he died at Naples, February 24, 1582.[42]

In his letters patent of December 10, 1575, Rossi instructs Tostado to enforce the statutes laid down by the visitators of Pius V and those of the general chapter of Piacenza, especially those ordered by Gregory XIII. There are two restrictions to his powers: Tostado may not grant permission to join the contemplatives or allow them to found houses in the future. This right Rossi reserved to himself.[43]

The career of this friar speaks for itself. His long association with Rossi, the confidence he shared with him, made Tostado the ideal choice as his representative. His task was a hopeless one, and his mission was a failure before it started. He was preceded by the rumor that he had come to destroy the reform. To Teresa–and through her to the general reading public since– he is the *bête noire* of the reform, "the sole cause" of its ills.

Tostado arrived on August 5, 1576; by August 29 he was already on his way out of Andalusia.[44] The timing of his visit was unfortunate. The Minim general had just been refused permission to visitate by king and president, because it was suspected that he had come to take measures against his vicar, Anthony Becerra, who was greatly esteemed for the reform he had carried out in his Order. As he had done in the case of the general of the Minims, Ormaneto advised Tostado to postpone his visit of Andalusia and to pass on to Portugal.[45]

"God has delivered us from Tostado," Teresa exclaimed.[46]

Tostado's patents did not apply to Portugal, but apparently he had subsequently received a commission for that province. On September 30, 1576, he presided at the chapter "and contributed much to its peaceful realization."[47]

The Abortive Discalced Province

Meanwhile Gracián proceeded with his plan to found a province. In letters patent of August 3, 1576, he created a separate province and congregation of Discalced Carmelites, consisting of the Discalced friaries and nunneries in Castile and Andalusia, as well as those to be founded in the future. He confirmed the three Discalced friaries in Andalusia, "since the faculties of apostolic visitors are greater than those of the Most Reverend Father General." Friars and nuns are to keep the same constitutions and manner of living; that is, the directives laid down by the Dominican visitors and himself. The Discalced are immediately subject to the prior general, who alone may visitate and then only in company with a Discalced friar. If he cannot personally visit, he may delegate only a Discalced who must be accompanied by the Discalced provincial. The Discalced may not transfer to the old Order under pain of apostasy. Priors and their *socii* are to meet in chapter at Almodóvar de Campo on August 26 to elect a provincial and definitors.[48]

The chapter of Almodóvar met in due course under the presidency of Jerome Gracián. Francis of St. Mary provides an account complete with speeches, but how much is Francis and how much is Clio is difficult to tell. St. John of the Cross is supposed to have been there, but Gracián summoned only the priors and *socii* of the Discalced houses. These were nine: Mancera, Pastrana, Alcalá Altomira, La Roda, Granada, La Peñuela, Seville, Almodóvar. It was decided among other things to send two friars to Rome to lobby for the reform, expel a number of friars from the provinces who had joined the reform and appoint a provincial *zelator*, or overseer of observance.[49]

Gracián deferred the election of a provincial, as he explained to the assembled members of the chapter in a letter dated September 1, 1576, because he was still apostolic commissary and visitor, and another head or provincial would be a source of confusion in the province. The moment his commission lapsed through revocation or absence or death of the nuncio, the first definitor, Anthony of Jesus, should convene a chapter to elect a provincial who for this first time would not require confirmation by the prior general.[50] Thus of his own initiative Gracián separated the reform from the provinces and placed himself at its head.

In his letter of September 1 Gracián states that he knew "that it was the will of the said Lord Nuncio to make a separate province of the Primitive Discalced friars and nuns and that many times we heard him say it." The nuncio undoubtedly wanted a separate Discalced province, but to want it and

Chapter Three: "An Intolerable Kind of Feud"

to feel authorized to institute it are different matters. In any case he would not have decided so important a matter in such an offhand way. It was typical of Gracián's muddled thinking in the matter of his prerogatives.

In the same letter of September 1 Gracián observes that "the complete and only remedy that can be taken and established for the reform of this Order is that the said primitive Fathers should make progress and be safeguarded, for morally speaking it is impossible for those who have been brought up in abuses to change their ancient customs in the way they ought." The reform of the Order in Spain thus has described a complete circle. By appointing visitators the Holy See had originally sought to ensure that the Carmelites would faithfully observe their existing Rule and constitutions. Then one of the visitators had decided that "the complete remedy for this reform" could only be brought about through the services of the primitives. Now the visitator decides that the Carmelites are a hopeless lot, and that the only prospect for the future is the promotion of the Discalced.

St. Teresa was elated with the results of the chapter of Almodóvar. "The Fathers have come back from it in the highest spirits," she wrote to Gracián from Toledo on September 20, 1576, "and I am extremely pleased to know how much good was done at it ... It is all your work, though perhaps, as you say, our prayers have had a lot to do with it. I was extremely glad about the appointment of a *zelator* for the houses ... I have urged him (John of Jesus Roca) to lay a great deal of stress on manual labor, which is of the very first importance. I told him I should write to your Paternity about it, as he says it was not discussed in the Chapter. I replied that it was in the Constitutions and Rule, and asked him what he was there for if not to see that they were obeyed. I was glad beyond belief, too, that those members of the Order have been expelled from it."[51]

Evidently the high-spirited Fathers had not bothered to tell the Mother of their attempt to erect a province. "I was also very glad," she writes in the same letter, "that the plan for getting our Father General to have us made into a separate province is being pursued in every possible way, for it is an intolerable kind of feud when one is on bad terms with one's superior." Later she consulted with Fray Peter Fernández. "He thinks the commissaries cannot make us into a separate province or nominate definitors unless they have more authority now than they had before," she wrote to Mariano on February 16, 1577.[52]

Ormaneto Under Fire

The reform of the religious orders in Spain was Ormaneto's personal devotion, catered to by the Holy See with increasing reluctance. "His Beatitude," Galli wrote on September 19, 1576, "is kept so busy listening to and answering the complaints that many religious orders in Spain are continually making. . . that, to tell the truth, he is being caused too much inconvenience. . . His Beatitude wants you to proceed less drastically, so that (religious) have no more reason to run here and cry out the way they do. Don't say that His Holiness need not listen to such complaints, because his office won't allow it; besides, the complaints are such that they cannot always be said to be wrong."53

The pope's secretary enclosed a sample submitted by the Carmelites. The pope, the memorandum states, has freed the Spanish provinces from the visit of the Dominicans and granted to the general chapter of Piacenza a brief authorizing the punishment of the disobedient, the closing of houses taken without the general's permission and the appointment of visitators and reformers. The nuncio has made provincial, visitator and reformer of the Andalusian province a Discalced friar named Fray Gracián who lacks the ten years of profession required for the office by the constitutions. He is disobedient to the general and has no fear of excommunications, because his brother is secretary to the king. The nuncio in making him provincial has done something not even done by the pope who has the power. The very Discalced are rebelling against Gracián's tyrannical ways. A copy is enclosed of the nuncio's faculties for Gracián derogating from papal briefs or decrees of the prior general or general chapter. A brief of recall of this visitator is requested. The order has ordained that the Discalced should be under the prior general to whom they make profession, that those who do not fear excommunication be punished, and that the Discalced do not accept all sorts of persons. Those who have been punished for some misdeed in the provinces join the Discalced, "not out of devotion but to rebel against their head, for under color of wearing rough cloth and going barefoot they say whatever they please; people do not everywhere know that they have been punished as miscreants and fugitives."54

The following January 15 Galli again wrote to Ormaneto: many Carmelites have left Spain for Rome and do nothing but complain about Gracián, the commissary deputized by him. The pope has never liked the idea that one order be visited by members of another order or Rule. He orders his nuncio to suspend Gracián's authority for the time being and to give complete liberty to Tostado, who being of the same Rule, will be better informed of the ordinances and needs of the Carmelites and consequently more apt to reform them. If the visit does not produce the desired fruit, Ormaneto is to report to the pope who will issue further instructions.55

Ormaneto had been seriously ill, but on February 5 he was able to reply. According to what is said hereabouts, he writes, Tostado "has come for no other reason than to suppress the Discalced, especially in Andalusia." He does not want the "Calced," as they are called, to oppose the Discalced who follow the primitive Rule. The Calced have noised it abroad that the Discalced are excommunicated by the general for founding houses against his will. He investigated the matter and discovered that the houses had been founded in obedience to an order of the former apostolic commissary who had the most ample faculties. It was he who had made Gracián provincial. The Discalced live very holy lives and give great edification. They are highly esteemed by the people; would to God the same could be said about the others. The Discalced will be very much favored and defended by the magistrates and men of good will; not so the others. Therefore Tostado had better tread lightly, as he (Ormaneto) hopes he will, for he seems a man of intelligence and discretion. If Tostado tries to harm the Discalced, he (Ormaneto) fears he will be sent away. The nuncio does not want the Discalced to be hindered from growing and founding houses with the permission of the ordinary according to the decrees of the council. Since the Discalced do not beg, but live by their own labor, they harm no one. "When Tostado returns, I shall see to it that he accepts them as sons, takes them into account and helps them to spread."[56]

In October of 1576 Gracián had resumed his visitation of the province of Andalusia.[57] On April 6, 1577, he was able to announce to Ormaneto that he had visited almost all the houses of the province; he asked his advice on certain problems and listed the decrees of reform to be published at the provincial chapter. The decrees correspond to those made for the friary of Seville.[58] The visitator also listed the abuses he encountered and the frequency of their occurrence and suggested a 44-point program of reform.[59]

With regard to the nunneries in the province, "the only remedy is to place in each monastery three Discalced nuns as porter, sacristan and prioress."[60] Gracián took occasion of a scandal which had arisen in Paterna, where four nuns were rumored to be pregnant, to reform this monastery through the Discalced. In October, 1576, Isabelle of St. Francis and Isabelle of St. Jerome, were sent from nearby Seville, the former as prioress. After her profession, January 1, 1577, Margarita of the Conception, a lay sister, joined them. The four nuns were shown to be innocent, but according to Gracián they showed their gratitude by calumniating him. The Discalced nuns met with much resistance; unfortunately they themselves lacked emotional stability and were inadequate for their task. Nevertheless they managed to improve fidelity to common life, choir and refectory. When Gracián ceased to be visitator, Teresa quickly withdrew her nuns, December 4, 1577.[61]

In due course Tostado returned from Portugal. On May 28, 1577, Teresa mentions that he was in Madrid, having passed through Toledo three or four days previously. Gracián was in Toledo on that day with the intention of visiting the nuncio who had summoned him.[62] At this critical moment Ormaneto died, June 18, after an illness of ten days, without settling the question of the Carmelite visitation. Certainly he left nothing in writing about this matter. His instructions from Rome had been to suspend Gracián's faculties and to allow Tostado to visitate.

Tostado's faculties did not depend from the nuncio, although in practice he could not exercise them without the king's *placet*. Gracián denied that Ormaneto had altered his status.[63] The opinion was sought of theologians and lawyers at Alcalá, Madrid, and Toledo. They concluded that Gracián's patents continued to be valid *re non integra*—as long as the business for which they had been granted was not finished. The president of the royal council, Bishop Diego de Covarrubias, a loyal friend of the Discalced, told Gracián to continue his commission.[64] From a letter of St. Teresa to Anna of St. Albert, July 2, 1577, it appears that the Discalced did not wait for the opinion of the experts to conclude that Gracián was still at the helm—or else they lost no time in collecting all those learned briefs.[65] Gracián continued to visitate the Discalced friaries in Castile.[66]

Gracián *versus* Tostado

In a rather strange ceremony the bishop of Avila, Alvaro de Mendoza, turned over the monastery of St. Joseph to the Order in the persons of St. Teresa and Jerome Gracián.[67] In the document solemnizing the occasion, August 2, 1577, the bishop does not specify the part of the Order to which he is committing the monastery. The provincial of Castile does not enter into the picture; presumably the monastery was to belong to the putative province Gracián had created the previous year.

On August 23, Gracián assigned Teresa conventuality at St. Joseph in Avila.[68]

Balthasar of Jesus chose this particular moment to revert to form. Due to a difference with Gracián, he abandoned his priorate of Almodóvar and went to Madrid where he placed himself under the jurisdiction of Tostado.[69] He composed a letter defamatory of Gracián and the Discalced which he induced Fray Michael de la Columna, a dim-witted cleric, to sign and present to the king. Fray Ferdinand de Medina, who had beautiful handwriting, kindly obliged and made the fair copy. Other Calced friars, present in Madrid, were alleged to be involved, and Tostado was said to be privy to the plot.[70]

In his letter Michael accuses Gracián of conducting the visitation of Andalusia in an insolent and exorbitant manner unbefitting a religious. Although the Discalced renounced the use of meat, Gracián, "like a secular bishop," had the Discalced nuns serve him sumptuous meals of chicken, turkey and partridge. He entered the cloister, and the nuns sang and danced for him. He wrote sonnets and *romanzas* for the nuns to sing. At Beas a nun, "young and very beautiful," dressed up in the silk ornaments of the sacristy, "so that she seemed more a prostitute than a nun," and danced before him. On one occasion Gracián and he stayed until ten o'clock at night and occasioned much scandal returning through the town to their lodgings in the home of a cleric who naturally wondered what they had been doing in a nunnery until that hour. Some of the houses of the Discalced were very lax, and certain of their practices resembled those of the *alumbrados*.[71] Obviously Balthasar had lost none of his flair.

Gracián's friends rallied round and wrote to the king and other influential persons on his behalf.[72] Teresa, horrified, begged the king not to dignify the accusations with an investigation. She blamed all on the devil and the Calced Fathers.[73] The devil had a lot to do with it, but the rest surely is feminine logic. The accusations were brought by two Discalced friars—one of them, Balthasar, an outstanding member of the reform. Later they retracted their accusations, implicating in the plot several Calced friars, including Tostado himself.[74] Certain Calced friars may have been pleased to help the malcontents, but if so, the initiative was not theirs. It is unlikely that Tostado had anything to do with the letter to the king, unless he believed it contained the truth. Strange how readily people credited the accusations against the Calced of those two proven liars.

With the arrival of the new nuncio, Philip Sega, on August 29, 1577, the policy of the nunciature in Madrid suffered a sea change. Rome had already formulated this policy during the last months of Ormaneto's life. Gregory XIII was weary of the state of continual turmoil into which the religious of Spain bad fallen because of reform. Ormaneto was commended for his zeal, but not for his prudence. His heavy hand caused the friars to yell so loud their cries were often heard in Rome. The reform of the Carmelites was to be confided to the commissary appointed by the prior general.[75]

When Sega made known to the king his instructions regarding the Carmelites, he received a visit on September 23, 1577, from the recently named archbishop of Toledo and supporter of the Discalced, Caspar de Quiroga, who held among other offices that of councilor to the king. Philip was absent from Madrid and asked Sega not to take any definite steps until they had a chance to talk. This suited the nuncio, because it allowed him to temporize until he had specific instructions from Rome.[76]

On October 14 Galli sent the nuncio his instructions. "With regard to the business of the friars, His Beatitude says that he intends that their charge be left to the officers appointed by their generals for their reform and for all that may be necessary to reduce the religious to a life conformable to their profession and obligations. This they will be more easily able to do, since they are assisted and armed with the authority of His Beatitude by means of special briefs." Only if the superiors are negligent of their duty or prove insufficient for their task is the nuncio to interfere and then only with the consent of the king. Without the king's consent nothing is to be undertaken.[77]

In other words the time of extraordinary visitations was past. The secretary's reference to the papal authorization of the Order's visitators shows that the Discalced's contention that the powers of apostolic commissaries were greater than these of the general was a bit simplistic and hints at a motive for resistance besides reluctance to be reformed.

On November 25 Sega wrote to Rome acknowledging the instructions of October 14. He had meanwhile had an audience with the king who referred him to Quiroga concerning a project for a reform of the Orders by theft own members. He had withdrawn the patents of six or seven commissaries appointed for reform by Ormaneto without further manifesting his intentions. In this way he hoped to scare the religious into bettering themselves. The Carmelites and Cistercians, because of the discord among them, required special consideration. He hoped that the Carmelite protector, the secretary of state, and the pope between them would provide him with a course of action. Meanwhile he would do what he could to maintain peace.[78]

The nuncio forbade Gracián to visitate any more. Gracián went first to Alcalá then to Pastrana where he lived in a cave.[79] He improved his time by directing memoranda to the king in which he pointed out "the great disadvantages that accrue to the religious orders of Spain when nuncios issue briefs contrary to the ordinances of theft superiors." This "beatific candor," to borrow Silverio's phrase, needless to say, did little to endear the former visitator to the nuncio. "I considered myself as good as dead," Gracián later recalled, "and feared I might be burned at the stake."[80]

As to Tostado's status during the next months, Francis of St. Mary states that on November 5, 1577, the royal council forbade him to visitate in Andalusia and Castile.[81] By that he did not forfeit his power to bind in conscience those to whom his commission was directed. He was recognized in the convents of the provinces and there surreptitiously exercised his authority—as the Discalced did not fail to tattle to the court.[82]

Trouble in Avila

At the Incarnation of Avila three years had passed since Teresa's successful superiorship, and many of the nuns were anxious to have her back. On October 7, 1577, the election of prioress was held under the presidency of the provincial of Castile, John Gutiérrez de la Magdalena. Before the balloting Gutiérrez let it be known that candidates outside the community were ineligible. In spite of this instruction fifty-four nuns voted for Teresa. These ballots were declared null, and the choice of the remaining forty-four nuns, Dona Juana del Aguila, became prioress. When the fifty-four pro-Teresian nuns insisted that their candidate had been validly elected and refused to acknowledge Dona Juana as prioress, the provincial excommunicated them. Tostado upheld the provincial's conduct of the election.[83]

All this did not take place without heated passion on both sides. The Discalced side of the controversy is well known to posterity, especially through the agile pen of St. Teresa, but today after the smoke of battle has cleared somewhat it may be safely said that the provincial, if not the perfect gentleman, was within his rights. Not to enter too deeply into the question, Teresa was not eligible because she was already prioress at St. Joseph's where she also had conventuality, granted to her by Gracián. Moreover, Teresa, unlike the community of the Incarnation, professed the primitive Rule. It was one thing for Pedro Fernández, as apostolic visitator, to appoint a Discalced nun prioress for purposes of reform, another for the community in a normal situation to elect her. Finally, unpalatable as it may be to our democratic tastes, presidents of elections in those days often had wide discretionary powers, and Gutiérrez claimed to have them.[84]

Nevertheless "learned men" declared that the nuns were not excommunicated, and that the president had acted against the council of Trent which required a majority of votes for an election.[85] The relatives of the excommunicated nuns united and appointed procurators to appeal to the royal council. The council ordered the provincial to absolve the nuns from excommunication. The provincial, on instructions from Tostado, signified his eagerness to obey the king, his "natural Lord," and ignoring the appeal of the nuns' procurator, of his own accord granted the absolution. The nuns continued to object to the election, but in this they received no support; the validity of the election was not in question.[86]

The provincial deputed Ferdinand Maldonado, prior of Toledo, to absolve the nuns, December 2-3, 1577. At the same time he was commissioned to remove the Discalced confessors from the monastery. It is generally said that he was under orders from Tostado, but there is no reason why the provincial could not have decided this measure on his own authority.

The Dominican visitator Fernández had placed Discalced friars at the Incarnation as confessors with great spiritual profit for the nuns. After Fernández had been recalled, the bishop of Avila, Alvaro de Mendoza, suggested to the nuncio turning the monastery over to the governance of the Discalced. In a letter of November 11, 1575, Ormaneto asked Gracián whether it was the policy of the Discalced to accept the governance of nuns. One thing he was sure of, they should not do so in places where they have no community of their own. "It never seemed to me to be good to have two or three friars in a house attached or not attached to a monastery." They should see about founding a convent of Discalced friars in Avila. Another matter he would like to mention: he does not like the way Mother Teresa, saint though she is, goes about founding and visiting monasteries. Religious women should stay in their monasteries and not travel about; that is the job of their superiors. However, the nuncio does not want his commissary to mention this opinion to a soul, as he does not wish to hurt "this good and holy Mother."[87]

Not long after this communication between the nuncio and his commissary, the prior of Avila, Alonso Valdemoro, created a commotion by removing the Discalced confessors, John of the Cross and Germain of St. Matthias, from the Incarnation, but Ormaneto ordered him to restore them.[88]

Now that Gracián's faculties had been suspended another attempt could be made to remove the Discalced confessors from the Incarnation. Since the Discalced had created their own province, it was unlikely that John and Germain would obey Gutiérrez, so they were forcibly removed. It is generally accepted that the incident took place the very night of Maldonado's unwelcome absolution of the nuns. St. John was imprisoned in Toledo until his escape in August 1578. Germain was confined at San Pablo de la Moraleja; he escaped in March.[89] (Conventual jails were notoriously insecure.) Teresa immediately wrote to the king in great distress, pleading that he command the Carmelites to set free their prisoners. "These friars have no respect either for justice or for God. It is a great grief to me to see our Fathers in their hands, where for a long time past they have wanted to get them. I would rather see them among the Moors, for they might well show them more pity."[90] Philip did not interfere.

The importance of this distressful incident has been blown up out of all proportion. Biographers and novelists have spared neither imagination nor descriptive skill on the story of St. John's imprisonment and treatment in prison. As a matter of fact little first hand information is available. Not all the punishments applicable by law are to be presumed to have been applied to the prisoners. Imprisonment, flogging, fasting on bread and water were standard penalties in religious orders of the time, Discalced as well as others. This is not to deny that in this case the accused were treated with severity, given the inflamed state of feelings that by this time existed between Carmelite brothers.

One bright ray in this dark picture: in his prison cell in the convent of Toledo St. John of the Cross composed a number of poems including most of the *Spiritual Canticle* and the *Dark Night*.[91]

Sega Takes the Initiative

Tostado could tarry no longer. In May 1578, he passed on to Aragon and Catalonia which the king allowed him to visitate.[92]

His departure was the signal for Gracián to return to the scene. The new president of the royal council, Anthony Maurice Pazos y Figueros, ordered Gracián to resume the visitation; on June 19, he obtained for Gracián the king's consent to use the secular arm.[93]

Chapter Three: "An Intolerable Kind of Feud"

Gracián was now in desperate straits. Neither pope nor nuncio would have any part of his apostolic powers. He was operating only on the strength of the royal mandate.

If it is true that the king and his council as a matter of policy supported the reform movements in religious orders, the Discalced operated a powerful lobby at court. Through his father and two brothers, Antonio and Thomas, Jerome Gracián had good connections there. Mariano Azaro, whose contribution to the early growth of the reform is difficult to overestimate, had the ear of the king and spent much time at court. Antonio de Jesús, as well as St. Teresa, was a close friend of the Duchess of Alba. Other influential friends of the Discalced included the noted Tridentine theologian, Diego de Covarrubias, president of the royal council, 1574-1577; Roque de Huerta, secretary of the royal council, who had a daughter among the Discalced; Cardinal Caspar de Quiroga, archbishop of Toledo and *oidor* of the royal council, who had a niece among the Discalced; Diego de Montoya, king's agent in Rome in the matter of religious reform, whose mother was a warm friend of St. Teresa; Leonor de Mascareñas, governess of King Philip and his son Don Carlos; Luis Hurtado de Mendoza, Count of Tendilla, and captain general of the Kingdom of Granada.[94]

Teresa and her friars also made use of the services of the Licentiate John Calvo de Padilla, a cleric who for some obscure reason concerned himself with the reform of religious orders in Spain. His methods were not always above reproach, and he ended up in the gaol of the Inquisition of Toledo.[95] The pope's secretary, Ptolemy Galli, had already had to warn Ormaneto against granting authority to certain imprudent persons such as Padilla who had written letters in his name.[96] Teresa remained loyal to Padilla after his disgrace.

Sega, reporting an audience with the king on July 17, 1578, tells of the fall of Padilla. "He set before the king whatever capricious notion came into his head, and it seemed that His Majesty gave him ready credence. Of the same sort as this man were two others—a certain Fray Mariano from Calabria, a Discalced Carmelite, and a certain Fray Maldonado, a Discalced Franciscan." The latter he managed to have removed from court: "I am not without hope of also being able to embarrass the other in some way, for truly these friars have been the means of keeping disturbed all these religious orders in Spain, because the matter of visitations and reforms has not been hitherto treated in the way demanded by the nature of the times, place, and persons."[97]

The friars of Andalusia, hearing that Gracián was in Valladolid preparing to visitate the south, appealed against him. They denied that he had an apostolic commission; if he ever had one, it had been taken away by the nuncio because of his misdeeds, especially in monasteries of nuns.[98]

The nuncio who had forbidden Gracián to visitate could hardly overlook the contravention of his command. On July 23, 1578, he formally deprived Gracián of his commission, ordering him under pain of communication to present himself within six days and surrender all documents concerning his visitations and reforms. Mincing no words, the nuncio declares that Gracián was led by a spirit of presumption and arrogance in continuing to exercise his faculties after Ormaneto's death, even after he had been expressly forbidden under censure to do so, "to the detriment of your honor and your soul and to the prejudice and scandal of the whole Order."[99]

Teresa was shocked by the nuncio's tone when she was served with his letter on August 9. Realist that she was, she set about at once to mend her fences: the next day she sent the chaplain of St. Joseph's, Julian de Avila, to Madrid to make an act of obeisance and to beg the nuncio not to put the Discalced under the provincials.[100] At the same time she composed a memorandum, to be distributed among "various people" in Madrid, justifying Gracián's conduct and showing "the injustice of the Brief's harsh treatment of him."[101]

The intervention of influential friends had its effect. At the instigation of the Count of Tendilla, Louis Hurtado de Mendoza, who explained that the nuncio "was trying absolutely to undo" the reform, the king's council sequestered Gracián's papers in order to review Sega's action. The nuncio complained to the king about Tendilla's interference, accusing him of hiding the Discalced friars wanted for questioning and comparing him to the Lutheran nobles who obstructed the action of the Holy See in Germany.[102] Francis of St. Mary states that Philip published an edict, dated Aug. 8, ordering authorities in all cities, towns and places to seize any orders of the nuncio regarding the governance of religious, because he had not shown his right over them.[103] There is no record of so drastic an action of the king, nor do extant documents show evidence of disaccord between Philip and Sega.

Eventually Sega succeeded in acquiring Gracián's papers as visitator. His decree of July 23 went unchallenged. Next he set about investigating "the life of this Gracián and the manner of living of these Discalced ... to see what manner of man he is, what sort of religious these are, what Rule they profess, in what manner they are governed, since they object to being governed by the Calced." To assist him in this investigation he diplomatically requested of the king the help of two religious of other orders.[104]

At this moment Gracián's time bomb, set in 1576, went off. As arranged then, at the lapse of Gracián's commission Anthony of Jesus, first definitor of the alleged Discalced province, convened a chapter at Almodóvar, October 9, 1578, to elect a provincial. Anthony himself emerged as provincial.[105]

Sega's reply, on October 16, was to declare the whole procedure null and void and to forbid Anthony under pain of excommunication to act as provincial. He furthermore placed the Discalced friars and nuns under the jurisdiction of the provincials of Castile and Andalusia, Diego de Cardenas and John Gutierrez de la Magdalena.[106] The nuncio thought he had discovered evidence to show that Gracián's arrangement for subsequently electing a provincial, allegedly made in 1576, had in reality been drawn up in Seville after Gracián had been deprived of his faculties. He branded the affair as "new ... extravagant and ... full of injustice and falsehood."[107]

Besides Antonio, Gregory Nazianzen, Mariano Azaro, and Gabriel of the Assumption were placed under arrest in various convents. Gracián was confined to the Carmen of Madrid.[108]

The Discalced Reunited to the Provinces

At the Discalced nunnery of Seville Cardenas ran into big trouble. During a visitation two nuns brought such accusations against St. Teresa, Jerome Gracián, and the prioress, Mary of St. Joseph, as would have made Balthasar Nieto blush.

Mary of St. Joseph whose surname was Salazar had been in the service of Dona Louise de la Cerda at the time of St. Teresa's visit in 1562. She entered the Order at Malagón in 1570. Able, intelligent, and spirited, Mary was a favorite of the foundress with whom she carried on a voluminous correspondence and even had her differences. Like Teresa too, Mary was close to Gracián but their relationship from the beginning was beclouded by rumor and gossip.[109]

From its difficult beginning–comparable in Teresa's opinion only to that of Avila[110]–had experienced problems. In December 1585, only a few months after the foundation of the monastery, Mary del Corro, "a great *beata* already canonized by the whole city," in the prioress' phrase, left the novitiate and accused the community of being *alumbradas*, thus bringing down on the house the unwelcome ministrations of the Inquisition.[111] On March 28, 1578, Teresa warned Mary of St. Joseph against the nuns writing on prayer.[112] One of the nuns went insane; writing to the prioress on June 4, 1578, Teresa offers advice on her treatment, suggesting whipping her to keep her quiet–a standard remedy of the time. In the same letter Teresa expresses concern over two sisters who were having spiritual experiences of doubtful origin.[113]

The first girl to enter the Seville monastery was Beatrix of the Mother of God, recommended by Gracián and clothed by Teresa herself. Teresa devotes a whole chapter of the *Foundations* (ch. 26) to the marvelous story of the girl's vocation–so marvelous in fact as to arouse suspicion.[114] When Beatrix began to have doubts about her vocation, Teresa advised Gracián to profess her and end her temptations.[115] The confessor of the community was Don García Alvarez, a priest who had been a friend in need at the foundation of the monastery. Beatrix and Margarita of the Conception, a lay nun, spent hours in his confessional. Alvarez believed the accounts of the irregularities in the monastery with which she filled his ears, as did the Jesuits, Diego Acosta and Caspar Hoyas, whom he brought in as consultants. The reputation of the community also began to suffer outside, and the prioress felt herself increasingly isolated. She got rid of Alvarez, but the provincial reinstated him.

Then at the provincial's visitation the most sensational revelations surfaced, the products of Beatrix's unbalanced mind. Teresa and other nuns had gone out dressed in secular clothes. She had told the nuns to confess to each other. Gracián had undressed in front of the nuns. He advised the nuns that they need not confess mortal sins. Because Beatrix alone did not volunteer to give up her habit when one was needed at Paterna, Mary of St. Joseph caused her to be stripped, so all could see whether she was "white, black or fat." Cardenas grilled the whole community and drew up a canonical process to be presented to the nuncio. He deposed Mary of St. Joseph and made Beatrix vicaress. The nuns later disclaimed the allegations of the process in a memorial to Gracián. Mary accused Alvarez and Cardenas of deliberately confusing the nuns, most of them novices, and of twisting their words out of context in order to discredit the Discalced reform. This is almost a more charitable interpretation than to believe that Cardenas could credit the ravings of the psychopathic nun, but mental illness was not so often recognized as such in those days. Again, the trouble came from within the reform and had been brewing for a long time.[116]

Teresa was not surprised at the conduct of the "black vicaress," as she nicknamed her. "That wretched vicaress," she wrote to Gracián in April of 1579, "was always making up such dreadful calumnies: for a long time I have been afraid this would happen."[117] Teresa readily forgave Beatrix, and urged the others to do the same, but after things had calmed down she wanted her punished and was shocked that she had been allowed to receive Holy Communion by July 1580.[118] Beatrix died in 1624, aged 86. Margarita accompanied Mary of St. Joseph to Lisbon and died in ripe old age in 1647.[119]

To assist him in his investigation of Fray Jerome Gracián and the Discalced, Sega received the services of Don Louis Manrique, royal chaplain; Hernando Castillo, Dominican; and Laurence de Villavicencio, Augustinian. Gracián was required to answer fifteen objections to his conduct of the visitation. To the accusation that he did not frequent refectory and choir, Gracián answered rather weakly that he had been afraid he would be poisoned and had no time to go to choir; besides he couldn't sing. He had not abstained from meat because he was ill. He had made no decrees which were not in conformity to the councils and the primitive Rule; he admitted going against the Order's legislation which was lax. He had founded houses in Andalusia with authorization of the apostolic visitator, Francis Vargas. If anyone claimed Vargas did not have the power, that was his business; it was not the subject's place to judge the superior's authority. Ormaneto had ordered him to continue his visitation in spite of the general chapter of 1575, confirmed by the pope; indeed had expressly ruled it out in his patents. As to his continuing the visitation after the nuncio's prohibition, he did not recall Sega's forbidding it under censure. When the president of the royal council, Pazos, had ordered him to proceed, he had thought he had the power to do so. He had divided the province and held the chapter on orders from Ormaneto who had told Fray Mariano orally "to hold the chapter and the rest."[120]

Sega issued his verdict on December 20, 1578. He absolved Gracián from all censures, but deprived him *in perpetuum* of the office of reformer, sent him to the convent of Alcalá, imposed penances of fasts and scourgings and forbade him to write or receive letters, especially from nuns, or otherwise interfere in the affairs of the Order.[121] When the rector, Elias of St. Martin, suffering from the quartan ague, asked Gracián on several occasions to hold the conventual chapter, three members of the community reported him to the nuncio, alleging that he was again governing the Discalced.[122] As this incident shows and later history was to bear out, Gracián was by no means as acceptable to the friars as he was to the nuns. He was not long confined to Alcalá. On February 19, 1580, he was elected prior of Seville. On March 10 Salazar confirmed his election and a month later named him visitator for the Discalced friaries and nunneries beyond the Sierra Morena in Andalusia.[123]

On January 21, 1579, on Sega's request for another member of his commission Philip appointed the Dominican Peter Fernández, former visitator and dear friend of Teresa who gave a sigh of relief.[124]

The nuncio now had the reins of authority firmly in hand. Although he was never able to obtain recognition for the visitor from Rome, he did manage to bring Gracián to heel and to insert the Discalced into the normal administrative channels of the Order. His constant purpose was not to "undo" the reform, as its members somewhat hysterically claimed, but to put a stop to "the noise of the friars," to bring peace to the troubled waters of religious reform in Spain. His subjection of the Discalced to the provincials, as he had written to Buoncompagni on November 13, was "provisional, until otherwise determined."[125]

In fact, on April 1, 1579, Sega withdrew the Discalced from the jurisdiction of the provincials and placed them under a special vicar general, Angel de Salazar, prior of Valladolid.[126] Teresa's choice, of course, was Gracián but knowing this would not be done, she would have preferred Anthony of Jesus, John of the Cross, or anyone, provided he was not Calced or Andalusian.[127] Teresa had no use for any Calced friar in Spain; Fray Angel was only the best of a bad lot. "May God grant that he may enjoy that office only for a short time," she commented to Gracián.[128]

On June 29, Salazar restored Mary of St. Joseph to the office of prioress of Seville. "It was evident," he wrote to her privately, "that the judge had tried to draw blood where there was none."[129]

By this time John Baptist Rossi, "the spiritual father of the Order," had died in Rome, September 4, 1578.[130] A devout and learned man, deeply committed to reform, it had been his fate to run afoul of the great reforming movement which had risen in the Order, corresponding to the new spiritual force at work everywhere in the church. In the parlor of St. Joseph's at Avila, St. Teresa's vision of Carmel had found sympathetic resonance in his soul. "I was intensely grieved at the news which I received about our Father General," Teresa wrote to Gracián. "I feel deeply moved by it. On the day I heard it I wept and wept–I could do nothing else–and I felt very much distressed at all the trouble we have caused him, which he certainly did not deserve; if we had gone to him about the matter everything would have been smoothed out. God forgive the person who has continually put obstacles in the way; for, though you had little confidence in my suggestion, I could have come to an understanding with your Paternity."[131]

To the end Teresa remained the obedient daughter of the prior general. This constant loyalty to its head may be taken to mean that Teresa's desire was to maintain the unity of the Order.

Chapter IV

A SEPARATE PROVINCE

The question of an independent province was a different matter. Not long after she found in Fray Jerome Gracián a leader for her reform St. Teresa began urging separation from "those of the cloth."[1] The erection of a separate province had become a necessity. The Discalced movement had become something more than a matter of a few contemplative houses attached to the provinces of the Order. On the other hand it could not be expected to absorb the unreformed (or less reformed) houses of the provinces, because the Discalced professed the "primitive" Rule, to which others of a different profession could not be obliged. In the case of the nuns the need for independence was even more acute. The nuns needed understanding of their way of life and freedom of action which often were not forthcoming from friars accustomed to traditional ways.

The Discalced Appeal to Rome

The bootleg chapter of Almodóvar, 1578, dispatched two friars, Peter of the Angels and John of St. Diego, a lay brother, to Rome to plead the Discalced cause. When Gracián's chapter of two years previously had decided (without result) to send emissaries to Rome, Teresa had heartily approved; after Rossi's death she opposed their going, fearful they would end up in jail.[2] With Gracián *hors de combat* Teresa set on foot her own negotiations, carefully planned to avoid the pitfalls she feared the others chanced.[3] John of Jesus (Roca) and Diego of the Trinity donned secular clothes and assumed the names John Bullón and Diego de Heredia respectively. They embarked from Alicante in mid-May 1579. The Discalced nuns, organized by St. Teresa, supplied the money for their journey and sojourn in Rome.

Teresa also helped support Peter of the Angels, the delegations working simultaneously.[4] Another negotiator for St. Teresa was Canon Diego de Montoya of Avila, agent for the Inquisition in Rome, "who has been fighting for our lives." He was already back in Spain in July, when he brought the cardinal's hat to Teresa's friend, Archbishop Caspar de Quiroga, of Toledo.[5] Peter of the Angels was also eliminated when he defected to the old observance, of which he had originally been a member. "Words cannot describe the treachery committed against the Saint and her sons," comments Silverio of St. Teresa.[6] John of Jesus and Diego of the Trinity, posing as Spanish gentlemen, spent a year in Rome winning influential friends for the reform and urging the erection of a Discalced province.[7]

In the end it was not this cloak and dagger caper that won the day. On July 15, 1579, Philip Sega and his commission reported to the king on the second phase of their investigation–the manner of living of the Discalced. St. Teresa's sons and daughters passed this test with flying colors, and for their benefit and for the sake of peace the nuncio recommended the erection of a separate province of Discalced friars and nuns.[8]

The way now lay open by which the Discalced might attain their desired freedom. A request to the new vicar general, John Baptist Caffardi, produced the reply that they should await the coming general chapter, but they had little hope of obtaining their wish from that body, especially since the degree of autonomy they intended to propose far exceeded that of an ordinary province. Instead they turned to the king, their last resource, and petitioned him to obtain their independence from the pope.[9]

The king supplied the pope with a rough draft, or minute, of a proposed brief, drawn up by the Discalced themselves, according to which the pope was to concede, besides the erection of a province and the approval of the Discalced way of life, the right of the king to nominate "an upright and suitable man" in Spain who would have wide powers "to make every provision for the good government of this Order without the need for recourse to the general chapter." This person would be able to found houses, make laws, decide the binding force of the visitations of provincials, generals or their vicars and of the decrees of the general chapters. Finally the brief should contain a clause of irrevocability, to protect it against less favorable successors of Gregory XIII.[10]

The nuncio was not edified by the initiative of the Discalced. In a letter to the cardinal protector of the Carmelites, Philip Buoncompagni, he enclosed a copy of the report by his commission to the king. The report did not enlarge on the sorry state in which the mitigated found themselves. Their reform had made so little progress that the king had considered making the same request of the Holy See in their case as he had in that of the Conventual Franciscans. However, some progress was being made. The Discalced are "a good and holy innovation," but there are four or five among them "who pride themselves on being founders and as it were Fathers of the Primitive Church and who have not attained the mortification they profess." These are Anthony of Jesus, Mariano of Calabria, Jerome Gracián, John of Jesus and Diego of the Trinity. They tried to separate themselves from the mitigated by a pack of lies and had received the punishment which was their due.

They continue to be restless, "dissatisfied at being cast out of their empire, the beginning of the ruin of the very birth of this holy reform," and have drawn up a rough draft of a *motu proprio* which the king is to present to his

Holiness as though it were his own idea and which suggests not only that they be separated from obedience to the provincials, as approved, but also to the general, the nuncio and, one would almost say, to the pope himself. Sega suggests the erection of a normal province with the power to make laws subject to confirmation. The Discalced houses should all be confirmed, but no more should be founded until those existing have sufficient members, because their "one ambition is to found many houses and gradually settle in all the places where the mitigated have convents in order to destroy them." None of their houses have enough friars, especially priests; instead of building up the order they create confusion.[11]

There should be one novitiate, candidates should not be received without the provincial's consent, no house should be founded without the decree of the provincial chapter and confirmation by the nuncio. The province should be placed under the nuncio with certain limitations to avoid separation from the general which the Discalced are procuring. The chapter should be held at Pastrana near the court under the presidency of the nuncio. The five who were punished should not be eligible for election as provincial.

Efforts to Maintain Unity

Angel de Salazar pleaded with Caffardi not to permit the erection of a separate province, even though "the endless business of the government of the primitives so afflicts me as to leave me dead." At the chapter of Castile, November 15, 1579, the Discalced priors had been present at the nuncio's request, and one of them, Gabriel of the Assumption, had been elected definitor. Salazar had caused the designation of Discalced prior and lectors to be entered in the book of provincial acts, but secretly, so as to avoid contention. The nuncio had drawn up decrees of reform, but some of the delegates had expressed certain reservations. Sega wanted them to wear habits of undyed wool (*bixo*), as is done in Italy, "to avoid the high cost of black cloth, which is very expensive, and the great pomp which many of us show by our black garments with much scandal, and to conform to the dress of the primitive or Discalced Fathers, whom God has sent us in this province to exercise us in good works and to keep us from any further wrongdoing." Salazar approved this decision of the nuncio: "I have decided to start wearing this color in a very few days."[12]

King Philip no doubt made his request for a Discalced province through his temporary representative in Rome, Abbot Bernardine Briceño, who in any case continued to report the progress of the affair. Pope Gregory XIII turned it over to a committee of six cardinals of the Congregation for Religious and Bishops. In the course of their deliberations these consulted the opinion of the Order's protector, Cardinal Philip Buoncompagni, and of the procurator general, Timothy Berardi.[13]

In the Order's reply to the Congregation, the latter is asked, first of all, to allow the general chapter to decide the issue. Failing this, the cardinals should inquire whether the Discalced are really going back to the primitive Rule, because it makes no provision for the austerities the Discalced practice, such as going barefoot. Secondly, it might be asked, was their institution by the former general licit? After the mitigation by Eugene IV the general chapter ordered all houses of the Order to conform, "in order to avoid division, the most essential beginning of all ruin of religious orders,"[14] and because the mitigation was "not far from the first life." Granted that the proposed way of life is Carmelite and properly instituted, their eminences should still consider whether the Discalced deserve to be heard. In requesting separation they are violating the promise made at their institution to remain united to the Order. They are new in religion and have no one apt to govern them. Their request comes from rebellious spirits condemned by the nuncio and the king's delegates, who ran to the king after having been asked by their superior to wait. The Discalced want freedom in order the better to molest the Order as they have always done, giving such false information about the Order to the king that he nearly suppressed it. Granting the request of the Discalced would appear to favor rebellion, for though excommunicated they continued to found houses.[15]

In a lengthy appeal to their protector, Cardinal Philip Buoncompagni, the Carmelites brand the request of the Discalced as unjust and founded on irrelevant and false reasons. The primitives were founded under the special condition that they would remain united to the province. Moreover it was not the general's intention to found a separate group, but simply to give the more fervent members of the province the opportunity to live lives of penance and contemplation. The Discalced request is unjust because it seeks to take away houses from the province and compromises the authority of the general when it denies that he can give permission to his sons to live the primitive contemplative life under the provincial. The Discalced lie when they say they were mistreated by the mitigated; at first the relationships were good, and many members of the province joined them. This friendly treatment they repaid by getting themselves named visitators by commissaries of another Order. Their petition is unjust because they attempt to absolve themselves from obedience to the provincial, general, and even the pope and to place themselves under a secular judge.

The Discalced plea that they need a superior of their own observance who will lead them with understanding and good example applies to the local prior not necessarily to the provincial, more so because the difference between the two observances is slight and reduces itself to a remission of the fast and abstinence and permission to leave the convent once or twice a week—matters which do not affect true religious virtue. The Discalced were not restoring the primitive Rule by such austerities as going barefoot, because such things are not found in it; rather they are founding a new Order, and it would be better if they were reduced to the old one. According to true profession, primitive and mitigated life is very similar and there can be perfect understanding between its practitioners, because after all it was the old Order that gave birth to the reform. The differences between the two observances will only be accentuated under different superiors. Religious orders have never fallen under such censure of the world as when they broke up into different congregations. Both Pius V and his Catholic Majesty tried to reduce religious orders to one way of living.[16]

One positive effect of the controversy was that the Discalced forced the old Order to turn back to its origins and for the first time to reflect on its identity. What was meant by "the primitive Rule"? Was the Order still true to its origins? Interestingly the friars of the old observance did not challenge the primitives on their insistence on the contemplative vocation of the Order. Somewhat too facilely they objected to austerities like going barefoot, wearing a rough habit, sleeping on boards, living by work and by not begging as novelties that did not affect the essence of the Carmelite vocation but tended to promote division—the worst thing that can happen to the Order. (When one thinks of the centuries of bad feeling and unedifying rivalry between the two orders, one must agree that this emphasis on the primacy of the unity of brotherly love was not misplaced.)

The mitigated friars painted an overly optimistic picture of conditions in the Order and minimized the real obstacles in the path of cohabitation, yet their insistence that the two groups did not differ fundamentally in their vocation represented an insight which unfortunately could not be implemented under the circumstances, to the ultimate disadvantage of Carmel. The friars of the old Order had the medieval concept of religious life as itself contemplative and of the contemplative life as inclusive of all elements of religious life. They could not see why they were not to be considered contemplatives too, but in fact the Order needed to be renewed in its spirit which was one of preoccupation with God. Yet by emphasizing and isolating the contemplative element of religious life, the Discalced—and Counter Reformation piety generally—created a dichotomy between contemplation and activity that continued to plague spirituality until recent times.

The Discalced did not manage to get a decision from the pope before the general chapter, but the fact that the question was *sub judice* with the Holy See prevented this body from making any decision. At the chapter which met at Traspontina, Pentecost, May 22, 1580, the definitors left the "case of the primitive Discalced to the wisdom and vigilance of the Most Reverend Father."[17] But already on April 18 Briceño had reported to Philip that the pope in a meeting with the cardinals had conceded the erection of a

Discalced province; on May 2 he related that the bull was almost ready and would be expedited at the next meeting of the cardinals.[18]

On June 22, 1580, Pope Gregory XIII in his brief, *Pia consideratione*, acceded to the request of King Philip II and the Discalced, "who were the object of a number of molestations and hindrances disturbing to their institute from the friars... called mitigated," and erected a separate province of Discalced friars and nuns. They were to be immediately subject to the prior general who had the right to visitate only in person or through a Discalced delegate. The provincial required the confirmation of the general. Only the permission of the provincial was needed to found new houses. Recourse to the pope or the cardinal protector is expressly declared to be licit.[19]

The Discalced had not won consent to all their requests, most importantly for that "upright and suitable man" who in effect would have cut them off from all influence outside Spain, but their province was given privileges above the common and in fact was already a congregation.

The *datarius* Cardinal Mark Anthony Maffei won the king's gratitude for his special efforts in obtaining the brief.[20]

The Chapter of Alcalá - 1581

In the ordinary course of events, the first chapter of the province and election of the provincial would have been presided over by a representative of the prior general, but this procedure might have led to complications, and Philip was careful to keep the Order at arm's length. At his request Gregory XIII on November 20, 1580, named the Dominican John de las Cuevas president of the forthcoming Discalced chapter.[21] St. Teresa who was keeping a close watch over events, now that her work was reaching its consummation, did not hesitate to make her preferences known to the president on the choice of a provincial. Gracián–"there is no one like my Father Gracián"–was of course her first choice, followed by Nicholas of Jesus and Mary Doria and John of Jesus Roca. Roca, she admits, she added to the list only so that she might not seem to be limiting her choice. Anthony of Jesus definitely would not do.[22]

Gracián as a matter of fact was elected provincial. At the provincial chapter which met at Alcalá, March 3, 1581, Gracián received eleven out of twenty votes; Anthony of Jesus, seven.[23] Not exactly a landslide, considering Gracián's outstanding role in the growth of the reform and Teresa's enthusiastic endorsement of him and disapproval of Anthony. The four definitors were respectively Nicholas of Jesus and Mary, Anthony of Jesus, John of the Cross, and Gabriel of the Assumption. Ambrose Mariano delivered an eloquent sermon in Latin.[24] The chapter members decreed special suffrages for the king in token of their gratitude, as indeed they had reason to do. By turns the convents and monasteries of the province would offer Mass and perpetual prayers day and night for this intention.²⁵

Caffardi confirmed the new provincial, June 29, 1582.²⁶

An important task of the chapter was to provide legislation for the reform.

As apostolic commissary for the Discalced in Castile and Andalusia, Gracián in 1575 or 1576 had composed constitutions or ordinances for the friars who up to then had been governed by the constitutions of Duruelo approved by Rossi. Gracián's constitutions consist of fifteen brief chapters and presume the general legislation of the Order in so far as it is not contrary to the "primitive" Rule. The chapters concern the election of the prior, reception of novices, reception of *beatas* (or rather, prohibition to do so), cloister, poverty, divine office, Mass stipends, care of the sick, clothing, chapter of faults, manner of travel, mental prayer and discipline, recreation, humility of the prior. Except in rare and serious cases no one is allowed to leave the house besides preachers, confessors, officials on business. Begging is abolished; the religious are to earn their bread by the work of their hands. No one may possess anything, however insignificant. Superiors should supply all their subjects' needs and may not tell them to fend for themselves. There should be community libraries, community supply rooms, community infirmaries. The divine office should be recited *sin punto*. All should eat in the common refectory, partaking of the same food; furnishings should be plain. Habits should be brown (*burial*), of serge (*sayal* or *xerga*), feet should be bare in open sandals. Travel is done on foot, on longer journeys on an humble beast of burden. Meditation is to be made two hours daily, the discipline is to be taken three times a week. After meals there is an hour recreation "from the spiritual labors of the Rule." All privileges of masters are abolished as well as titles of honor and other differences among the brethren.²⁷

The constitutions issued by the chapter for the friars form a complete body of legislation, at least at the provincial level, and replace the constitutions of the Order, of which they preserve Soreth's basic structure of five parts and many juridical elements not affecting the reformed way of life. Without repeating what has already been pointed out concerning the Teresian way of life, it may be said that the constitutions canonize its characteristic elements of confinement to the cell, liturgical and mental prayer, silence, austerity in dress, perpetual abstinence from meat, common life of poverty, manual labor, study.

Only a few kinds of apostolate are admitted: preaching, catechesis, hearing confessions. Confessions of the laity are generally heard within the convents. Preaching is limited to the nuns, though later constitutions (1590, 1592) provide for preaching to the faithful on Sunday. The care of parishes is forbidden; missions are not yet contemplated.

The complete Latin text of the constitutions was printed at Alcalá by

Hernan Ramírez with a sixth part containing decisions of the chapters of Almodóvar (1583) and Pastrana (1585). A Spanish translation of the Alcalá constitutions, reduced in part, appeared at Salamanca, printed by Pedro Lasso, 1582.[28]

Another concern of the chapter was the legislation of the nuns. On May 7, 1576, Jerome Gracián, "provincial and apostolic visitator," had issued a decree designed to organize the life of the Discalced nuns. They were to follow the constitutions made by the prior general and Pedro Fernández. The former had ordained that the visitator of the nuns should be a friar of the primitive Rule, if possible. Since such friars were now to be had in abundance, Gracián forbade the nuns under pain of rebellion to admit a Calced visitator.[29] The chapter now undertook to issue definitive constitutions for the nuns.

In the weeks before the chapter St. Teresa engaged in a brisk exchange of letters with Gracián about this business so vital to her. Suggestions for modifications, carefully censored by the mother foundress, were sent from all the monasteries. The chapter retained the nuns' constitutions intact with only a few additions and modifications of a stylistic and juridical nature. Teresa's comments were also generally followed. The sisters were placed under the direct jurisdiction of the provincial, thus eliminating interference by the local prior. Communities without income were limited to thirteen or fourteen nuns; those with income to twenty. Teresa preferred all houses to have income, but the chapter decided to recommend poverty when possible. There was to be no difference in life-style in the two sorts of houses. The chaplain, chosen by the prioress and provincial in consultation, should be a secular priest. He could also be confessor (not recommended by Teresa). The prioress was free to call in other confessors besides the ordinary one. The same freedom applies to preachers. She did not need permission from the provincial. This structure, unusual in an age of male chauvinism, gave the nuns needed freedom to grow in the Spirit according to God's calling for each individual. The constitutions of Alcalá comprised twenty chapters and were printed in Salamanca by the heirs of Mathias Gast, 1581.[30]

The new province numbered twelve friaries and twelve nunneries with almost four hundred friars and two hundred nuns.[31]

Teresa could now sing her *"Nunc dimittis"*— her lifework was secured. "This," she wrote about the chapter of Alcalá, "proved to be one of the most joyful and satisfying experiences that I could ever have in this life, and I had been suffering trials, persecutions, and afflictions for more than five-and-twenty years ... When I saw that they were all at an end, only those who know the trials we had endured can understand what joy filled my heart and how I longed that the whole world should praise Our Lord and that we should pray to Him for this holy King of ours, Don Philip, through whose mediation God brought everything to such a good end, for the devil had used such crafts that, had it not been for the King, all our work would have come to nothing. Now, Calced and Discalced alike, we are all at peace, and no one hinders us in Our Lord's service.[32]

But the troubles of the reform were not yet at an end. Times were coming when the battles with the fathers of the cloth would seem child's play. Teresa however was to be spared the internecine wars which would have wounded her mother's heart even more deeply. This marvelous woman, so heavenly yet so human, died on October 4, 1582.

Chapter V

CARMEL AFTER TERESA: THE DIVISION OF THE ORDER

Nicholas of Jesus and Mary Doria

Recent years had seen the rise of a man who was now to challenge Gracián's leadership and ideas. Nicholas Doria (1539-1594), the scion of a merchant family of Genoa, settled in 1570 in Seville, trading center of the Indies. He had amassed a comfortable fortune when he decided to embrace the ecclesiastical state. After studies at the Dominican College of St. Thomas in Seville he took priestly orders. He came to know Fray Mariano, a fellow Italian, at the Discalced convent of Los Remedios. Even as a priest his talent for business continued to serve him. He saved from the hands of creditors the palace of the archbishop of Seville, Don Christopher Rojas y Sandoval, who became his grateful friend as a result. He likewise gave valued advice to Philip II on financial matters. The grateful king, Gracián declares, "would have given him any bishopric or archbishopric in Spain."[1]

Nicholas was also known to the Discalced nuns of Seville and gave them practical advice in temporal matters and in the *affaire* Beatrix; he was Mary of St. Joseph's confessor. The foundress herself knew and esteemed him for his virtue and sound sense. Eventually he joined the Discalced reform, pronouncing his vows on March 25, 1578. A mature man of affairs, his talents were immediately put to use; within months of profession he became superior at Los Remedios. As such, on December 1, 1578, he wrote a letter of filial submission in answer to Caffardi's announcement of Rossi's death and his own appointment as vicar general of the Order.[2] By this diplomatic gesture–the sort of thing Teresa had been urging for years, which Gracián had never had the sense to make–Doria made himself spokesman for the reform at a time when it lacked a head, Gracián being in disgrace with the nuncio. His letter, allegedly written on behalf of the Seville community, was signed by friars from other houses as well, among them John of the Cross, vicar of El Calvario.

During that difficult time for the Discalced Doria made himself very useful to their cause, taking up residence in Madrid to be nearer the court. St. Teresa praises the astuteness with which he lived at the Carmen of Madrid, all the while unbeknownst to his hosts promoting the interests of the Discalced: "He is so discreet that, when he was at the Calced monastery in Madrid, he dissembled his purpose as though he were there on other business, and they never knew that he was working on our behalf and so allowed him to remain. We wrote to each other frequently. . . and we used to discuss the best methods of procedure."[3] With Gracián, Mariano, and Roca he formed a commission to help Las Cuevas prepare the chapter at Alcalá. At the chapter itself he was elected first definitor.[4]

Teresa hoped Doria would become Gracián's right hand. The two men complemented each other in temperament and talent; with such a combination the future of the reform seemed doubly assured. A letter to Gracián of July 7, 1579, expresses her desire, at the same time betraying her misgivings: "It was a great comfort to me to know your Paternity has someone now whom you can discuss matters concerning the Order with and who can help you in a way that gives me great satisfaction. It has worried me dreadfully to see you quite alone in the Order, as you have been. I thought him really sensible, and a good person to go to for advice, and a servant of God, though he has not that graciousness and serenity that God has given to Paul (Gracián)–there are very few to whom He has given so many gifts all at once as He has to him. But Father Nicolao is certainly a sound man, full of humility and penitence, with a great regard for truth and able to win others' good will. He will fully recognize how valuable Paul is and he is quite resolved to follow him in everything, and I was very glad to see that. In many respects, if Paul gets on well with him–and I believe he will, if only to please me–it will be very advantageous for them both to be of one mind, and it will be the greatest relief to me ... So your Paternity must not be distant with him, for, unless I am very much mistaken, he will be a great help in many ways."[5]

The constitutions provided for a *socius* of the provincial, to be chosen by the provincial from four names submitted by the chapter (pt. 5, ch. 6, n. 5). Gracián chose Doria, but made little use of him as companion on visitations. He sent him to Italy to report the results of the chapter to the prior general. The choice was natural: Doria was an Italian, and Caffardi no doubt recalled his gracious letter after Rossi's death. The meeting went off very well, and the general made Doria his procurator for the Discalced.[6] Nevertheless there were those who thought Gracián was deliberately trying to put his *socius* on the shelf. In her last letter to her beloved Gracián Teresa expresses her concern: "I have been told that your Reverence is notoriously disinclined to having anyone of consequence with you. I know, of course, that you have no choice in the matter, but as the Chapter is coming on, I should be sorry if there were grounds for imputing such a motive to you."[7]

Teresa's dream of close collaboration between Gracián and Doria was doomed to disappointment. Doria was one of many who felt that Gracián's conduct was not in keeping with the contemplative and penitential character of the reform. He was too much given to preaching and spent too much time with the nuns. As head of the reform he would soon lead it along the wide and easy path of laxity. The "super-hermits" (*muy heremiticos*) or "zealots"(*zelosos de retiro*) stressed observance as the way to safeguard the basic values of the reform. Gracián insisted on interior dispositions rather than outward forms and in this he had truly read the Mother's heart. "I like to lay great stress on the virtues, but not on austerity," Teresa wrote to the ex-hermit Fray Mariano, now one of the zealots.[8] On the other hand Doria and the zealots seem to be no less echoing the mother foundress when she wrote at the end of her life: "As for those who are to come after us ... let them, for the love of Our Lord, allow no practice which makes for perfection to fall into abeyance ... Let them keep watch over the most trifling things and realize that the devil is always boring little holes through which in time great faults may enter."[9] As frequently happens the lofty proclamation of principle was simply a reflection of temperament. The charming extrovert Gracián was drawn to ambitious schemes and service of neighbor; the austere unrelenting Doria found in external observance the seal of the enclosed garden of the order.

Jerome Gracián, Provincial, 1581-1585

As provincial, Gracián's policy was expansionist and activist.

On October 14, 1581, a foundation was made in Portugal at Lisbon. The Prudent King who had recently added Portugal to his extensive realms made no difficulties over a foundation by Spaniards under his loyal friend Fray Mariano. A monastery of nuns under Mary of St. Joseph followed in 1585.[10]

In Lisbon, the focus of Portugal's colonial enterprises, with its marvelous estuary opening on worlds beyond the sea, Gracián's imagination took fire at the prospect of converting the heathen. He had no time, he claimed, to notify the prior general, but he consulted with Doria, Roca, Azaro, and the Valladolid community.[11] As a result, on April 5, 1582, the first Discalced missionaries were dispatched from Lisbon to the Congo.

Unfortunately all of them—three priests, one deacon, and one oblate—were lost at sea when their ship was accidentally rammed by another of the fleet. A second group, dispatched to the Congo in mid-April, fell into the hands of English pirates. A third party which left on April 10, 1584, arrived safely and initiated the Discalced mission in Africa.[12]

The provincial held office for four years, but the chapter met every two years, when the definitors were elected (*Constitutiones 1585*, pt. 2, ch. 2, n. 1; pt. 5, ch. 1, n. 1). The chapter which convened at Almodóvar, May 1, 1583, elected as definitors John of Jesus Roca, Mariano Azaro, Augustine of the Kings, and Ambrose of St. Peter. It altered the constitutions in the matter of the election of priors and ordained that they should be elected by the provincial rather than the conventual chapter.[13]

According to early Discalced historians the chapter heard a report by Doria on his Italian mission, decided to send the third group of missionaries to Africa, approved the foundation of a house in Italy, ordered the solemnization of the feast of Our Lady on the second Sunday of July and of the feast of St. Joseph. Finally various decrees concerning the nuns were made. The *Liber provinciae* seems to be lost, but an existing partial list of the acts of this chapter makes no reference to these matters, except to confirm Doria as the general's agent in the province.[14]

When the time came for the accusation of faults at the chapter, Doria, according to Francis of St. Mary, faced Gracián with the allegation that he had "destroyed the Order by his easy ways and lack of rectitude in government." Nicholas' eloquence so inflamed the minds of the others that they wanted to depose the provincial then and there. Doria restored calm, and the chapter was satisfied to make a decree limiting Gracián's preaching engagements which caused him to be absent from choir and community acts.[15]

During his second term Gracián continued to expand the Discalced missionary effort. In Lisbon he met the Friar Minor, Martin Ignatius de Loyola, recently returned from the Far East. This veteran missionary and relative of the founder of the Society of Jesus turned his attention to China. On April 9, 1585, Gracián and Loyola signed an agreement, *Vinculo de hermandad misionera*, for the mutual collaboration of their orders "for the conversion of pagans in Ethiopia (Africa), the kingdoms of China, the Philippines and other parts of the East and West Indies." This remarkable document which betrays an open-mindedness and lack of self-interest unique in the competitive business of the missions of religious orders, was undoubtedly the work of Gracián.[16]

Mary of St. Joseph, no doubt inspired by Gracián, made a similar agreement with the Dominican nuns of the monastery of the Annunciation in Lisbon to share prayers, sacrifices, and good works for the benefit of the missions.[17]

Before the provincial could realize his plan the chapter opened in Lisbon, May 11, 1585. Nicholas Doria received all votes save two as provincial. The new definitors were respectively Jerome Gracián, John of the Cross, Gregory Nazianzen, and John Baptist "el Rondeño." Doria was away in Italy, engaged in making a foundation in his native Genoa, so the chapter was adjourned pending his return.[18]

Gracián used the interval to launch his missionary enterprise, availing himself of his position as first definitor and vicar in the absence of the provincial. A common missionary trajectory to China, ever since Columbus had mistaken Cuba for Japan, was over Mexico and the Philippines. On May 13, 1585, Gracián obtained royal patents for Fray John of the Mother of God and eleven other friars to cross the sea to the Indies. On May 17 he

Chapter Five: Carmel After Teresa: the Division of the Order

added the permission of the definitory. The courageous little band set sail for Mexico from Sanlucar, July 11.[19]

"It was by God's permission that they left at that time," Gracián piously remarks; "Had the opportunity passed, they would never have crossed to the Indies, as later events showed."[20] So they did indeed. Gracián's precipitous entry into the mission field is a typical example of the way he did the right things the wrong way–or as St. Teresa affectionately chided him, swam against the stream.[21] In his enthusiasm for the missions he did not sufficiently sound out the sentiment of the province. Though volunteers were not hard to find, many friars felt that missionary activity could not be reconciled with the contemplative vocation of the Carmelite. Gracián must have known that the newly elected provincial was one of these. This made his decision in the role of vicar all the more temerarious. The missionary effort of the Spanish Discalced was doomed to wither on the vine.

That Gracián's provincialate had been riddled with quarrels and opposition appears from the "Apology and Defense" of his office against calumniators.[22] The principal accusations against him were that he was remiss in correcting faults with the result that the Order was being ruined, that he spent too much time in preaching and study to the neglect of his duties as provincial, that he had accepted many of his own sisters and relatives into the Order, that he played favorites, that he acted on his own without consulting older members of the province, that he had sent Doria to Italy to rid himself of one who was zealous and observant, that he was too attentive to the nuns.

Some of his enemies had broadcast the fact that his preaching had been restricted by the Almodóvar chapter, thus lending credibility to the calumnies and lies he had suffered from the Calced in defense of the province.

The most charitable judgement one can make about Peter of the Angel, Gracián continues, is that he is either mad or possessed by the devil. This plausible old friar presented a memorial to the king against the provincial which caused much trouble. When Mariano stripped him of the habit as incorrigible, he spread such tales at the court that he had to be taken back to quiet him down. Sent to La Roda, Peter again dispatched "horrible and abominable memorials" to the king who commissioned John de las Cuevas to investigate. Fray Gregory Nazianzen was able to reassure him. Peter also reported the Order to the Inquisition of Cordova.

Other calumnies against him were sent to the prior general from Seville. Gracián accuses the malcontents Anthony of Jesus "and his itch to command," Peter of the Mother of God, Bartholomew Baptist, and other Andalusians. The general reported the matter to the pope. Fray Mariano himself was taken in, and certain open letters he wrote to Gracián seemed to justify the calumniators.

Finally, Gracián lists by name a number of apostates to Rome who justified themselves by calumniating him.

The airing of these complaints at the chapter shows little judgement on Gracián's part, but he could never resist the temptation to justify himself.[23]

Nicholas Doria, Provincial, 1585-1588

On December 1, 1584, Nicholas Doria had founded the first Discalced house outside Spain in his native city of Genoa.[24] From this seed the other houses in Italy and Europe were to spring.

On his return from Genoa, Doria reconvened the chapter at Pastrana, October 17, 1585. Under Gracián the province had come to number nineteen friaries in Spain, Italy, Africa, and the Indies, as well as twenty nunneries.[25] The chapter decided to divide the province into four vicariates, each in charge of a definitor dependent on the provincial: Old Castile, New Castile, Andalusia, and Portugal. St. John of the Cross was given the care of Andalusia; Jerome Gracián, of Portugal. Genoa, Africa, and Mexico remained under the jurisdiction of the provincial. The four vicars and the provincial constituted the diet or *consulta* which met annually and carried on the business of the province. Decisions were made by three out of five votes. The *consulta* could not make constitutions, otherwise it had all the powers of the chapter. If for some reason a vicar lapsed from office, the provincial could name another. The office of *socius* to the provincial, elected by the chapter, was abolished; the provincial could choose a *socius* without right to vote. Provincial and vicars could not be re-elected. Calced friars could be received in the reform. Only nunneries and student houses could have fixed incomes.[26]

Thus originated the famous *consulta*, source of much controversy in the future. Its critics objected to the decisive vote of the consultors, as a result of which the province was ruled by a commission not a single person, while it was precisely this feature that appealed to Doria and was doggedly defended by him.

Unforgettable was the fiery exhortation to observance of the new provincial. The reform, he declared, had departed from its pristine fervor and had started down the broad and easy path of laxity. In vain one pretends to perfection and perseverance in it without the most powerful virtue of observance. Nicholas served notice that observance was to be the concern of his provincialate. Because it was morally impossible for superiors to enforce observance unless they too bore the burden of the Rule he would insist on the common life. The superior, the preacher, the lector, the favorite ate meat without need, were absent from choir, wandered about outside the convent, while the poor subject gnawed his codfish at home, attended Matins, went about poorly attired, uncared for in illness. How could there be peace amid such inequality? Superior and subject should bear the burden of the Rule together, the former having the greater responsibility. No better way to success than the punishment of misdeeds. The dead wood, Doria assured his spellbound listeners, would be pruned from the tree of Carmel.

The provincial also touched on the matter of excessive freedom between friars and nuns, entering the monasteries for frivolous reasons, meals in the parlors, intimate correspondence. He decried the freedom the nuns had to choose confessors according to their own whims.

"So loud were the roars of the noble cub of Carmel, now become a strong lion," writes the admiring Francis of St. Mary, "that not only the flock and the pastures trembled, but the shepherds as well."

"Even after my death," Doria declaimed, "my bones, clashing together in the tomb, will cry out: 'Observance, observance!'"[27]

Francis observes that Doria in fact stemmed the tide toward laxity that had set in and placed the reform firmly on the path of exemplary observance which was to be its hallmark from that time onward. Perhaps historians should ponder more carefully this analysis of the situation. Doria doubtlessly exaggerated the low estate of the reform, but his alarm must have had some foundation. It is not unlikely that controls had begun to slip a bit under the charismatic leadership of Jerome, engaged in a thousand concerns of the apostolate, and that if conditions were not yet critical, they might become so unless proper measures were taken.

Gracián tied a knot in the lion's tail by circulating a tract entitled, *Apology for Charity Against Some Who Under Color of Observance of the Law Cause Charity to Grow Cold and Disturb Religious Orders.*[28]

A meeting of the definitory beginning August 13, 1586, resulted in several important decisions confirmed by Sixtus V September 20. The independence of the Discalced province was confirmed, the Discalced were given permission to adopt the Roman breviary and to have a procurator in Rome. John of Jesus Roca became the first procurator.[29]

Gracián Under a Cloud

Relations between Gracián and Doria worsened after Pastrana which created the *consulta*. Jerome now had a focus for his instinctive difference with the Genoese friar. From now on he was to carry on a relentless opposition to the government which he felt was replacing the spirit of simplicity and love Teresa had left to her heirs in Carmel by external formality. To the austere Doria Gracián was simply rationalizing an easy-going way of life that could not abide the contemplative and penitential character of the Order.

As a subject Doria had rightly confined his disapproval of the provincial to fraternal correction at the chapter. Gracián constantly criticized the superiors and their laws, urging others to opposition and himself showing little inclination to comply. He brought the conflict to a head in the question of the governance of the nuns.

Were it not so simplistic one might be tempted to say that Gracián had never learned to obey. He had jumped from novice to apostolic visitator. When he was no longer in charge of the Discalced movement, he could not refrain from driving the chariot of Elijah from the back seat.

In Portugal Gracián persevered in his zeal for the missions, producing a little treatise on their behalf, *Estimulo de la propagación de la fe* (Lisbon, Andrés Lobato, 1586), often reprinted and translated, the first missiological work by a Carmelite.[30] Carried away by enthusiasm, the author showed that missionary work was not alien to the reformed way of Carmelite life and referred to those who would not send laborers into the missions as "demons in the flesh who prefer to remain in Spain and live off the alms of the faithful." Perhaps for this reason he did not deem it advisable to obtain permission for publication.

In fact under Doria the opinion of the "super-hermits" prevailed, and missionary activity slacked off. The Congo mission was discontinued. The Mexican enterprise endured and became a province, but the friars abandoned the *doctrinas* and plans to expand into New Mexico.[31]

On April 18, 1587, the provincial chapter met at Valladolid. The new definitors were Elias of St. Martin, Anthony of Jesus, Augustine of the Kings, and John Baptist "el Remendado." Jerome Gracián was made vicar of Mexico.[32]

Mary of St. Joseph, prioress of Lisbon and Gracián's good friend, shared his diffidence to the rule of the *consulta*. Jerome and Teresa had harmoniously settled the affairs of the nuns between themselves; now this business was discussed and settled impersonally by a committee. Mary also had reason to believe that the *consulta* was planning to change the constitutions of the nuns. In a poem written in 1586 she issued a battle cry to Carmel:

> Your path is right, you need no other,
> For you have long experience.
> Resist with holy vehemence,
> To change you need not bother.[33]

On February 19, 1587, Gracián circulated a letter among the monasteries, instructing the nuns on what they were to petition the coming chapter. The Fathers were asked not to change the constitutions, not to make laws on the word of a few, not to read the protocol of the visitations in the chapter, not to punish the nuns' faults in the chapter, not to legislate for all the monasteries because of the needs of one.[34]

In reply the chapter declared its love and reverence for St. Teresa and denied that it intended to change her constitutions. Some friar, the chapter suspected, must have disquieted the nuns.³⁵ Certainly the nuns seemed to know a great deal about the inner workings of the *consulta*. This underhanded action by Gracián, himself a member of the *consulta*, weakened the harmony of the province.

On July 23, 1587, Gracián received his orders to depart for his vicariate in Mexico with nine other friars, but it turned out that no fleet sailed that year for fear of Drake.³⁶ Not long afterwards Gracián appears in the diocese of Jaén to found a friary in Ubeda. He also made himself useful to the bishop, Don Francisco Sarmiento.³⁷

Actually he had been sent there by Augustine of the Kings, vicar provincial of Andalusia, as much to get him away from the nuns of Seville as to use his help in Jaén. It would take some doing, Augustine wrote to Doria, to get him away from Seville, due to the influence of Don Pedro Cerezo, wealthy friend of Gracián, and others. The two had spent a few nights in the church of the nuns. In the chapter nothing had been done about Gracián's frequenting the monasteries because his departure for the Indies was imminent, but now that his departure had been postponed for a year, he had shown no improvement. After Augustine's letter Doria decided to get the *consulta's* consent to call Gracián to order.³⁸

On October 18, 1587, Elias of St. Martin, first definitor, was dispatched to Gracián at Ubeda with a list of ten allegations against him to which he was requested to reply. At Lisbon Gracián was supposed to have visited the nuns daily in spite of correction at the conventual chapter. In Seville he did the same. In both places the nuns washed his laundry and sent him sheets and linen shirts. In Lisbon the sisters sent him food. He often stayed in the monastery until one or two o'clock in the morning. He visited the nuns without a companion; corrected about this by the definitory he had shown no betterment. His relationship with the nuns has caused disturbance in the whole province; he knows this and will not change. Besides, Gracián is accused of ordinarily eating meat, wearing linen, sleeping on a mattress, and using sheets of serge on the excuse of ill health. Often told to stop using the sheets, he has not obeyed. In the company of seculars and while travelling he eats meat. In Seville he left the house every day and ate outside the convent. Often he ate meat with seculars in the garden by night. Other accusations he already knew: he published a book (*Estímulo*) in which he called the fathers of the province who were not of his opinion very indecent names; moreover he had not withdrawn the book as he had been told. He had given voice and place to Fray Balthasar (Nieto). Without the provincial's permission he had disposed of moneys from Guinea.³⁹

Gracián replied that as superior he had the right to visit the nuns in Lisbon. Also he went there to say Mass and hear confessions and to oversee the construction going on. The house chapter had agreed he should go. In Seville he had the prior's permission to say Mass for the nuns, hear their confessions and to preach to them. They were preparing the friars' outfits for the journey to the Indies. Gracián saw nothing contrary to the constitutions in the fact that the nuns did his laundry. In sending him sheets and shirts they were performing an act of charity. It was no sin for the poor to accept food from the sisters or seculars. That his conduct disturbs the whole province is a generalization: to refute it, it is enough to find one friar who is not disturbed. As to his visiting the monastery in Lisbon without a companion, the conventual chapter had agreed it could be done because of lack of members and the proximity of the monastery. After the definitory forbade it, he took a companion, sometimes seculars. In the course of construction in the monastery of Lisbon he had sometimes remained late, but never as late as alleged. He ate meat and used a mattress and sheets because of illness. He could produce doctors' testimony to his condition. In Seville he left the house and ate outside, but not every day. He never ate in the garden at night. His remark in his book about those who frustrate the vocation of missionaries did not apply to members of the Order; as vicar he did not need the provincial's permission to publish. It was impossible to recall copies of the book; besides it would have caused scandal and aroused the curiosity of the Inquisition. Balthasar had been given voice and place by Cardinal Albert. He had distributed the money from Guinea among the friaries and nunneries, as it was his right to do as vicar.[40]

At the invitation of the provincial, Gracián adds suggestions on how the investigation is to be carried further. Also, asked to indicate the witnesses and judges he considers prejudiced, he confesses that he has little confidence in any justice meted out by Doria who is blinded by passion.[41]

On November 28, 1587, the provincial and his councillors sent Gracián a formal admonition. Witnesses had testified out of a desire for his betterment and that of the province, but he had reacted with poor grace, characterizing them as melancholic, malicious, false. The province had always striven to lead the regular life, observe the laws, and practice restraint in dealings with the nuns. Gracián of all people should observe the laws, as he himself helped to make them. Great danger lurked in not observing the laws, not leading the common life, frequently visiting the nuns. The religious should see in the commands of his superior the voice of God and if he fails, should admit his guilt and request correction. As to the charges made against him, Gracián in effect admits them and seeks to excuse them.

Whatever happened in the past, the *consulta* commands him for the future to lead the common life in clothing and cell, to remain at home, to exercise prudence in visiting the nuns, no matter how beneficial these visits are considered to be. Gracián is reminded that the nuns are no longer his charge and he should not meddle in their affairs any more than the province wishes.

As to recognizing his fault, Gracián has done just the opposite, misrepresenting the purpose of the charges against him. The witnesses do not accuse him of sinful actions, but only of not conforming to the laws. Still less do they accuse the nuns of wrongdoing, as Gracián claims.[42]

Among the additions the chapter of Alcalá, had made to St. Teresa's constitutions was a series of decrees severely limiting visits to the nunneries.[43] For that matter this legislation no way differs from general post-Tridentine practice. Almost certainly Gracián was not responsible for the additions. The friars' constitutions, purporting to restore the primitive Rule, stress remaining in the cell and limit the apostolate.

On April 1, 1588, Doria wrote to Gracián in Jaén, permitting him to visit Madrid briefly; afterwards he was not to stir from Seville until departing for Mexico.[44]

Encouraged perhaps by the mild tone of the *consulta's* admonition, Gracián on May 2 wrote a letter of humble submission. He acknowledges that he has been guilty of carelessness out of simplicity of nature not maliciousness. He urges the provincial to enforce prudent visiting of the nuns and the equal observance of the regular life by all. He expresses willingness to resign as vicar of Mexico, if Doria thinks it best. He asks to be assigned to a convent where without any responsibilities he can devote himself to prayer and study. He is willing to renounce active and passive voice.[45]

Thus it looked as though Doria had at last won the battle of reducing Gracián to the ranks.

On May 12, 1588, the *consulta* ordered Jerome to Seville before leaving for Mexico and assigned six priests, two professed clerics, and one lay brother as his companions.[46]

The Discalced Congregation

With the growth of the Discalced reform the division into provinces and the erection of a congregation was simply a matter of time. On July 10, 1587, by his brief *Cum de statu* Sixtus V raised the Discalced reform to the status of a congregation headed by a vicar general who had all the powers over the congregation the prior general had over the entire order. The latter had the right of visitation, but only in person and accompanied by two *socii* and a secretary elected from the congregation. More serious and severe matters (*graviora et atrociora*) also required confirmation by the prior general. The *consulta* remained, but whereas it had previously been composed of the vicars provincial, it now constituted a body over and above the provincials.[47]

In contrast to the creation of the province, the congregation–theoretically at least, a more important step–came into being with very little fanfare, as far as can be judged by the present state of information. The text of the papal brief reveals that King Philip II again sponsored the request, and the Congregation for Bishops and Religious was duly consulted. The Discalced procurator, John of Jesus, would have expedited the transaction.

Doria used the occasion to obtain papal confirmation of the *consulta*. It is this aspect of the event that has engaged the attention of Discalced historians, rather than the creation of the congregation. Gracián was later to claim that the chapter of Valladolid in 1587 had rejected government by the *consulta*, and that Doria had obtained papal approval in spite of this. Had this been so, it seems unlikely that complaints would have been limited to Gracián alone.

Shortly before the issuance of the brief *Cum de statu* Roca obtained another, *Decet Romanum pontificem*, dated June 27, concerning admission to and leaving the congregation. Among other privileges the Discalced were granted the faculty, bestowed on the prior general by Clement VII and Pius V, of expelling incorrigible members.[48] In a society in which religious remained irrevocably fixed in their state in life expulsion from the Order was a last resort and implied entrance into another order equally strict or stricter.

On February 13, 1588, the papal nuncio, Caesar Speziano, ordered the execution of the brief erecting the congregation. In another letter of the same date he explained certain points that might give rise to doubt: the vicar general needed the collaboration of the *consulta* also in taking punitive measures, for the time being definitors could also be consultors, the nuns were to be governed by the vicar general and the *consulta*. On February 22 the nuncio explained that the term *graviora et atrociora* was to be taken in the sense given it by canon law not the constitutions of the Order.[49]

In a letter to the friars and nuns dated March 8, 1588, Doria reported the reception of the *Cum de statu* and explained its provisions.[50]

The chapter to implement the brief *Cum de statu* met in Madrid on June 19, 1588. Nicholas Doria was elected first vicar general of the new congregation by the not very convincing number of thirty-two out of fifty-eight votes. Obviously his popularity had considerably eroded since his unanimous election as provincial. Francis of St. Mary provides the detail about the balloting: it would be interesting to know how many of the dissident votes went to Gracián. Definitors were respectively: John of the Cross, Augustine of the Kings, Anthony of Jesus, Elias of Saint Martin. The six members of the *consulta* were: John of the Cross, Anthony of Jesus, Mariano Azaro, John Baptist "el Andaluz," Louis of St. Gregory, Bartholomew of Jesus. Five provincials were elected for the five newly constituted provinces: John Baptist "el Remendado" for Old Castile, Elias of St. Martin for New Castile, Augustine of the Kings for Andalusia, Gregory of Nazianzen for Portugal, John of Jesus Roca for Aragon. In the future the local priors were

Chapter Five: Carmel After Teresa: the Division of the Order

to attend only the provincial chapters, though they continued to be elected by the chapter of the congregation or by the *consulta* when there was no chapter. The *consulta* in fact carried out most of the day by day business of the congregation, leaving very little to the discretion of the provinces. The vicar general was elected for six years, the other officials for three.[51]

Two decrees of the chapter Doria considered so important that he obtained apostolic confirmation for them from the nuncio: all matters are decided collegially by the *consulta* which also governs the nuns in the same manner.[52]

The rule by the *consulta* was cumbersome and unpopular. Doria does not seem to have introduced the system out of personal ambition, because he would have had greater freedom under the traditional system. His motive seems to have been to spread authority, and as a matter of fact he was accused of running the congregation like a republic–bad marks in the Spain of Philip II. It would have been natural for him to regard his native government of Genoa as ideal, a conviction not shared by all his Spanish brothers. To this may perhaps be added a trait of character: Teresa had already divined that he feared sole responsibility.[53]

On the eve of the chapter, on June 17, the *consulta* replied to Jerome's letter of submission of May 2, ordering it implemented in every detail, except that as an alternative to withdrawing to a house for recollection he might go to Mexico, but no longer as vicar.[54]

The same day, June 17, 1588, the nuncio Caesar Speziano, no doubt at Doria's request, added the weight of apostolic authority. He ordered Jerome to lead the same regular life as the others in matters of clothing, food, cell and leaving the convent. Gracián was forbidden to treat with persons outside the Order or to write to them without permission of his superiors, as the constitutions ordain. He should not air his complaints to laymen, but to his superiors or to him, the nuncio.[55]

The royal chaplain, García de Loaysa, on June 23 in more friendly fashion urged Gracián to bend his will to the regulations made by the chapters. Rule by the *consulta* is an excellent system of government; by it the vicar general does not depend on his own judgment alone. The statute which limits converse with the nuns is also most holy. The only favor the superiors of the congregation ever ask his majesty is the enforcement of observance. They are motivated by love of Gracián, as is he, Loaysa.[56]

Gracián seems to have decided not to attend this important chapter which constituted the congregation. According to Archbishop Braganza he was already in Portugal–at Evora, where the delegates on their way to the chapter met him and urged him to attend.[57] Gracián's reversal to his old habits which blatantly gave the lie to his protestations of May 2 would have so exacerbated the *consulta* that it decided to hold Gracián to his own proposals.

In what was evidently intended as a gesture of good will, clumsy as it was, Doria made Gracián his *socius* on June 20. Protesting himself to be Gracián's brother in all things, Nicholas declared himself desirous of reciprocating Gracián's act when he had become first provincial.[58]

But Teresa's good friend, Teutonio de Braganza, archbishop of Evora, urgently wanted Gracián in his diocese. Archduke and Cardinal Albert, governor of Portugal, also asked him to return to Lisbon. Through the king these worthies put pressure on Doria who a week after appointing Gracián his *socius* found himself on June 27 signing patents ordering him to report to Evora. A month later, on July 27, 1588, he repeated this directive, adding on obedience to serve the cardinal.[59]

Once more Gracián was off and running.

Mary of St. Joseph and Anne of Jesus

Mary of St. Joseph had been implicated with Jerome Gracián in the nuns' appeal to the provincial chapter at Valladolid in 1587. Gracián's failure to satisfy the *consulta* in the matter of his excessive familiarity with nuns also involved Mary as prioress of Lisbon and former prioress of Seville. It was now her turn to undergo investigation.

On August 12, 1588, Mary answered six questions, though she doubted whether she would be believed any more than she had been previously. At the time of Cardenas' visitation in Seville she had not been punished by Gracián nor had St. Teresa held her responsible. She gave a detailed account of the voyage from Seville to Lisbon to show that all due propriety had been observed. She had to account for her actions in connection with the settlement of a group of Flemish *beatas* in Lisbon which she had undertaken at the Cardinal's request. Gracián came to offer Mass and hear confessions accompanied by a *donatus*. It was not true that he stayed to midnight. She had not pulled strings to get Gracián assigned to Lisbon. She was not guilty of double dealing with the mother foundress.[60]

Three days later Mary received a prohibition to communicate in any way with Jerome Gracián. On October 16 the community requested a thorough investigation to clear its name.[61] Mary claimed that one of the friars wrote to her for three years trying to compromise her and Gracián, especially attempting to trap her into asking that Jerome stay in Lisbon instead of going to Mexico.[62]

Doria fondly thought that this sort of Inquisition by mail in which testimony was carefully examined and weighed by the *consulta* at Segovia was the most equitable and efficient way of maintaining discipline.

Another person besides Mary and Gracián who came to oppose Doria's system of government was the prestigious Anne of Jesus, prioress of Madrid.

Chapter Five: Carmel After Teresa: the Division of the Order

Born at Medina in 1545 Anne entered the Order at Avila in 1570 and was professed at Salamanca the following year. She was one of St. Teresa's most distinguished daughters. Comparing her to St. Teresa, Bañez declared that she was in no way inferior in supernatural gifts and in natural gifts had the advantage. St. John of the Cross dedicated his *Spiritual Canticle* to her. After functioning as prioress in a number of monasteries in Spain, she went on to found the Order in France and the Low Countries.[63] Anne collaborated with the noted Augustinian humanist, Louis de León, in producing the *editio princeps* of St. Teresa's works (Salamanca, G. Foquel, 1588).

Anne was concerned about the changes which Doria's system of governing through the *consulta* might bring in the lives of the nuns. In a visit to the parlor in Madrid Doria assured her that the sisters' affairs would be handled by his *socius* Gracián.[64] But Doria had already the previous week freed Gracián to work in the archdiocese of Evora. Moreover, three days later, on July 5, 1588, he published a circular letter to the nuns in which he notified them of the decision of the chapter, confirmed by the nuncio, that the government of the nuns should be the prerogative of the *consulta* as a body. The *consulta* will name confessors and a procurator for each monastery. Besides these no friar may speak to the nuns without permission of the *consulta*—even those assigned to offer Mass or preach. All untoward familiarity between friars and nuns is to be avoided. They should not give each other food, clothing or other things. Anyone infringing on these directives is to be deprived of voice and place for a year. The *consulta* will also appoint visitors. Until the opinion of the nuns can be heard by the next chapter, prioresses may not be re-elected.[65]

On the other hand on August 15, 1588, the *consulta* authorized the monastery of Madrid to reprint the nuns' constitutions. They appeared the same year (Madrid, Pedro Madrigal, 1588), bearing the confirmation of Speziano who at the same time warned that he had no intention of derogating from his letter of February 13 subjugating the nuns to the *consulta*. The constitutions changed the time of compline. In all this there is no hint yet of a clash between Doria and Anne.[66]

Meanwhile from Evora Gracián was escalating his attack on the government of the congregation. He had been bidden by Speziano to air his complaints to his superiors or to himself, the nuncio, but neither alternative offered very promising prospects. On November 2, 1588, Jerome appealed to the king against Doria. The devil, he stated, had invented three ways to destroy the charity, sincerity and simplicity which hitherto characterized the Discalced brotherhood. The first way was through "a new government in the form of a republic" imposed by a Genoese friar. The chapter at Valladolid in 1587 had rejected government by the *consulta*, nevertheless the provincial, ingratiating himself with the king, obtained a papal brief to make provinces without consulting the chapter. The same brief confirmed the government he had previously wanted. At the chapter of Madrid in 1588, the provincial by means of certain devices was elected vicar general in order better to introduce his way of governing. The chapter approved the government for three years, but the vicar general got it confirmed *in perpetuum* by the nuncio.

Gracián complained secondly that the vicar general was arranging to meet with the Calced to elect a prior general according to his own taste, "which is the total destruction of the Discalced Congregation." Jerome seems to be alluding here to preparations for a general chapter which for some reason did not eventuate. No general chapter had been held since 1580, and none would be held until 1593, when Doria's choice was Michael Carranza.

Finally Gracián claimed that Doria had punished and discredited persons who did not agree with his government. He asked the king, "as the protector and true refuge of religion after God," to appoint one or two persons to examine Doria's government, its laws, and all that had been done in its name.[67]

Doria, alerted to Gracián's attack, did not wait for the king to invite a reply. Fray Jerome, he writes, objects to the governance of the nuns by the *consulta* which imposes restraint on the relations of the friars with the nuns. This measure was commanded by the nuncio at the request of the definitory which considered it most salutary. The nuns will be treated with much more prudence, reserve, and respect by seven absent persons than by one person who is with them every day. The nuns suffer now, but will change with time. Fray Gracián argues that the vote of the councilors is only consultative. The words of the pope are that the vicar should use "the counsel and intervention" of the six councillors, but he cannot do this if their vote is not definitive. The nuncio declared this to be so. For years the definitors have had decisive voice with the provincial; Gracián was first definitor when this was decided and he was the first to concur. The *consulta* is nothing more than a permanent definitory. Such a system prevents the vicar general from acting arbitrarily.

Doria concludes by asking the king to prevent a friar or individual nuns from upsetting the Order by presenting petitions against their superiors and the laws; the place for this is in the chapter.[68]

On February 20, 1589, Fray Nicholas was officially notified by the royal chaplain, Garciá de Loaysa, of the king's satisfaction with the laws and mode of governing decreed by the chapter of Madrid. Specifically the king approved of the decisive vote of the six councilors, the governance of the nuns by the *consulta* and the prohibition of the re-election of prioresses. Doria may be assured that anything that favors observance and the perfection of religious life will always enjoy the support of the king.[69]

Gracián Returns to Lisbon

Early in 1589 Jerome Gracián returned to Lisbon, summoned there by

Chapter Five: Carmel After Teresa: the Division of the Order

the Cardinal Archduke Albert, Philip II's twenty-five year old nephew and governor of Portugal. The cardinal's confessor was the Dominican John de las Cuevas, an old friend of the Discalced.

Lisbon before and during the raid of Sir Francis Drake, May 1589, offered ample opportunity for Gracián's fervor. He did much good work preaching, hearing soldiers' confessions, founding a refuge for fallen women who were especially numerous and without means in the war-torn city.

The Cardinal Archduke also found Fray Jerome useful for political ends. The spirit of Nuño Alvarez Pereira was still very much alive in the Carmo of Lisbon. Don Antonio numbered many sympathizers in the Carmelite community of 100 friars, in Gracián's phrase "perhaps the most restless in the kingdom."[70] The prior, Antonio Calderón, was placed under arrest by the Spaniards, another friar had been one of Don Antonio's captains, others had broken bread with him. It was rumored that six thousand arquebuses were hidden in the fort-like Carmo, against which the artillery of the castle across the valley was constantly trained. Archduke Albert entrusted Gracián with the "reform" of the Carmo.

The scope was purely political, Jerome assured Michael de Carranza, vicar general for Spain and Portugal, who appeared on the scene; he did not concern himself with the regular observance of the friars, "for in this no province of the whole Order of Calced Carmelites exceeds them." The rumor about the weapons proved unfounded. Gracián sent to other convents some of the more politically dangerous members of the community. During the battle the Portuguese friars were locked in an upper dormitory, while the convent was occupied by two thousand destitute refugees. Gracián and his Discalced friars went about hearing the confessions of soldiers. After the battle he sallied forth with a company of arquebusiers to identify the dead–"since I knew the Castilian soldiers"–so that the Catholics could be buried and the heretics burned. Three hundred Catholics were placed face up with their arms crossed; eight hundred Lutherans were turned face down, "looking at hell, where their souls were burning."[71]

All this was far removed from the studious and prayerful retirement which Gracián had elected and to which he had been consigned. Gracián's return to Lisbon also once more brought him close to Mary of St. Joseph. Doria tried in vain to get him back to Spain. Poor Jerome seemed always to be hindered by higher authority from obeying his religious superiors.

As appears from a letter of Fray Nicholas to the king, November 28, 1589, the former had asked Philip three months previously to recall Jerome to Spain. The king had expressed a desire that Gracián live under obedience. Two things only the definitory and *consulta* had ever asked of Gracián: that he live a regular life, as did others older and less healthy than he, and more importantly that he give up his familiar way with the nuns, especially with one living in Lisbon. In the past this conduct had caused great inconvenience to the Order, but in spite of the fact that he had been sentenced on this account, he had continued unchanged, thereby causing much complaint and scandal.

"Although I am convinced," Doria writes, "that no personal sin is involved, nevertheless the sin of scandal remains." The fathers feel they would be guilty of grave sin, if they took no steps to provide a remedy. The remedy they request of the king is very simple: that he tell Gracián to live the regular life and give up his relationship with the nuns. If the king deems it advisable for Gracián to remain in Portugal, it will be necessary to remove the above-mentioned nun under pretext of making a foundation.[72]

Evidently the king delivered the requested admonition, for on December 23, 1589, Gracián wrote to Philip's secretary, Gabriel de Zayas. He had Doria's permission to be in Lisbon, whither he had been summoned by the Prince Cardinal. No one desired regular observance more than he, Gracián. If any laws had not been perfectly observed, it was not without the necessity which the Rule allows. True, he had advised the chapter of Madrid against certain laws in the manner of a republic, which, he was convinced, replaced peace, sincerity, interiority, and obedience by an exteriority based on a multitude of precepts and punishments. Likewise he was all in favor of restraint in the relationships of friars to nuns, but the particular case of which he stands accused does injustice "to a spouse of Jesus Christ [Mary of St. Joseph] who is one of the purest and holiest souls in our order." When friars want to discredit someone, Zayas should be told, they spread malicious gossip which causes calumnious rumors, investigating which leads to vague accusations of scandal, bad example, and similar generalities. It would be a service to God to investigate this case and punish either the wrongdoing of the accused or the calumny of the accusers.

Finally, the sentence against him was passed so that the vicar general could be elected. He, Gracián, had signed his letter of submission at the advice of a friend, John López de Velasco, as a gesture of humility for the sake of peace, but it had been used as a juridical confession of guilty. Jerome requested an investigation and for information recommended Zayas to John Vázquez de Mármol and his brother Dr. Barnaby del Mármol, both exemplary priests. (Barnaby was also the brother-in-law of one of Jerome's sisters.)[73]

The Prudent King took no further action at the moment, perhaps because he found Gracián useful in Portugal. Jerome remained in Lisbon for another year and a half.

The same day, December 23, Las Cuevas wrote to Jerome's mother, Dona Juana Dantisco, apparently in answer to an appeal on behalf of her son. The

Dominican's attitude is worth noting and offers a key to one who wishes to arrive at the truth between Gracián and Doria. Both are "very weighty personages and of much virtue." Jerome did not solicit the visitation of Carmel. "Other matters too should not be imputed to him, as I consider him very religious and esteemed." When the visitation is over soon (actually Jerome finished it much later), the "other matters" can be settled, but only if Gracián acts the part of subject and son, and Doria of superior and father, and if both sacrifice something, either of their rights or opinions.[74]

Las Cuevas' counsel unfortunately went the way of too much good advice.

It seems to have been around this time that Gracián appealed to the pope against the rule of the *consulta*. Authorized by Cardinal Albert and the protector of the Order, he dispatched to Rome a loyal supporter, Peter of the Purification, living in Genoa.[75] Peter's trip may have been made in connection with the nuns' recourse to Rome.

The Revolt of the Nuns

Doria felt constrained to explain once more the workings of the *consulta* and the question of the re-election of prioresses. This he did in a circular letter to the congregation, January 24, 1590. Gracián followed with a rebuttal.[76]

In Madrid Anne of Jesus had been won to the cause against the *consulta*. According to Mary of the Incarnation (Yolante de Salazar), lady-in-waiting to Empress Maria, sister of Philip II, who had entered the Order in 1586, Anne had wrung from Nicholas the admission that it would be a good thing to obtain papal confirmation of the nuns' constitutions. This was not yet authorization to do so, nor above all to request changes in the government of the congregation.[77]

Sent secretly to Rome, Barnaby del Mármol succeeded in obtaining from Pope Sixtus V his brief *Salvatoris*, June 5, 1590. It contained all that the sisters' hearts desired. The constitutions of Alcalá with slight changes received papal approval. The pope moreover recalled the power of the chapter and the vicar to change the constitutions and revoked changes already made. He placed the nuns directly under the jurisdiction of the vicar general who every three years was to depute a commissary general having voice and place in the chapter after the vicar general. He prohibited provincials, councilors and bishops from interfering in the affairs of the nuns. Finally he instructed bishops to defend the interests of the nuns when they appealed.[78]

It was no accident that Sixtus in a brief of June 21 should appoint as executors of the *Salvatoris* Gracián's friend, Archbishop Teutonio de Braganza, and Anne's friend, Fray Louis de León. Within a month of receiving their commission they were to convene a chapter of the congregation, publish the papal brief, and elect a commissary general for nuns.[79]

In due course Louis de León, acting also for Braganza, gave notice of his commission and ordered Doria to convoke a chapter and elect a commissary, meanwhile suspending the vicar general's jurisdiction over the nuns. Francis of St. Mary states that León proposed Gracián and St. John of the Cross for commissary. In 1625 Mary of the Incarnation remembered that the name of John of the Cross had been suggested to the pope.[80] The pope specifies no names, either in his brief or his letters of execution.

Before the brief reached Spain Doria, on June 10, 1590, convened an extraordinary chapter in Madrid. The purpose of the meeting among other things was to raise to the level of constitutions the acts and other decisions made since the province had become a congregation and to make corresponding revisions in the existing constitutions of 1588. The new *Constitutiones* (Madrid, Pedro Madrigal, 1590), comprising thirty-two chapters, canonized such disputed points as the decisive vote of the consultors, the governance of the nuns by the *consulta*, etc. Permission was given to add two new houses to the three existing in Mexico and to create a province. The friars were not to work in *doctrinas*, or catechetical centers, or to live outside the convent (ch. 28, nos. 2, 4). Nicholas thus consolidated the position of his innovations which he could now claim were the law of the congregation.[81]

The chapter also considered the case of Jerome Gracián. In view of letters written by Fray Jerome, certain nuns and laymen, the chapter decreed on July 22 that no friar or nun should write to Gracián without permission of the *consulta*, nor should they write to anyone else about his affairs. All letters and papers regarding him are also to be turned over to the *consulta*. Gracián for his part wrote a detailed criticism of the constitutions of the chapter.[82]

At the time of the chapter Doria had not yet heard of the existence of the sisters' papal brief, but on August 21, 1590, he addressed them a circular letter on the subject. In requesting the brief the nuns had not only acted without permission but had turned against the Order. He, Doria, could not in conscience accede to their wishes and so he was constrained either to appeal against the brief with hurt to many or relinquish the care of the nuns. Gracián too wrote to the nuns, "for it is good that they know the reasons they have in their favor."[83]

When Fray Nicholas made no move to convoke a chapter, Louis de León, on October 2, 1590, himself set the date for November 25. On that day only Elias of St. Martin (New Castile), Gregory of Nazianzen (Portugal), and Augustine of the Kings (Andalusia) appeared. Louis could only assign another date, February 2, with not much more chance of success.[84]

Both sides appealed to the king. The monastery of Madrid appointed the Mármol brothers its procurators. Louis de León also remained in the breach.[85]

Doria's threat to abandon them struck consternation into the camp of the nuns. It is not known how many monasteries had rallied to "the captain of the prioresses."[86] As time went on, the friars increased pressure on the monasteries to abandon Anne and her cause. Among eminent personages who remained faithful to the regime was Bl. Anne of St. Bartholomew, companion of Teresa, who later claimed that the saint had changed her mind about using the services of confessors other than Discalced.[87]

On January 26, 1591, the committee entrusted with the case under the Count de Barajas was able to report to the king. The Discalced friars should not renounce the care of the nuns. Anne of Jesus, one of two or three sisters who had "raised this dust," should be given to understand that her duty lay in obedience to superiors. She should desist from urging the implementation of the brief which will not be admitted. The same holds for Mary of St. Joseph about whom the king should write to the Lord Cardinal Archduke. Dr. Mármol and his brother should also be told to give up their efforts. One of them who is rumored about to leave again for Rome to obtain confirmation of the brief should be refused a passport. The *asistente* or regent of Seville should likewise caution Peter Cerezo who provided funds for obtaining the brief. Louis de León should be told to attend to his job of provincial of the Augustinians. Finally the king should instruct his ambassador in Rome, the Count de Olivares, to persuade the pope to revoke his brief.[88]

This last recommendation the Prudent King had already anticipated on August 17, 1590. From the king's letter to Olivares it also appears that Doria had a friar in Rome for the same purpose.[89]

Doria Wins His Case

The year 1590 witnessed the reign of three popes: Sixtus V died on August 27; Urban VII ruled from September 15-27, followed on December 5 by Gregory XIV. The latter on April 25, 1591, issued his brief, *Quoniam non ignoramus*. With regard to the burning issues, the provincials were given charge of the nuns as well as the friars with powers to correct all except the most grave faults specified in the constitutions. Punishing such faults remained the province of the vicar general and his consultors with decisive vote. Priors could punish grave or lesser faults. The office of commissary was specifically abolished. Prioresses could not be immediately re-elected, nor could they choose confessors, but provincials were reminded in the words of the council of Trent to provide an abundance of confessors.[90]

Neither side obviously had dictated the terms of the solution; it was a genuine compromise devised by the Roman curia. The nuns did not realize their dream of being under one head as in the idyllic days of Gracián's rule. Still they had escaped the cold impersonal bureaucracy of the *consulta* and could treat on a personal basis with the provincials. Doria had been right:

the day was past when all the Discalced monasteries could be properly administered by one person. The *consulta* had had its tail bobbed, but at least the commissary was no more. It should be noted that Fray Nicholas who is generally considered to take contradiction poorly submitted without demur.

There remained the culprits to be punished. Any other course to the severe Doria would have been dereliction of duty: this had been a fault for which he had reproved Gracián. It was not so much that the rebels had appealed to the Holy See; they had gone about it the wrong way (subreptiously and obreptiously). In the course of a visitation of the monastery in Madrid Anne of Jesus was deprived of active and passive voice, confined to a cell, and denied communion except monthly for three years. The prioress of Madrid, Mary of the Nativity, was deposed. A new prioress, Mary of St. Jerome, cousin of St. Teresa, and the lay sister, Bl. Anne of St. Bartholomew, were imported from Avila, which in the words of Bl. Anne "had not taken part in any revolt, and matters had remained in the state in which the saint had left them."[91] To her credit Anne of Jesus did not fill the air with lamentations. Fray Louis de León at her encouragement finished the commentary on Job he had begun in 1578 and dedicated it to her. It was an appropriate gift, and she no doubt made abundant use of it.

Mary of St. Joseph was deprived of vote for two years and sentenced to one year in a locked cell; she was not permitted to communicate with others by written or spoken word or to assist at Mass except Sundays. She was allowed to confess and communicate once a month.[92]

It is not certain whether Gregory's brief was known when the chapter of the congregation met at Madrid, June 1, 1591. The new consultors were Blaise of St. Albert, Thomas of Aquinas, Bartholomew of St. Basil, Gregory of the Holy Angel, Diego Evangelista, Philip of Jesus. Provincials were: John of St. Albert (Old Castile), John Baptist "el de Ronda" (New Castile), Anthony of Jesus (Andalusia), Louis of St. Jerome (Portugal), Dominic of the Presentation (Aragon). No doubt the delegates worked at the new version of the constitutions which soon appeared, but their activity would have been hampered, if the outcome of the appeal to Rome still remained unknown.[93]

With the controversy settled Doria produced his constitutions, the term of half a dozen years' evolution. Separate editions appeared for the friars (Madrid, Peter Madrigal, 1592) and the nuns (Madrid, Peter Gómez, 1592).[94] Oddly enough Doria's constitutions for the nuns was a Spanish translation of the Latin text published in Gregory's brief. Thus was lost the spontaneity and freshness of expression of the Teresian constitutions of 1588.[95] The latter at the initiative of Bérulle were adopted by the monasteries in France and Belgium.[96]

Gracián in Disgrace

Gracián finished his visitation of the Carmo of Lisbon, May 14, 1591.[97] His services were no longer required, he had to come out from behind the cardinal, and Doria—though not like the father of the prodigal son— was waiting for him with open arms. On June 3 the vicar general ordered Fray Jerome to report within twenty-five days to the Discalced convent in Madrid.[98] Exactly twenty-five days later Jerome walked in the front door, "like a desperado without humility or resignation," Gregory of the Holy Angel disapprovingly recorded.[99] Doria was not pleased when Gracián's brother-in-law, Peter Zapata del Mármol, almost immediately asked if Jerome might go out to visit his mother.[100]

Jerome was imprisoned in a cell, and—again in Gregory's words—"his affairs began to be considered."[101] Charges against him had already been gathered, it was only a question of hearing his replies. Although Gracián's part in the revolt of the nuns did not help to endear him to Doria, his trial at this time should not be judged to be merely a vendetta for this act. The charges against Jerome were mainly the old ones for which he had been sentenced, June 17, 1588, and had never accounted, having been absent ever since in Portugal. Neither should it necessarily be thought that Gracián was brought to trial in order to expel him from the Order. This outcome was the result of his eventual decision not to submit to punishment. This brought him the note of incorrigibility, the *gravissima culpa*, the sanction for which was expulsion from the Order (*Constitutiones*, 1592, pt. 3, ch. 8, para. 6, no. 1).

The king added two judges to the bench: Francis de Segovia, Jeronimite, prior of Madrid, and Francis Muñoz, rector of the Dominican College of St. Thomas. The unanimous opinion of the judges was read on February 17, 1592. Fray Jerome Gracián was declared guilty of sixty proven charges, most of which he admitted, "of excess in his conduct with the nuns as well as excessive familiarity with one of them, laxity, and defect in the regular observance of his profession, and of other faults for which our Order was on the point of being destroyed." He had also sown discord in the Order and against his superiors. For these faults he had been repeatedly but vainly corrected and now he refused to accept sentencing and punishment. As incorrigible, he was accordingly expelled from the Order. Before communicating the sentence to Jerome, Gregory urged him to reconsider. By way of answer Gracián silently cast off his capuce. After sentencing, his monastic tonsure was removed and he was given the garb of a secular priest, "new and of very good quality," and sent on his way.[102]

It was a shocking disgrace and an incredible end for the favorite of St. Teresa and collaborator with her in the establishment of the Discalced friars.

At stake here were two divergent concepts of the Carmelite vocation. Doria was profoundly convinced that Gracián's activism was threatening the very existence of the reform, just as Gracián believed that Doria's rigid asceticism was destroying its Teresian character of joyful service of the Lord. Gracián's conviction, real or self-induced, that he must in conscience oppose the regime and encourage others to do so led him to a course of continuous obstructionism and finally induced him to refuse correction. In Doria's eyes Jerome was rebellious and incorrigible.

In the end Gracián's fears proved unfounded. Doria, as it turned out, did not live forever, and the Discalced reform was not destroyed. In fact, its stern novitiate under Doria impressed it for all time with the seal of meticulous observance which has been its characteristic and the safeguard of its vocation. On the other hand Gracián is not at all convincing in the role of contemplative in the sense of the primitive Rule. He resisted with all the force of his nature attempts to make him live a life of prayer in solitude. "They would have buried me in some convent," he later remembered, "where I would have had no other occupation but to confess an occasional *beata* and to follow the choir."[103] One can only guess where Gracián might have led the reform.

The rest of Gracián's extraordinary career can be briefly summed up. He travelled to Rome to make a fruitless appeal to the pope. Later, he had the bad luck to be captured by Turkish pirates and spent two years in captivity in Tunis. In the end, his old enemies, the Calced, took him back into their ranks. He comforted himself with the reflection that after all he was returning to the profession he had originally made to the prior general, that the Rule, which is the essence of the Order, was the same for both Orders, and that the constitutions of the Discalced had been altered in a way that made it impossible for him to observe them.[104]

"I clearly perceived," he wrote, "that the perfection I so much desired did not consist only in external and corporal austerity, since St. Paul says, 'If I should deliver my body to be burned,' etc., 'it profits me nothing'; and when he lists the signs of charity, saying, 'Charity is patient, kind,' etc., he does not include external austerity among them; and the twelve he names can be acquired in the habit of the Calced as well as in other orders, though they do not go barefoot."[105] He concludes: "Having returned to the Calced, I have experienced greater peace, and they have treated me with greater love, honor, and charity than when I was with the Discalced."[106] Nevertheless his heart remained in the reform founded by his beloved Mother Teresa. Gracián spent his last years in Flanders, where his old patron, Archduke Albert, was now regent. He died in the Carmelite convent of Brussels, September 21, 1614.

St. John of the Cross

Little has been said in this narrative about St. John of the Cross for the

Chapter Five: Carmel After Teresa: the Division of the Order

simple reason that he hardly enters into the external course of events. "I cannot think why that saint is so unfortunate that no one remembers him," Teresa once exclaimed.[107] Attempts to make St. John the "Father of the Reform" are based on the dictates of the heart rather than on sober fact.

Not that he was insignificant. To say nothing of the influence of his writings, St. John of the Cross was undoubtedly held in high esteem by his contemporaries for his role as one of the first members of the reform, his strength of character, and the authority of his unquestioned sanctity. He was several times elected prior and from the first functioned as definitor and consultor.

Apart from the mere score of letters mostly dating from the last years of the saint's life, primary sources contemporary to events are scarce. Knowledge of St. John's life rests mainly on early biographies and the processes of beatification and canonization. These yield a rich harvest of *fioretti* which contain much information but have to be used with greater caution than has generally been done.

There is little hard evidence for Doria's alleged "persecution" of St. John. The relationship of the two men seems to have been one of mutual reverence and esteem.

On the other hand John cannot be shown to have been particularly favorable to Gracián and his ideas. Fray John Evangelist, beloved disciple of the saint, recalled forty years later that St. John began to avoid the meetings of the *consulta* at the end of his term of office when that body was discussing Gracián's case, not out of sympathy for Jerome, but because the affairs of the Order were being broadcast outside it. "Now that the prey has been flushed," St. John is supposed to have said, "we should run it to ground without help from anyone else."[108] Among the friends whom Gracián claimed Doria favored unfairly were Augustine of the Kings and John of the Cross; they had heard friars' confessions without permission of the ordinary and the required age, yet Doria had not punished them. St. John would also have qualified for Gracián's criticism that Doria accumulated offices on his favorites. John was definitor and consultor and was in charge of the convent in Segovia (it is not clear whether this house as the seat of the *consulta* had a prior).[109]

As to Gracián's ideas, there is a passage in the *Spiritual Canticle* that would appear to be a shoe to fit his foot: "Let those, then, that are great actives, that think to girdle the world with their outward works and their preachings, take note that they would bring far more profit to the Church and be far more pleasing to God (apart from the good example which they would give of themselves) if they spent even half this time in abiding with God in prayer."[110]

At the chapter of 1591 St. John retired from office as definitor and consultor. Gregory of the Holy Angel, elected to the *consulta* at the chapter, recalled in 1627 that John had been left without office so that he could not be elected commissary of the nuns.[111] At least in one detail Gregory's memory played him false: the commissary did not have to be a superior. Moreover John, like the other definitors and consultors, was not eligible for re-election to the same office (*Constitutiones* 1590, ch. 10, n. 2).

In spite of his close relationship to Anne of Jesus, John of the Cross as a member of the *consulta* almost certainly did not approve of the surreptitious acquisition of the papal brief. Under its prioress, Mary of the Incarnation (Bracamonte), Segovia, where St. John was confessor, remained loyal to Doria.[112]

One thing is certain. As John wrote to Anne of Jesus (Jimena), July 6, 1591, Doria wanted him to continue in charge of Segovia (a sign, incidentally, that this house had no prior, for priors could not serve two terms in the same place), but the saint wanted urgently to remain without office.[113] Apparently he managed to persuade the vicar general to leave him free.

Evidently by this date John's assignment to Mexico—a curious episode—had already been cancelled. The saint's first biographer, Joseph of Jesus and Mary Quiroga, states that the definitory on June 25, 1591, ordered John to Mexico with twelve companions.[114] Two years after the appearance of Quiroga's book John Evangelist informed Jerome of St. Joseph that he could not recall any such decree. While it was thought that St. John might have been involved in the revolt of the nuns, John Evangelist declared, there was a rumor in the province that a decree had been made, but the rumor had ceased when John's neutrality had been established.[115]

Nevertheless when Jerome published his biography of St. John in 1641, he verbally quoted the book of acts, June 2 (not June 25), 1591, to the effect that the chapter accepted St. John's offer to go to Mexico with eleven others. John commissioned John of St. Anne, his companion, to gather volunteers in Andalusia.[116] When John of St. Anne later reported to St. John the completion of his task, the latter answered after much delay, "that the expedition to the Indies had fallen through and that he had gone to La Peñuela to embark for better Indies."[117]

There is about all this something that does not ring true. For St. John of the Cross at this point in his life to embark on the apostolic life of a missionary flies in the face of all that is characteristic of him as a profound contemplative and dedicated solitary. If the chapter at which he was present assigned him to Mexico on June 2 (or June 25), why was he concerned on July 6 about being put in charge of Segovia? It is hardly likely that it was a question of a temporary assignment, as has been opined.[118] For some reason the decree may have been a dead letter from the start: Fray John Evangelist

Chapter Five: Carmel After Teresa: the Division of the Order

had never heard of it. If so, why had John of St. Anne proceeded with the rounding-up of volunteers? In fact it is odd that the *consulta* did not itself name the friars who were to go to the Indies. If it were not for the fact that John of St. Anne testifies that he had collected the volunteers, one would be tempted to say that the decree of the chapter never existed. It would not be the first time that a seventeenth century historian quoted a document that did not exist.

At the time of the chapter St. John was a very sick man; he had only months to live. He was eventually assigned to the province of Andalusia–not his favorite place on earth–where his old companion in the foundation of the reform, Anthony of Jesus, had been elected provincial. On August 10, 1591, St. John arrived at the remote convent of La Peñuela, the first house in Andalusia en route from Castile.[119] Anthony left him free to choose a convent, but John insisted on being given an obedience.[120] The upshot was that John remained at La Peñuela, where he happily devoted himself to solitary prayer. But the saint of the cross was not to be left off so easily.

In Madrid Gracián's trial was in progress. Fray Diego Evangelista, newly elected member of the *consulta* who was investigating Gracián's case, thought he had struck a scent leading to John of the Cross, like Gracián much involved in the direction of nuns. There followed the usual cross-examinations and signed statements. The nuns complained that Diego distorted and falsified their testimony. Diego's zeal was misplaced and yielded no results. Besides, John was no Gracián; he did not rush to his own defense and would have accepted punishment without a word. "Son, let this not grieve you," the saint is supposed to have written to John of St. Anne, "for I am quite prepared to amend my ways in all wherein I have strayed, and to be obedient, whatsoever penance they give me."[121] It was a sad note on which to end his life.

History has not been kind to Diego Evangelista, but unlike ourselves he could not have known he was dealing with a saint. He should be given credit for being sincere, if unwise. "He was young, of little prudence and choleric," a contemporary, Ferdinand of the Mother of God, remembered.[122] In 1594 Diego was elected provincial of Andalusia, but died on the way to his province, aged 34.[123]

On September 21, only a month and a half after his arrival in La Peñuela, St. John wrote to his friend, Dona Anne del Mercado y Peñalosa in Segovia: "Tomorrow I go to Úbeda to cure a slight bout of fever, for as I have been suffering from it daily for over a week, I think I need medical aid; but I go with the intention of returning here again, for in truth I am deriving great good from this holy retreat."[124] But John never saw La Peñuela again. The "slight bout of fever" was erysipelas and claimed his life. After painful and unavailing surgery St. John of the Cross died at Úbeda, December 14,

1591.[125]

It is an irony of history not often noted that both St. Teresa and St. John of the Cross lived and died as members of the old Carmel. The Discalced reform had not yet become a separate order. This final step was not long in coming.

The Order of Discalced Carmelites

At the general chapter of Cremona which convened on June 6, 1593, the Discalced Congregation was represented by its vicar general, Nicholas Doria, his two *socii* and three provincials with their *socii*.[126] Doria's candidate for prior general, and Philip II's as well, was Michael de Carranza. Carranza, as a matter of fact, was present at the chapter by special mandate of Clement VIII.[127] Carranza (d. 1607) was certainly a worthy candidate for the Order's highest office, and in the light of the tragic career of John Stephen Chizzola, who was actually elected, it is a pity that Philip II's wishes for once were not honored by the Order. One of the outstanding Carmelites of all Spain, Carranza earned the king's esteem for his zeal for reform. He would have suited the mood of Clement VIII. Anne of Jesus refers to Carranza as "a great friend of our Discalced friars."[128]

The general chapter of Cremona of 1593 is mostly remembered for the division of the Order. John Baptist, procurator of the Discalced Congregation, proposed the complete independence of the Congregation from the Order to be confirmed by the pope. By secret vote the chapter agreed on the condition *sine qua non* that the Discalced would not accept houses in places where the Order already was represented.[129] On December 20, 1593, Clement VIII in his constitution *Pastoralis officii* confirmed the decree of the chapter and erected the Order of Discalced Carmelites under a preposite general. Doria was nominated to this office until the first general chapter of the new order.[130]

On March 16, 1594, Clement was presented a petition on the part of "several who noted with the zeal of God" that it would be well if the preposite general could be continued in office at the coming general chapter. He had introduced the pristine observance from which the Order had already fallen due to the doctrine and life of a certain superior whom the pope had expelled from the Order. Certain lovers of a more lax way of life, especially nuns who aspired to more humane ways and more frequent communication with the friars were doing all they could to bring about the election of a preposite general after their own desires. Since the preposite general was opposed to the protraction of his term of office, the pope's brief should be addressed to the nuncio in Spain. On March 30 Clement VIII acceded to this request.[131]

All these fears and precautions were in vain. On May 9, 1594, the Lion of Carmel passed to his reward. It is to be hoped that his bones in fact found rest in the tomb. With blind stubbornness he battled the most brilliant and imaginative spirits of the reform; this was one time the bull won the *corrida*.

Doria was skilled at manipulating the law and never transgressed anyone's legal rights. Had he instead of Gracián been in charge of the Discalced from the start, the separation of the reform from the Order might equally have taken place, but it would have been brought about with less hysterics.

In any case the rift in the unity of Carmel, inevitable under the circumstances, can only be regretted.

NOTES

For complete references see list of *Abbreviations* and *List of Authorities Cited*.

Chapter I: John Baptist Rossi and Teresa of Jesus

1. *Bullarium carmelitanum*, II, 124.
2. *Foundations*, 2; *Works*, tr. Peers, III, 5.
3. ACG, I, 368
4. On Ristori, see *Bibl carm.*, 11, 208-210.
5. Steggink, *La reforma*, 125-134. This chapter is mainly based on this work to which the reader is referred for sources in each case.
6. *Bullarium carmelitanum*, II, 124-125.
7. Arch. ord., II Neapolitana 2 (no pagination).
8. Rossi *Regesta*, ed. Zimmerman, n. 2.
9. *Ibid*, n. 7.
10. Steggink, *La reforma*, 135, note 60.
11. Arch. ord., II Romandiolae et Piceni 1: 1563.
12. Steggink, *La reforma*, 113.
13. *Ibid.*, 114-115.
14. "Institutiones et sanctiones comitiorum generalium huius anni 1564"; ACG, I, 457-470.
15. Steggink, *La reforma*, 95-102, 119-123.
16. Borromeo became protector of the Order, May 5, 1564; *Bullarium carmelitanum*, II, 126-127. 7. See also Marcellinus, "Cronotaxis," 121-123.
17. ACG, I, 447.
18. On Carranza see *Bibl. carm*, II, 431-432.
19. *Bullarium carmelitanum*, II, 137-141.
20. *Ibid.*, 141-143.
21. Catena, *Traspontina*, 23-26; Steggink, *La reforma*, 152, 156.
22. Steggink, *La reforma*, 152, 156.
23. *Ibid.*, 155.
24. Rossi, *Regesta*, ed. Zimmerman, n. 65; Wessels, "Sancta Teresia," 183-184. See also Steggink, *La reforma*, 45.
25. *Bullarium carmelitanum*, II, 134-135. See also Saggi, "Questioni connesse," 180-181.
26. Steggink, *La reforma*, 148-151, 137-139.
27. *Ibid.*, 169-175.
28. *Ibid.*, 178.
29. *Ibid.*, 181-229.
30. *Ibid.*, 66-68.

31. Arch. ord., II Baetica 5, f. lr-59v. See also Steggink, *La reforma*, LIII, 181.
32. ACG, I, 453.
33. Steggink, *La reforma*, 183 and note 8.
34. On the Nieto brothers, see Steggink, *La reforma*, 207-212.
35. Wessels, "Sancta Teresia," 200.
36. Steggink, *La reforma*, 206.
37. *Ibid.*, 182.
38. *Ibid.*, 231-239. The acts of the chapters of Andalusia have been lost, but some account of them can be had from the history of the province written 1804-1807 by Michael Rodriguez Carretero, O. Carm., *Epytome historial de los Carmelitas Calzados de Andalusia*; Madrid, Biblioteca nacional, Ms. 18.118.
39. Steggink, *La reforma* 239-267. A copy of the *Institutiones*, bound with a similar booklet of decrees for Aragon, is found at Zaragoza, Biblioteca Universitaria, A-39-39.
40. Wermers, *A ordem carmelita*, 187-188. For the visitation of Portugal, see Steggink, *La reforma*, 271-276.
41. *Ibid.*, 100.
42. AGC, I, 429.
43. *Ibid.*, 453.
44. Steggink, *La reforma*, 276-280.
45. *Ibid.*, 281-289 and note 67.
46. *Ibid.*, 289-311.
47. *Ibid.*, 311-326.
48. Rossi, *Regesta*, ed. Zimmerman, n. 435.
49. Wessels, "Sancta Teresia," 191-193.
50. *Documenta primigenia*, appendix 2, 1-2.
51. *Documenta primigenia*, n. 18.
52. AGC, I, 466-467.
53. Steggink, *La reforma*, 326-331.
54. *Ibid.*, 331-339. The *Liber provinciae* (Acts of Chapters) of Castile seems lost. Extracts from it, covering the years 1567-1586, are found at Madrid, Biblioteca nacional, Ms. 2711, ff. 420r-lv. These in turn were partially reproduced by Zimmerman in his edition of Rossi's *Regesta*, pp. 245-248.
55. Rossi, *Regesta*, ed. Zimmerman, p. 245-247.
56. Recent and most thorough: Efrén de la Madre de Dios (Montalvo), O.C.D., Otger Steggink, O. Carm., *Tiempo y vida de Santa Teresa*, Madrid, 1968, which is extensively used in this chapter. Other lives: Silverio de Santa Teresa, O.C.D., *Vida de Santa Teresa de Jesus*, Burgos, 1935-1937, 5 v.; B. Allison Peers, *Mother of Carmel*, New York, 1946; Marcel Lepde, Sainte Th díAvila, Bruges, 1947; William Thomas Walsh, Saint Teresa of Avila, Milwaukee, 1948; Marcelle Auclair, Teresa of Avila, Garden City, N.Y., 1959 (Image Books); Olivier Leroy, Sainte ThËr díAvila; biographie spirituelle, Paris, 1962.

The most comprehensive bibliography on St. Teresa remains that compiled by Otilio del Niño Jesús (Rodriguez), O.C.D., which prefaces the edition of the *Obras completas*, ed. Efrén de la Madre de Dios, O.C.D., Otger Steggink, O. Carm., Madrid, 1951-1959, 3 v. For editions of the works of St. Teresa, see Simeón de la Sagrada Familia, O.C.D., *Bibliographia operum Sanctae Teresiae a Jesu typis editorum (1583-1967)*, Roma, 1969. For writings on St. Teresa and editions of her works since 1953, see the BCA and the BCT (since 1956).

57. Efrén, *Tiempo y vida*, 20 and note 4.

58. *Ibid.*, 4. See also Jiménez Salas, *Santa Teresa*, 37, section on ancestors; Petersson, *The Art of Ecstasy*, 3-4, and his bibliographical note, p. 142-143.

59. *Life*, ch. 4; *Works*, tr. Peers, I, 20.

60. *Life*, ch. 3; *ibid.*, 19.

61. *Life*, ch. 4; *ibid.*, 22.

62. *Life*, ch. 6; *ibid.*, 32.

63. *Life*, ch. 4; *ibid.*, 21.

64. *Ibid.*, 23.

65. *Life*, ch. 7; *ibid.*, 38.

66. *Ibid.*, 38-39.

67. *Life*, ch. 8; *ibid.*, 48-9.

68. *Ibid.*, 51.

69. Efrén, *Tiempo y vida*, p. 101, n. 158.

70. *Life*, ch. 9; *Works*, tr. Peers, I, 54.

71. *Ibid.*, 56.

72. For Teresa and the Jesuits, see Alban Goodier, S.J., "Saint Teresa and the Society of Jesus," *The Month*, 168 (1936), 395-405.

73. *Life*, ch. 23 and 24; *Works*, tr. Peers, I, 152-153.

74. Efrén, *Tiempo y vida*, p. 110, n. 176.

75. *Life*, ch. 24; *Works*, tr. Peers, I, 154. For this paragraph, see Efrén, *Tiempo y vida*, p. 102-110, n. 159-173.

76. Efrén, *Tiempo y vida*, p. 110, n. 179.

77. *Ibid.*, p. 111-112, n. 179; p. 114-115, n. 185-187.

78. *Life*, ch. 24; *Works*, tr. Peers, I, 155.

79. *Ibid.*, 155-6.

80. Efrén, *Tiempo y vida*, p. 112-113, n. 181-184.

81. *Ibid.*, p. 117, n. 191-192.

82. *Life*, ch. 27; *Works*, tr. Peers, I, 177.

83. "El ideal de Santa Teresa," 210. On St. Teresa and St. Peter of Alcantara, see René de Nantes, O.F.M.Cap., "Saint Pierre di Alcantara et Sainte Thérèse," *Etudes franciscaines*, 10 (1903), 162-168, 384-394. For references since 1953, see BCA and BCT (since 1956).

84. *Life*, ch. 32; *Works*, tr. Peers, I, 217.

85. *Vida de Santa Teresa de Jesús*, bk. 4, ch. 10; ed. Jaime Pons, S.J., Barcelona, 1908, 436. In 1565 Salazar dispensed her from the vow; *Documenta primigenia*, 13.

86. *Life*, ch. 32; Works, tr. Peers, I, 217.

87. Efrén, "El ideal de Santa Teresa," 216-218.

88. *Life*, ch. 32; *Works*, tr. Peers, I, 218-219.

89. *Life*, ch. 31; *Ibid.*, 209. It is not certain which monastery Teresa is referring to; see Efrén, *Tiempo y vida,* p. 126, n. 109 and Wilderink, *Les Constitutions*, 27, for some educated guesses.

90. Steggink, *La reforma*, 357-362. The 15th century manuscript copy of the *Institution* in Latin and Spanish used by St. Teresa is found in the General Archive of the Carmelite Order in Rome, Cod. II C.O. II 35. See also Graziano di Santa Teresa, O.C.D., "Il codice di Avila," *Ephemerides Carmeliticae*, 9 (1958), 442-452.

91. For this account of the famous meeting drawn from various sources, see Steggink, *La reforma*, 357, 362-363. Teresa's account is found in her *Life*, ch. 32; *Works*, tr. Peers, I, 219.

92. *Ibid.*, 219-220.

93. *Ibid.*, 220-221.

94. *Life*, ch. 32; *Works*, tr. Peers, I, 221, 222-223. For St. Teresa and the Dominicans, see Felipe Martín, *Santa Teresa de Jesús y la orden de Predicadores*, Avila, 1909; M.J. Savignol, *Sainte Thérèse et l'ordre de St. Dominique*, Toulouse, 1930; Alban Goodier, S.J., "St. Teresa and the Dominicans," *The Month*, 168 (1936), 247-256; Raimondo Spiazzi, O.P., "Riforma domenicana e riforma teresiana nel secolo XVI," *Memorie domenicane*, 80 (1963), 152-170, 212-225; Alvaro Huerga, O.P., "I Domenicani nella vita e nella riforma di S. Teresa," *Rivista di vita spirituale*, 17(1963), 458-474.

95. *Life*, ch. 33; *Works*, tr. Peers, I, 223-224, 226-227.

96. *Ibid.*, 224.

97. *Ibid.*, 225-6. For St. Teresa and the Inquisition, see Enrique Llamas Martinez, O.C.D., *Santa Teresa de Jesús y la Inquisición española*, Madrid, 1972

98. Efrén, *Tiempo y vida*, p. 138-142, n. 228; text of the *Dictamen*, p. 139-142, n. 229.

99. *Life*, ch. 33; *Works*, tr. Peers, I, 231.

100. For this paragraph and respective references see Steggink, *La reforma*, 367-368.

101. *Life*, ch. 35; *Works*, tr. Peers, I, 242. Text of Spanish version of the Rule: Tomás, *La reforma*, 93-96, 110-120. See also Saggi, "Questioni connesse," 163-164.

102. *Life*, ch. 35; *Works*, tr. Peers, I, 243.

103. Efrén, *Tiempo y vida*, p. 154-155, n. 251.

104. *Documenta primigenia*, n. 3; *Bullarium carmelitanum*, II, 119-120.

105. *Documenta primigenia*, n. 7; *Bullarium carmelitanum*, II, 123. Papal approval of both rescripts by Pius IV followed, July 17, 1565: *Documenta primigenia*, n. 15; *Bullarium carmelitanum*, II, 135-137.

106. Steggink, *La reforma*, 373-374; Efrén, *Tiempo y vida*, p. 161-165, nn. 260-267.

107. *Life*, ch. 36; *Works*, tr. Peers, I, 249-250.

108. *Ibid.*, 252. For this paragraph, see Efrén, *Tiempo y vida*, p. 168-170, nn. 273-276.

109. *Life*, ch. 36; *Works*, tr. Peers, I, 253.

110. Efrén, *Tiempo y vida*, p. 170, n. 177.

111. *Life*, ch. 36; *Works*, tr. Peers, I, 254.

112. St. Teresa and Bañez, see Marcel Lepée, *Bañez et Sainte Thérèse*, Paris, 1947.

113. Efrén, *Tiempo y vida*, p. 171-180, nn. 279-295; Steggink, *La reforma*, 376-379.

114. Efrén, *Tiempo y vida*, p. 180-182, nn. 297-299, p. 183-184, n. 1; Steggink, *La reforma*, 346-348, 379. For the authorizations by Salazar and Crivelli, see *Documenta primigenia*, n. 9 and 11.

115. See references provided by Steggink, *La reforma*, 380.

116. *Way*, ch. 3; *Works*, tr. Peers, II, 12 (ms. E).

117. *Life*, ch. 36; *ibid.*, I, 259.

118. Saggi, "Questioni connesse," 163-164, 172.

119. *Life*, ch. 36; *Works*, tr. Peers, I, 260.

120. *Way*, ch. 13; *ibid.*, II, 56 (ms. V).

121. *Mansion V*, ch. 1; *ibid.*, 247.

122. *Foundations* ch. 2; *ibid.*, III, 5.

123. *Way*, ch. 27; *ibid.*, II, 110-113 (ms. V).

124. For a description of the way of life at St. Joseph's and an evaluation of St. Teresa's work as foundress, see Steggink, *La reforma*, 393-408.

125. *Way*, ch. 4; *Works*, tr. Peers, II, 15 (ms. V).

126. Steggink, *La reforma*, 396-367; Saggi, "Questioni connesse," 175-176.

127. Teresa, *Obras*, ed. Efrén, 633-649; Tomás, *La reforma*, 96-101. Some idea of Teresa's primitive constitutions may be had from a rough draft of constitutions for the friars, still extant. The friars' constitutions were taken with requisite changes in gender and other alterations from those of the sisters.

128. *Way*, prologue, *Works*, tr. Peers, II, 1.

129. *Way*, ch. 1; *ibid*, 3.

130. *Way*, ch. 3; *ibid*, 10.

131. *Foundations*, ch. 2; *ibid*, III, 4-5.

132. *Ibid.*, 5.

133. *Ibid.*

134. *Vida*, pt 2, ch. 8; ed. La Fuente, 239.

135. *Documenta primigenia*, n. 129.

136. *Ibid.*, n. 12.

137. *Foundations*, ch. 2; *Works*, tr. Peers, III, 5-6.

138. *Documenta primigenia*, n. 19; see also the commentary by Steggink, *La reforma*, 413-416.

139. *Foundations*, ch. 27; *Works*, tr. Peers, III, 146.

140. *Foundations*, ch. 1; *ibid*, 3-4.

141. *Foundations*, ch. 2; *ibid*, 6.

142. *Letters*, tr. Peers, II, 817.

143. *Foundations*, ch. 2; *Works*, tr. Peers, III, 6.

144. *Ibid.*

145. *Documenta primigenia*, n. 21; see also the commentary by Steggink, *La reforma*, 419-422.

146. *Foundations*, ch. 2; *Works*, tr. Peers, III, 6.

Chapter II: The Discalced Reform

1. Steggink, *La reforma*, 423-424.

2. *Ibid.*, 424-427.

3. Wessels, "Sancta Teresia," 194-195. See also *Documenta primigenia*, n. 17.

4. Steggink, *La reforma*, 427-429.

5. *Ibid.*, 429-430. The acts of the chapters of Aragon for the years 1558-1628 are found at Valencia, Archivo General del Reino de Valencia, Ms. 1425.

6. Montañes, *Espejo*, ed. Garrido, appendix 1.

7. Steggink, *La reforma*, 429-433. A copy of the *Instituta*, bound with those of Andalusia, is found at Zaragoza, Biblioteca universitaria, A-39-39.

8. Wessels, "Sancta Teresia," 202-204; Rossi, *Regesta*, ed. Zimmerman, n. 149; Steggink, *La reforma*, 433-434. The following chapter acts are extant: Barcelona, Biblioteca provincial y universitaria, Ms. 1039: Acts of chapters, 1476-1566. Barcelona, Archivo de la Corona de Aragon, Fondos monacales procedentes de la Universidad, n. 21: Acts of chapters, 1567-1711.

9. Steggink, *La reforma*, 434-438.

10. Rossi to the nuns of Medina del Campo, Jan. 8, 1569; *Regesta*, ed. Zimmerman, p. 88-89.

11. A copy of the Memorial, or memorandum is found at Geneva, Bibliothèque Publique de l'Université, Collection Edouard Favre, vol. 82, ff. 5r-6v. Quoted by Steggink, *La reforma*, 438-440.

12. Cardinal Jerome Rusticucci, protector of the Order, to the nuncio of Spain, no date; Rossi, *Regesta*, ed. Zimmerman, p. 221.

13. *Informationi della visita fatta in Spagna alli frati carmelitani dal generale dell ordine e poi da reverendissimi ordinarii con gli assistenti deputati dal Conseglio Reale, per virtù d'un breve ottenuto da sua Beatitudine* (1568). Published by Steggink, *La reforma*, 469-473; see esp. p. 472.

14. Rossi, *Regesta*, ed. Zimmerman, p. 219-220.

15. *Ibid.*, 218-219.

16. *Informationi della visita*; Steggink, *La reforma*, 472.

17. Wessels, "Sancta Teresia," 205-207.

18. *Documenta primigenia*, I, 79, note 3.

19. *Ibid.*, I, 470-471; *Bullarium carmelitanum*, II, 165-166.

20. *Documenta primigenia*, n. 25. See also nn. 26-28.

21. Vargas' brief is found in the Archivio Segreto Vaticano, Secretaria brevium, v. 12, f. 222; Hebrera's in *Bullarium ord. frat. Praed.*, V (Roma, 1733), 219-221. See *Documenta primigenia*, I, 84, note 6.

22. *Documenta primigenia*, n. 29; Wessels, "Sancta Teresia," 208-209.

23. *Foundations*, ch. 2; *Works*, tr. Peers, III, 7.

24. *Foundations*, ch. 3; *ibid.*, 7-15.

25. Teresa, *Obras*, ed. Silverio, V, 339-340; Rossi, *Regesta*, ed. Zimmerman, p. 88-89.

26. *Foundations*, ch. 27; *Works*, tr. Peers, III, 146.

27. *Documenta primigenia*, n. 24.

28. *Ibid.*, n. 34.

29. Letter of Sept. 24, 1570; *Documenta primigenia*, n. 32.

30. Letter to her brother, Don Lorenzo de Cepeda, in Quito, Jan. 17, 1570; *Letters*, tr. Peers, I, 75.

31. *Foundations*, ch. 27; *Works*, tr. Peers, III, 146.

32. *Obras*, ed. Efrén, 732. Peers translates the last part: "except when I got a definite command from the General." *Letters*, I, 170.

33. Peers, *Handbook*, 237-238.

34. Rossi, *Regesta*, ed. Zimmerman, p. 88-89.

35. *Foundations*, ch. 3; *Works*, tr. Peers, III, 14-15.

36. Noteworthy among many biographies: Bruno de Jésus Marie, O.C.D., *Saint John of the Cross*, London, 1932; Crisógono de Jesús Sacramentado, O.C.D., *The Life of St. John of the Cross*, New York, 1958.

For a bibliography on St. John, see Pier Paolo Ottonello, *Bibliografia di S. Juan de la Cruz*, Roma, 1967. See also *Bibliographia carmelitana annualis*, 1953- and *Archivum bibliographicum carmelitanum*, 1956-

37. Bruno, *St. John*, 1-51; Crisógono, *Life*, 1-44 and note 5 of ch. 5.

38. *Foundations*, ch. 13; *Works*, tr. Peers, III, 61-64.

39. Silverio, *Historia*, III, 203-207. See also *Documenta primigenia*, n. 23.

40. *Foundations*, ch. 14; *Works*, tr. Peers, III, 66-67.
41. Silverio, *Historia*, III, 230.
42. *Documenta primigenia*, n. 72.
43. Fortunatus, *Constitutiones*, 13*-28*, 3-14; see also the book review by L. Saggi, *Carmelus*, 15 (1968), 278-80.
44. Silverio, *Historia*, III, 235-236.
45. *Ibid.*, 309-312.
46. *St. John*, 96. On Narducci, see Silverio, *Historia*, III, 312-315.
47. *Foundations*, ch. 17; *Works*, tr. Peers, III, 83-85. See also Bruno, *St. John*, 96-99; Crisógono, *Life*, 58.
48. Teresa, *Obras*, ed. Efrén, III, 993.
49. *Documenta primigenia*, 31.
50. María de San José, O.C.D., *Libro de recreaciones*, 110; qu. by Silverio, *Historia*, III, 353.
51. Rossi, *Regesta*, ed. Zimmerman, p. 46 (n. 112), 55 (n. 146), 246-247.
52. Francisco, *Reforma*, I, 345-346. According to Francis, the apostolic commissary, Peter Fernández, authorized the foundation. See also Silverio, *Historia*, III, 348-370.
53. *Documenta primigenia*, n. 38, 48, 53, 58, 72. See also Silverio, *Historia*, III, 498-534, 746-747.
54. On Fernández, see Alfaro Huerga, O.P., "Pedro Fernández, O.P., teólogo en Trento, artifice en la reforma teresiana, hombre espiritual," in *Il Concilio di Trento*, II, 647-665.
55. Arch. Ord., Il Castella 2: Statuta et constitutiones quas edidit visitator apostolicus in provincia Castellae Ordinis Carmelitarum (1571).
56. Wessels, "De patribus Discalceatis," 455.
57. Madrid, Biblioteca Nacional, Ms. 2711, f. 420r-lv: Extracts from the liber provinciae, 1567-1586.
58. Andrés de Ia Encarnación, O.C.D., *Memorias historiales*; Madrid, Biblioteca nacional, Ms. 13483, f. 107-108. Quoted by Steggink, *La reforma*, 446, note 6.
59. Procesos, I, 11.
60. Ribera, *Vida*, 264-265. Francisco, *Reforma*, I, 366, states that Teresa held the election and that Agnes was elected.
61. *Documenta primigenia*, n. 35, 39.
62. *Ibid.*, n. 36.
63. Yepes, *Vida*, bk. 2, ch. 25; II, 97. According to Maria Pinel, chronicler of the Incarnation who entered the monastery in 1640 and died in 1707, Fernández was tricked by the provincial who wanted to revenge himself on the nuns for not accepting his candidate for prioress and to impede Teresa from founding more monasteries. This account is accepted by Silverio, *Historia*, II, 442, and Efrén, *Tiempo y vida*, 438-441.
64. Teresa to Dona María de Mendoza, sister of the bishop of Avila, March 7, 1572; *Letters*, tr. Peers, I, 100-101.
65. *Ibid.*, 113.
66. *Ibid.*, note 3. See also *Documenta primigenia*, n. 47.
67. Testimony of Julian de Avila, whom Teresa sent to Fernández; *Procesos*, I, 223.
68. *Letters*, tr. Peers, I, 110; see also *ibid.*, 113-114, 115-116.
69. Bruno, *St. John*, 124-134; Crisogóno, *Life*, 71-79; Efrén, *Tiempo y vida*, p. 464-469, n. 321-323.

70. *Letters*, tr. Peers, I, 91-92. Date from *Obras*, ed. Efrén, 697. Frs. Efrén and Otger Steggink confuse González and Salazar. They owe the latter's restless shade an apology for the sinister motives mistakenly attributed to him.

71. *Letters*, tr. Peers, I, 86.

72. Wessels, "De patribus Discalceatis," 457.

73. Teresa, *Letters*, tr. Peers, I, 114, note 2.

74. Francisco, *Reforma*, I, 388.

75. *Procesos*, II, 3.

76. *Documenta primigenia*, 37.

77. Hebrera's acts for Aragon, published at Sariñena, are found in the Vatican Archive, Nunziatura di Spagna, v. 2, f. 302-313.

78. *Ibid.*, f. 245v; quoted by Carmelo, "Gracián y Sega," 377, note 67.

79. *Documenta primigenia*, n. 40.

80. Vargas' decrees are reproduced in J. Gracián's report to N. Ormaneto, April 6, 1577, of his visitation of Andalusia; *Documenta primigenia*, n. 127, pp. 353-354.

81. Francisco, *Reforma*, 398-399.

82. *Documenta primigenia*, n. 41.

83. See also Saggi, "Questioni connesse," 182-183. For a defense of Vargas' powers, see Victor, "Un conflicto," 439.

84. Francisco, *Reforma*, I, 399-400; Silverio, *Historia*, III, 655-656.

85. *Documenta primigenia*, n. 50.

86. Francisco, *Reforma*, I, 413, 433; Silverio, *Historia*, III, 667, 678.

87. *Documenta primigenia*, n. 54.

88. On Gracián, see Antonio Fortes Rodriguez, O.C.D., "Bibliografia del P. Jerónimo Gracián de la Madre de Dios," *Archivum Bibliographicum Carmelitanum*, 15 (1975), 173-203.

89. Francisco, *Reforma*, I, 469-476; Silverio, *Historia*, III, 693-701.

90. *Documenta primigenia*, n. 83.

91. *Ibid.*, n. 61.

92. *Ibid.*, n. 65.

93. P. Galli to N. Ormaneto, Dec. 16, 1573; *ibid.*, n. 56.

94. *Ibid.*, n. 57; see also n. 59, note 1.

95. On Ormaneto, see Francesco Carini, *Monsignore Nicoló Ormaneto*, Roma, 1894; Cuthbert Robinson, *Nicoló Ormaneto*, London, 1920; Alberto Monticone, "L'applicazione a Roma del Concilio di Trento; le visite del 1564-1566," *Rivista di Storia della Chiesa in Italia*, 7 (1953), 225-250, esp. 242-50; *idem*, "L'applicazione del Concilio di Trento a Roma; i riformatori e l'Oratorio," *Rivista di Storia della Chiesa in Italia*, 8 (1954), 23-48, esp. 23-31; Carlo Marcora, "Nicoló Ormaneto, vicario di S. Carlo (giugno 1564-giugno 1566)," *Memorie de diocesi di Milano*, 8 (1961), 209-590.

96. *Documenta primigenia*, n. 60. See also Rossi, *Regesta*, ed. Zimmerman, p. 224.

97. Rossi, *Regesta*, ed. Zimmerman, n. 576, 577, 589.

98. *Documenta primigenia*, n. 62. On the continuing validity of Vargas' patents after four years see Victor, "Un conflicto de jurisdicción," 437.

99. *Documenta primigenia*, n. 62, 64.

100. *Ibid.*, n. 67.

101. *Ibid.*, n. 71.
102. *Ibid.*, n. 75.
103. *Ibid.*, n. 73.
104. *Ibid.*, n. 74.
105. *Ibid.*, n. 76.
106. *Ibid.*, n. 79.
107. *Ibid.*, n. 78, 80; Teresa, *Obras*, ed. Silverio, VI, 319.
108. *Letters*, tr. Peers, I, 135.
109. *Foundations*, ch. 23; *Works*, tr. Peers, III, 120.
110. Gracián, *Peregrinación de Anastasio*, dial. 13; *Obras*, ed. Silverio, III, 200.
111. *Letters*, tr. Peers, I, 175.
112. Gracián, *Peregrinación de Anastasio*, dial. 13; *Obras*, ed. Silverio, Ill, 200.
113. *Letters*, tr. Peers, I, 179, 181.
114. Martino, *Monasteri femminili*, 294.
115. *Letters*, tr. Peers, I, 178-184.

Chapter III: *"An Intolerable Kind of Feud"*

1. ACG, I, 486-487; *Bullarium carmelitanum*, II, 183-184. See also Saggi, "Questioni connesse," 181-182; *idem*, "Santa Teresa," 186; Victor, "Un conflicto de jurisdición," 448-452.
2. ACG, I, 509-515. See also Saggi, "Santa Teresa," 186.
3. Wessels, "De patribus Discalceatis," 454-463. See also Saggi, "Santa Teresa," 187-188.
4. Wessels, "De patribus Discalceatis," 456.
5. *Letters*, tr. Peers, I, 224-225.
6. *Documenta primigenia*, n. 128, p. 360.
7. Letter of July 19, 1575; *Letters*, tr. Peers, I, 188.
8. *Documenta primigenia*, n. 84.
9. Letter of February 5, 1577; *Documenta primigenia*, n. 125.
10. ACG, I, 498; Wessels, "De patribus Discalceatis," 455. See also Victor, "Un conflicto de jurisdición," 473, note 208.
11. ACG, I, 530.
12. Letter of September 27, 1575; *Letters*, tr. Peers, I, 197. Translation revised by the author.
13. *Relation* 59; *Works*, tr. Peers, I, 364.
14. Gracián, *Obras*, ed. Silverio, III, 245.
15. Relation 60; Works, tr. Peers, I, 364-365. See also Mary of St. Joseph, *Libro de recreaciones*, 112.
16. Complaints against Gracián's visitation and his replies, Dec. 1, 1578; *Documenta primigenia*, n. 175, p. 62-63. Gracián, *Relación sumaria... de la visita de la Orden del Carmen*; *ibid.*, n. 128, p. 361-362. N. Ormaneto, *Litterae declatoriae*, Nov. 6, 1575; *ibid.*, n. 86. N. Ormaneto to the provincial and province of Andalusia, Dec. 8, 1575; *ibid.*, n. 92. N. Ormaneto to P. Galli, ca. 11 December, 1575; *ibid.*, n. 93.
17. *Letters*, tr. Peers, I, 208.
18. J. Gracián to J. Calvo de Padilla, Dec. 13, 1575; *Documenta primigenia*, n. 95, p. 252.
19. Teresa to Gracián, November 1575; *Letters*, tr. Peers, I, 208.

20. December 22, 1575; *Documenta primigenia*, n. 97 and note 3.

21. Gracián, Relación sumaria; *Documenta primigenia*, n. 128, p. 360.

22. Complaints against Gracián's visitation and his replies, Dec. 1, 1578; *Documenta primigenia*, n. 175, p. 68 (complaint 11).

23. *Obras*, ed. Silverio, Ill, 209.

24. N. Ormaneto to J. Gracián, February 18, 1576; *Documenta primigenia*, n. 105.

25. Marcora, "Nicoló Ormaneto," 282-283.

26. J. Gracián to N. Ormaneto, February 9, 1576; *Documenta primigenia*, n. 101. J. Gracián to J. Calvo de Padilla, December 13, 1575; *ibid.*, n. 95. For the date of the visitation, see Gracián, Relación sumaria; *ibid.*, n. 128, p. 363. For Rossi's visit to the monastery ten years previously, see Steggink, "Beaterios," 175-176.

27. *Documenta primigenia*, n. 99.

28. Gracián, Account of visitation; *Documenta primigenia*, n. 107, p. 290.

29. *Ibid.*, p. 291.

30. *Constitutiones 1524*, Isagogicon, ch. 4, n. 2.

31. Accounts of visitation; *Documenta primigenia*, n. 107 and 110.

32. Complaints against Gracián's visitation and his replies, December 1, 1578; *Documenta primigenia*, n. 175, vol. 2, p. 63.

33. *Ibid.*, p. 69.

34. *Bullarium carmelitanum*, II, 188; *Documenta primigenia*, n. 42.

35. Teresa to Mariano Azaro, May 9, 1576; *Letters*, tr. Peers, I, 235-237.

36. Silverio, *Historia*, IV, 124, 129.

37. Rossi, *Regesta*, ed. Zimmerman, p. 247.

38. *Reforma*, I, 555-556; Silverio, *Historia*, IV, 119-121.

39. *Documenta primigenia*, n. 114, note 4. On Suriano, see Bibl. carm., I, 787-788; ACG, I, 476, note 1 and 499.

40. *Documenta primigenia*, n. 114.

41. *Bullarium carmelitanum*, II, 213-214.

42. Sá, *Memorias historicas dos illustrissimos arcebispos*, 198-201; *Bibl.carm.*, I, 656-657; ACG, I, 486, note 3.

43. Arch. ord., II, Extra 1578.1

44. Teresa, *Obras*, ed. Silverio, VII, 269, note 1.

45. N. Ormaneto to P. Galli, February 5, 1577; *Documenta primigenia*, n. 125.

46. Teresa to Mary of St. Joseph, September 7, 1576; *Letters*, tr. Peers, I, 271.

47. Sá, *Memorias historicas dos illustrissimos arcebispos*, 200.

48. *Documenta primigenia*, n. 115.

49. Francisco, *Reforma*, I, 556-560; Silverio, *Historia*, IV, 135-142.

50. *Documenta primigenia*, n. 118.

51. *Letters*, tr. Peers, I, 285-286.

52. *Ibid.*, 434.

53. *Documenta primigenia*, n. 119.

54. *Ibid.*, 120.

55. *Ibid.*, 124.

Notes

56. *Ibid.*, 125.
57. Silverio, *Historia*, IV, 133, gives no source and has 1577 by mistake.
58. *Documenta primigenia*, n. 127.
59. *Ibid.*, n. 107, p. 299, note 9. See also Efrén, *Tiempo y vida*, 602. The authors by an oversight fail to indicate their manuscript source, but it seems to be Madrid, Archivo Histórico Nacional, Clero, libro 8494, n. 33.
60. Efrén, *Tiempo y vida*, 602, note 3.
61. María de San José, *Recreaciones*, 345-346; Gracián, *Peregrinación*, dial. 1 and 16, *Obras*, III, 85, 246. For the three reformers, see Peers, *Handbook*, 172-173, 191; Teresa, *Obras*, ed. Efrén, III, 1012, 1018, and Teresa's references to them in both these works. See also Saggi, "Santa Teresa," 213-214.
62. Letter to Mary of St. Joseph; *Letters*, tr. Peers, I, 460. See also the testimony of Mariano Azaro, October 1, 1577; *Documenta primigenia*, n. 139.
63. Letter to an unknown correspondent, August 23, 1577; *Documenta primigenia*, n. 130.
64. Teresa to Roque de Huerta, August 1578; *Letters*, tr. Peers, II, 588.
65. *Ibid.*, I, 466, but see Carmelo, "Gracián y Sega," 374. For a defense of Gracián's faculties, see Victor, "Un conflicto de jurisdicción," 486-491.
66. Relación sumaria; *Documenta primigenia*, n. 128, p. 365.
67. *Documenta primigenia*, 129.
68. *Ibid.*, 131.
69. Testimony of Mariano Azaro, October 1, 1577; *Documenta primigenia*, n. 139.
70. Confessions of Michael and Balthasar, September 24 and October 8, 1577; *Documenta primigenia*, 138 and 140.
71. *Documenta primigenia*, n. 131.
72. *Ibid.*, n. 133, 135.
73. Letter of September 18, 1577; *Letters*, tr. Peers, I, 482-484.
74. *Documenta primigenia*, n. 136, 138, 140, 141, 143.
75. P. Sega, letter of September 14, 1577, Carmelo, "Gracia y Sega," 367; *Documenta primigenia*, n. 137, note 1; P. Galli to P. Sega, October 8, Rossi, *Regesta*, ed. Zimmerman, p. 234, n. 36.
76. P. Sega to P. Galli, September 23, 1577; *Documenta primigenia*, n. 137.
77. Carmelo, "Gracián y Sega," 369.
78. *Documenta primigenia*, n. 147.
79. Teresa to T. de Braganza, January 16, 1578; *Letters*, tr. Peers, II, 515.
80. *Peregrinación*, dial. 2; *Obras*, ed. Silverio, III, 91. Silverio, *Historia*, IV 296. It is not clear whether this imprudent action took place at this time or later.
81. *Reforma*, I, 655.
82. *Documenta primigenia*, n. 139.
83. Account by the dissident nuns, dated November 25, 1577; *Documenta primigenia*, n. 146. Teresa to Mary of St. Joseph, October 22, 1577; *Letters*, tr. Peers, I, 487-489 (date from *Obras*, ed. Efrén, 881.) Tostado to the nuns, October 9, 1577; *Documenta primigenia*, n. 142.
84. See further Hipólito de la Sagrada Familia, O.C.D., "La 'elección machucada' de Santa Teresa," *Ephemerides carmeliticae*, 20 (1969), 168-193.
85. Teresa to Mary of St. Joseph, October 22, 1577; *Letters*, tr. Peers, I, 489.
86. Instructio pro Castella provinciali in causa monialium conventus Incarnationis provinciae Castellae; *Documenta primigenia*, n. 148. See also *ibid.*, n. 145 (procurators named for the

defense of the nuns, November 3, 1577), n. 149 (nuns refuse absolution, December 2).

87. *Documenta primigenia*, n. 88.

88. Teresa to J. B. Rossi, end of January 1576; *Letters*, tr. Peers, I, 226 (date from Teresa, *Obras*, ed. Efrén, 754). See also Bruno, *St. John*, 147. Crisógono, *Life*, 93, accepts the opinion that John's companion was Francis of the Apostles.

89. Teresa to Mary of St. Joseph, December 10, 1577; *Letters*, tr. Peers, I, 504.

90. Letter of December 4, 1577; *ibid.*, 497.

91. Bruno, *St. John*, 173-177; Crisógono, *Life*, 108.

92. P. Sega to P. Galli, May 5, 1578; *Documenta primigenia*, n. 155. See also Teresa to J. Gracián, May 7 and 22; *Letters*, tr. Peers, II, 560, 570.

93. Teresa to R. de Huerta, August 1578; *Letters*, tr. Peers, II, 589. *Documenta primigenia*, n. 156. See also the complaints against Gracián's visitation and his replies, December 1, 1578; *ibid.*, n. 175, p. 69-70.

94. For the persons mentioned in this paragraph, see Peers, *Handbook*, 105-233; Teresa, *Obras*, ed. Efrén, III, 986-1041.

95. Vicente Beltrán de Heredia, O.P., "El licenciado Juan Calvo de Padilla y su proceso inquisitorial," *Ciencia Tomista*, 42 (1930), 169-198.

96. Letter of August 24, 1576; *Documenta primigenia*, n. 117.

97. P. Sega to P. Galli, July 24, 1578; *ibid.*, n. 160. On Maldonado, see Pedro Borges, O.F.M., "Un reformador de Indias y de la orden franciscana bajo Felipe II, Alonso Maldonado de Buendía, O.F.M.," *Archivo Ibero Americano*, 21 (1961), 53-97.

98. Petition by Luke Carrión, July 10, 1578; *Documenta primigenia*, n. 157.

99. *Ibid.*, n. 159.

100. Teresa to J. Gracián, August 9, 1578; *Letters*, tr. Peers, II, 583-587 (date from *Obras*, ed. Efrén, 924).

101. Letter of August 1578; *ibid.*, 588-590.

102. L. Hurtado to A. M. de Pazos, November 19, 1578; L. Hurtado to P. Sega, same date; *Documenta primigenia*, n. 174, 173.

103. *Reforma*, I, 656; Silverio, *Historia*, IV, 213.

104. P. Sega to P. Galli, October 16, 1578; P. Sega to P. Buoncompagni, same date; *Documenta primigenia*, n. 166, 167. John of Jesus Roca claimed he suggested the assistants to the king; Teresa, *Cartas*, III, 349 (note by Anthony of St. Joseph).

105. Francisco, *Reforma*, I, 662-665; Silverio, *Historia*, IV, 224-248.

106. *Documenta primigenia*, n. 165.

107. P. Sega to P. Buoncompagni, November 13, 1578; *ibid.*, n. 171.

108. Francisco, *Reforma*, I, 668; Silverio, *Historia*, IV, 228.

109. For Mary of St. Joseph Salazar, see the introduction to her writings by Simeón de la Sagrada Familia in *Humor*, 121-151 (with bibliography).

110. *Foundations*, ch. 26; *Works*, tr. Peers, III, 134.

111. María de San José, *Recreaciones*, 9, ed. Simeon, 128, 326-327.

112. *Letters*, tr. Peers, II, 544.

113. *Ibid.*, 574, 575.

114. *Works*, tr. Peers, III, 135-139.

115. Letter of June 18, 1576; *Letters*, tr. Peers, II, 249-250.

116. Mary of St. Joseph's account of the visitation and its antecedents, see her *Recreaciones*, ed.

Simeón, 334-40. Fr. Silverio published extracts from the nuns' disclaimer to Gracián, *Historia*, IV, 235-263.

117. *Letters*, tr. Peers, II, 639-640. See also her letter to Isabel of St. Jerome and Mary of St. Joseph, May 3, 1578; *ibid.*, 647.

118. Letter to Mary of St. Joseph, July 4, 1580; *ibid.*, 760. See also her letter to Isabel of St. Jerome and Mary of St. Joseph, May 3, 1578; *ibid.*, 647-653.

119. *Ibid.*, 647, note 2; Teresa, *Obras*, ed. Silverio, VIII, 310, note 2.

120. Complaints against Gracián's visitation and his replies, Dec. 1, 1578; *Documenta primigenia*, n. 175.

121. *Ibid.*, n. 179.

122. Gracián, *Peregrinación*, dial. 2 and 16; *Obras*, ed. Silverio, III, 93, 245-246.

123. *Documenta primigenia*, n. 196-198.

124. A.M. de Pazos to the king, January 21, 1579; qu. by Silverio, *Historia*, IV, 280, note 1. Teresa to R. de Huerta, May 2, 1579; *Letters*, tr. Peers, II, 645.

125. *Documenta primigenia*, n. 171.

126. *Ibid.*, n. 182. For Sega's instructions to Salazar, same date, see *ibid.*, n. 183.

127. Letter to R. de Huerta, October 1578; *Letters*, tr. Peers, II, 608-609.

128. Letter of April, 1579; *ibid.*, 637.

129. *Documenta primigenia*, n. 186 and note 1.

130. For this date, see Saggi, "Le prime pubblicazioni," 103.

131. Letter of October 15, 1578; *Letters*, tr. Peers, II, 614-615.

Chapter IV: A Separate Province

1. For a list of Teresa's letters on this subject see *Documenta primigenia*, II, 110, note 2.

2. Teresa to J. Gracián, September 20, 1576; *Letters*, tr. Peers, I, 286. Teresa to J. Gracián, Oct. 15, 1578; *ibid.*, II, 615-6.

3. Teresa to R. de Huerta, end of October 1578; *ibid.*, 620 (date from Teresa, *Obras*, ed. Efrén, 942).

4. Teresa to the nuns of Valladolid, May 31, 1579; *Letters*, tr. Peers, II, 653-654 (date from Teresa, *Obras*, ed. Efrén, 960).

5. *Ibid.*, 655; Teresa to L. de Cepeda, July 27, 1579, *ibid.*, 682.

6. *Historia*, IV, 277.

7. For the mission to Rome, see Francisco, *Reforma*, I, 719-25; Silverio, *Historia*, IV, 470-475.

8. *Documenta primigenia*, n. 187.

9. The requests to the superior of the Order and to the king are not at hand, but this course of events is described in a petition on the part of the order to the Congregation of Religious and Bishops; *ibid.*, n. 202.

10. *Ibid.*, n. 188. For summaries of the minutes, see n. 189-191.

11. *Ibid.*, n. 191.

12. A. Salazar to P. Sega, November 20, 1579; *ibid.*, n. 193.

13. B. Briceño to Philip II, May 2, 1580; *ibid.*, n. 207. G. Robuster to Philip II, no date, *ibid.*, n. 210.

14. See the general chapter of 1440; ACG, I, 193.

15. Undated, unsigned memorandum; *Documenta primigenia*, n. 202.

16. Undated, unsigned memorandum; *ibid.*, n. 201. See also part 2 of n. 200.

17. ACG, I, 557.

18. *Documenta primigenia*, n. 203, 207.

19. *Ibid.*, n. 209; *Bullarium carmelitanum*, II, 208-12.

20. Philip II to M. A. Maffei, August 15, 1580; *Documenta primigenia*, n. 212. See also Philip II to B. Briceño, same day, *ibid.*, n. 211.

21. Text in Antolín, *Constitutiones*, 675-681.

22. Teresa to J. Gracián, February 19, 1581; *Letters*, tr. Peers, II, 809-813 (date from *Obras*, ed. Efrén, 1038).

23. Official attestation to the election, dated March 4, 1581; *Documenta primigenia*, n. 238.

24. *Ibid.*, 237.

25. *Ibid.*, 241.

26. *Ibid.*, II, 284, note 18.

27. Antolín, *Constitutiones*, 15-23. See also *ibid.*, 29*-32*.

28. The Latin constitutions are reprinted by Antolín, *Constitutiones*, 25-298; see also *ibid.*, 33*-40*. The Spanish constitutions are reprinted in Teresa, *Obras*, ed; Silverio, VI, 447-523. For a study of the Discalced constitutions see Antolín, *Constitutiones*, 46*-56*

29. *Documenta primigenia*, n. 113.

30. Otilio Rodriguez, O.C.D., "El testamento teresiano," *El Monte Carmelo*, 78 (1970), 11-83, etc. Italian translation: *I testamento teresiano*, Roma, 1973. Fortunato Antolín, O.C.D., "Observaciones sobre las constituciones de las Carmelitas Descalzas promulgadas en Alcalá de Henares en 1581, *Ephemerides carmeliticae*, 24 (1973), 291-374.

31. J. Gracián's account of the chapter; *Documenta primigenia*, n. 244.

32. *Foundations*, ch. 29; *Works*, tr. Peers, III, 176.

Chapter V: Carmel After Teresa: the Division of the Order

1. *Peregrinación de Anastasia*, dial. 13; *Obras*, ed. Silverio, III, 186.

2. *Documenta primigenia*, n. 176. See also *ibid.*, n. 163-164.

3. *Foundations*, ch. 30; *Works*, tr. Peers, III, 179.

4. For this paragraph, see Silverio, *Historia*, VI, 103-118.

5. *Letters*, tr. Peers, II, 670.

6. Teresa to her niece, Tomasina Bautista, prioress of Burgos, August 3, 1582; *ibid.*, 953.

7. Letter of September 1, 1582; *ibid.*, 966-967.

8. Letter of December 12, 1576; *ibid.*, I, 376.

9. *Foundations*, ch. 29; *Works*, tr. Peers, III, 176-177.

10. Belchior, *Chronica*, I, 83, 123-128; Silverio, *Historia*, IV, 680, V, 428-436.

11. J. Gracián's patents for the missionaries, March 19, 1582; *Obras*, ed. Silverio, III, 480-482.

12. Belchior, *Chronica*, I, 106-113; Silverio, *Historia*, IV, 692-693; V, 259.

13. Gabriel, "Elecciones," 249; Antolín, *Constitutiones*, 282-286.

14. For an account of the chapter, see Silverio, *Historia*, V, 250-72; the fragmentary acts are published by Antolín, *Constitutiones*, 299-302.

15. Francisco, *Reforma*, II, 55-56; Silverio, *Historia*, V, 267-270.

16. Johannes Beckmann, S.M.B., "Missionarische Partnerschaft in fruhrer Zeit; ein karmelitisch-

franziskanisches Uebereinkommen zur Bekehrung Chinas von 1585," *Neue Zeitschrift für Missionswissenschaft*, 24 (1968), 81-93. See also Silverio, *Historia*, V, 451-452.

17. Text: Belchior, *Chronica*, I, 310-311.

18. "Elecciones," 250; Francisco, *Reforma*, II, 154-157; Silverio, *Historia*, V, 444-464.

19. Victoria, *Los Carmelitas Descalzos*, 13-17, 59.

20. *Pereginación*, dial. 13; *Obras*, ed. Silverio, *Historia*, I, 199.

21. Teresa to J. Gracián, October 15, 1578; *Letters*, II, 615.

22. A summary is provided by Silverio, *Reforma*, VI, 90-102.

23. See also Francisco, *Reforma*, II, 155-156; Silverio, *Historia*, V, 447-449; Bruno, *St. John*, 297.

24. Francisco, *Reforma*, II, 123-128; Silverio, *Historia*, V, 282-289.

25. Peers, *Handbook*, 257-258.

26. *Constitutiones 1585*, pt. 6, ch. 2, in Antolín, *Constitutiones*, 286-298.

27. Francisco, *Reforma*, II, 175-176; Silverio, *Historia*, V, 457-458.

28. Francisco, *Reforma*, II, 176-178; Silverio, *Historia*, V, 462-464.

29. *Bullarium carmelitanum*, II, 232-235. See also Francisco, *Reforma*, II, 338-340; Silverio, *Historia*, V, 570-576.

30. The Brussels 1609 edition is reprinted in Gracián, *Obras*, ed. Silverio, III, 1-37. See also Ambrosius, *Bio-bibliographia missionaria*, n. 22, etc. Gregory of St. Joseph had in hand the 1586 edition: Le père Jérôme Gratién, 47, note 3.

31. For the controversy over missions among the Discalced of Spain, see Tomás Alvarez, O.C.D., "Contemplación y espíritu misionero en el Carmelo teresiano primitivo," *El Monte Carmelo*, 64 (1956), 1-42.

32. Gabriel, "Elecciones," 250-251.

33. Redondillas, in *Humor*, 495-496. Translation by the author with apologies.

34. Text: Gracián, *Obras*, ed. Silverio, III, 293-295. See also María de San Jose, Ramillete de Mirra, in *Humor*, 398-400.

35. *Ibid.*, 274.

36. Gracián, Letter to unspecified confreres, February 8, 1588; *Obras*, ed. Silverio, III, 297. His orders to leave are published by Silverio, *Historia*, VI, 305-306.

37. Silverio, *Historia*, V, 598-602; VI, 306-307.

38. Letters of Augustine of the Kings to N. Doria and of N. Doria to the vicars provincial, reproduced without dates, *ibid.*, VI, 339-340, 340-341.

39. *Ibid.*, 308-312.

40. *Ibid.*, 312-326.

41. *Ibid.*, 326-344.

42. *Ibid.*, 344-347.

43. *Constitutiones 1581*, ch. 3; Rodriguez, "El testamento teresiano," 40-42.

44. Silverio, *Historia*, VI, 356, note 1.

45. *Ibid.*, 144-145.

46. *Ibid.*, 357-358.

47. *Bullarium carmelitanum*, II, 237-242; Antolín, *Constitutiones*, 721-733. See also Francisco, *Reforma*, II, 395-400; Silverio, *Historia*, VI, 131-137.

48. *Privilegia*, 149-151.

49. Texts in Antolín, *Constitutiones*, 737-742.

50. Text in Silverio, *Historia*, VI, 727-732 (appendix 2).

51. Gabriel, "Elecciones," 251-252; Francisco, *Reforma*, II, 426-429; Silverio, *Historia*, VI, 147-153.

52. Letter of C. Speziano, September 10, 1588; Antolín, *Constitutiones*, 743-744.

53. Teresa to Tomasina Baptist, prioress of Burgos, August 3, 1582; *Letters*, tr. Peers, II, 953.

54. Text in Silverio, *Historia*, VI, 359-360.

55. Text in Silverio, *Historia*, VI, 359-360. On August 7 Speziano allowed Gracián to communicate with Teutonio de Braganza, archbishop of Evora, Barnaby del Mármol Zapata and his brother John Vasquez de Mármol; *ibid.*, 372-373.

56. *Ibid.*, 361-363. Loaysa wrote again in the same vein on December 10; *ibid.*, 363-364.

57. *Ibid.*, 398-399.

58. Text: *ibid.*, 360-361.

59. Text: *ibid.*, 399, note 2.

60. Text: *ibid.*, 382-386.

61. María de San José, "Ramillete de mirra," in *Humor*, 411-412, 413-414. Another copy, dated September 25, is published by Silverio, *Historia*, VI, 388, note 1.

62. *Humor*, 401-406. Silverio opines that Mary's unnamed correspondent was Gregory: *Historia*, VI, 362, note 1.

63. Teresa, *Obras*, ed. Efrén, III, 990; Peers, *Handbook*, 116 (with bibliography). To Peers' bibliography might be added Louis van den Bosssche, *Anne de Jésus*, Bruges, 1958. For works published since 1953, see BCA & BCT.

64. Anne of Jesus to Mary of St. Jerome, prioress of Avila, July 2, 1588; Silverio, *Historia*, VI, 815-817.

65. Text: Moriones, *Ana de Jesús*, 160-162.

66. Antolín, O.C.D., "Precisiones sobre la edición de las Constituciones de las Carmelitas Descalzas hecha en 1588," *Ephemerides carmeliticae*, 20 (1969), 434-448.

67. J. Gracián to Philip II, November 2, 1588; Silverio, *Historia*, VI, 395-397.

68. Francisco, *Reforma*, II, 432-435 (no date, but Francis lists the letter under the year 1588); Silverio, *Historia*, VI, 171-177.

69. Francisco, *Reforma*, II, 436-437; Silverio, *Historia*, VI, 180-181.

70. Letter to G. de Zayas, December 23, 1589; *Obras*, ed. Silverio, III, 299.

71. *Peregrinación de Anastasio*, dial. 3 and 14; *Obras*, ed. Silverio, III, 99-104, 209-210. See also Silverio, *Historia*, VI, 404-414.

72. Silverio, *Historia*, VI, 437-439.

73. J. Gracián, *Obras*, ed. Silverio, III, 298-301. Gracián mentions John López' name in an undated memorial quoted by Silverio, *Historia*, VI, 424. This memorial, entitled "Cargos que se pueden poner al padre Fr. Nicolás de Jesús María Doria, vicario general de los Descalzos," is a much more lengthy litany of injusticies allegedly committed by Doria and apparently served as a source for Gracián's defense presented to the king by John Vázquez de Mármol, *ibid.*, 418-431. John López was secretary to the king; *ibid.*, 495.

74. Silverio, *Historia*, VI, 440-442.

75. Gracián, *Peregrinación de Anastasio*, dial. 4; *Obras*, ed. Silverio, III, 104. See also Peter of the Purification to Gregory Nazianzen, March 13, 1589; Silverio, *Historia*, VI, 431-436.

76. Doria's letter; Silverio, *Historia*, VI, 739-746 (appendix 4); Gracián's answer: *ibid.*, 801-804 (appendix 12).

77. Letter of September 30, 1625; Berthold Ignace, *Anne de Jésus*, 126-128, 329-330.

Notes

78. *Bullarium romanum*, IX (Torino, 1865), 203-228; *Bullarium carmelitanum*, III, 280-283.

79. Moriones, *Ana de Jesús*, 191; Silverio, *Historia*, VI, 217, dates the brief June 27.

80. Francisco, *Reforma*, II, 548; Silverio, *Historia*, VI, 217; Moriones, *Ana de Jesús*, 191.

81. Antolín, *Constitutiones*, 301-376. See also Simeón, "Bibliografía de los impresos," n. 15-16.

82. Decree of the consulta, August 8, 1591; Silverio, *Historia*, VI, 499-500; Gracián's criticism, *ibid.*, 804-813 (appendix 13).

83. Doria's letter: Silverio, *Historia*, VI, 747-753 (appendix 5). See also Simeón, "Bibliografía de los impresos," n. 19. Gracián letter: Silverio, *Historia*, VI, 787-799 (appendix 10).

84. Statement by a notary, December 14, 1590; Silverio, *Historia*, VI, 233, note 3.

85. Notary act, November 1, 1590; *ibid.*, 258. For the course of the process before the king, see *ibid.*, 235-248; Moriones, *Ana de Jesús*, 203-253.

86. For letters of nuns in support of both sides, see Silverio, *Historia*, VI, 253-273, 815-870.

87. Letter 60 to a Carmelite prioress, May 14, ca. 1621-1622; *Lettres*, ed. Sérouet, 140.

88. Silverio, *Historia*, VI, 240-246; Moriones, *Ana de Jesús*, 255-262.

89. Silverio, *Historia*, VI, 251, note.

90. Antolín, *Constitutiones*, 745-751; *Bullarium carmelitanum*, III, 283-286. See also Silverio, *Historia*, VI, 289-293.

91. *Autobiografía*, 80.

92. María de San José, "Ramillete de mirra," in *Humor*, 417.

93. Francisco, *Reforma*, II, 565-567; Silverio, *Historia*, VI, 277-283. The list of officials is from Gabriel, "Elecciones," 253, and differs from that presented by Francisco. Silverio, as usual, repeats Francisco, yet later (p. 759) publishes a document with the correct names as listed by Gabriel.

94. Text of the friars', Spanish and Latin, Antolín, *Constitutiones*, 378-603.

95. Moriones, *Ana de Jesús*, 284-287.

96. Berthold Ignace, *Anne de Jésus*, 232-270.

97. Francisco de la Crux, O.C.D., "Segundo dicho que me fue tomado en 1 de abril de 1590," Silverio, *Historia*, VI, 460.

98. N. Doria to J. Gracián, June 3, 1591; *ibid.*, 493, note 2.

99. *Relación of Gracián's trial and sentencing*; Francisco, *Reforma*, II, 602-605, esp. 603; Silverio, *Historia*, VI, 513-526, esp. 514.

100. J. Gracián, Crónica de lo que le acaeció a el P. Gracián cuando vino a este convento de San Hermenegildo desde Portugal y de la manera que fu tratado; Silverio, *Historia*, VI, 494-501, esp. 497-498.

101. *Relación*; Francisco, *Reforma*, II, 603; Silverio, *Historia*, VI, 515.

102. Text of sentence: Silverlo, *Historia*, VI, 519-525. See also Gregory's *Relación*, *ibid.*, 525-526; Francisco, *Reforma*, II, 605.

103. *Peregrinción de Anastasio*, dial. 10; *Obras*, ed. Silverio, III, 154.

104. *Ibid.*, dial. 9; *ibid.*, 151-2.

105. *Ibid.*, 153.

106. *Ibid.*, dial. 16; *ibid.*, 246.

107. Teresa to J. Gracián, August 19, 1578; *Letters*, tr. Peers, II, 597.

108. John Evangelist to Jerome of St. Joseph, July 2, 1630; Silverio, *Historia*, VI, 799.

109. Cargos que se pueden poner al padre Fr. Nicolás de Jesús María Doria, vicario general de los Descalzos; *ibid.*, 420, 423.

110. *Spiritual Canticle* (B), stanza 28; *Works*, tr. Peers, II, 328-329.

111. Process at Segovia, quoted by Crisógono, *Life*, 275, 380. Joseph of Jesus and Mary says the same, *Vida*, 417.

112. Mary of the Incarnation to N. Doria, October 10, 1590; Silverio, *Historia*, VI, 855.

113. *Works*, tr. Peers, III, 295. On the re-election of priors see *Constitutiones 1590*, ch. 10, n. 2.

114. *Vida*, 423.

115. John Evangelist to Jerome of St. Joseph, July 2, 1630; Silverio, *Historia*, VI, 800.

116. Jerónimo de San José, *Historia del Juan de La Cruz*, 699.

117. Testimony of John of St. Anne; Juan de la Cruz, *Vida y obras*, ed. L. Ruano, 312, note 29.

118. Hipólito, *La vida de San Juan*, 24-25.

119. St. John to Dona Anne del Mercado y Peñalosa, August 19, 1591: "I arrived here 9 days ago." *Vida y obras*, ed. L. Ruano, 383 (not in Peers' translation).

120. Testimony of of Alonzo of St. Albert; Juan de la Cruz, *Vida y obras*, ed. L. Ruano, 316; Crisógono, *Life*, 281.

121. José de Jesús María, *Vida*, 860-861; Juan de la Cruz, *Works*, tr. Peers, III, 298.

122. Juan de la Cruz, *Vida y obras*, ed. L. Ruano, 321, 324-325; Crisógono, *Life*, 286.

123. Gabriel, "Elecciones," 254; Peers, *Handbook*, 148.

124. *Works*, tr. Peers, III, 297.

125. Crisógono, *Life*, 289-305; Bruno, *St. John*, 340-359.

126. ACG, 1, 574, 576.

127. *Ibid.*, 574.

128. Anne of Jesus to Mary of St. Jerome, July 2, 1588; Silverlo, *Historia*, VI, 816.

129. ACG, I, 593-594.

130. *Bullarium carmelitanum*, II, 268-272.

131. Moriones, *Ana de Jesús*, 288-291.

ABBREVIATIONS

For complete references see *List of Authorities Cited*

ACG: Acta capituloruin generalium.

AOC: Analecta ordinis armelitaruin, Roma, v. 1, 1909-

AOCD: Analecta ordinis Carnielitarum Discalceatorum, Roma, v. 1-25, 1926-1953.

Arch. ord.: Archive of the Order, Rome.

Arch. Vat.: Archivio Vaticano, Cittá del Vaticano.

BCA: Bibliographia carmelitana annualis.

ECT: Bibliographia carmeli Teresiani.

Bibl. carm.: Vilhiers, Cosmas de, O. Carm., Bibliotheca carmelitana.

Bibl. carm. lug.: Bibliotheca carmelitana lusitana.

Bull. carm. Bullarium carmelitanum.

MHC: Monumenta historica carmelitana.

LIST OF SOURCES CITED

Acta capitulorum generalium ordinis fratrum B. V. Mariae de Monte Carmelo; ed. Gabriel Wessels, O. Carm., Roma, 1912-1934. 2v.

Alvarez, Tomás, O.C.D., "Contemplación y espíritu misionero en el Carmelo teresiano primitivo," *El Monte Carmelo*, 64 (1956) 1-42.

Alvarez, Tomás, O.C.D. *La reforma teresiana, documentario histórico de sus primeros días* [por]Tomás de la Cruz, Simeón de la S. Familia]. Roma, 1962.

Ambrosius a Sancta Teresia, O.C.D. *Bio-bibliographia missionaria ordinis Carmelitarum Discalceatorum (1584-1940)*. Roma, 1940.

Andrés de la Encarnacíon, O.C.D. *Memorias historiales*. Madrid, Biblioteca Nacional, Ms. 13483.

Antolín, Fortunato, O.C.D. *Constitutiones Carmelitarum Discalceatorum*, 1567-1600; ed. Fortunatus a Jesu, O.C.D., Beda a SS. Trinitate, O.C.D. Roma, 1968.

Antolín, Fortunato, O.C.D. "Observaciones sobre las constituciones de las Carmelitas Descalzas promulgadas en Alcalá de Henares en 1581," *Ephemerides carmeliticae*, 24 (1973) 291-374.

Antolín, Fortunato, O.C.D. "Precisaciones sobre la edición de las Constituciones Descalzas hecha en 1588," *Ephemerides carmeliticae*, 20 (1969) 433-448.

Archive of the Order, Roma.

II C.O. 1 (3). *Regestum Joannis Battistae de Rubbeis.*

II Baetica 5.

Castella 2. *Statua et constitutiones quas edidit visitator apostolicus in provincia Castellae Ordinis Carmelitarum (1571).*

II Romandiolae et Piceni 1.

Archivum bibliographicum carmelitanum; comp. Simeón de la Sagrada Familia, O.C.D. Roma, 1956. Includes the BCT.

Auclair, Marcelle. *Teresa of Avila*. Garden City, N.Y., 1959 (Image Books).

Beckmann, Johannes, S.M.B. "Missionarische Partnerschaft in frueherer Zeit; ein karmelitisch-franziskanisches Uebereinkommen zur Bekehrung Chinas von 1585," *Neue Zeitschrift fuer Missionswissenschaft*, 24 (1968) 81-93.

Belchior de Santa Ana, O.C.D. *Chronica de Carmelitas Descalcos, particular do reyno de Portugal*. Lisboa, 1657-1753. 3 v. Vol. 2, 1721, by Joaõ do Sacramento, O.C.D.; vol. 3, 1753, by José de Jesus Maria.

Beltrán de Heredia, Vicente, O.P. "El licenciado Juan Calvo de Padilla y su proceso inquisitorial," *Ciencia Tomista*, 42 (1930) 169-198.

Berthold Ignace de Sainte Anne, O.C.D. *Anne de Jésus et les constitutions des Carmélites Dechaussées*. Bruxelles, 1874.

Bibliographia Carmeli Teresiani; comp. Simeón de la Sagrada Familia, O.C.D. Roma, 1956- . Appears irregularly, covers only the Discalced Carmelites.

Bibliographia carmelitana annualis; comp. Pius Serracino-Inglott, 1953- Appears serially in the review *Carmelus*, covers both Carmelite Orders.

Bibliotheca carmelitana lusitana, historica, critica, chronologica. Romae, 1754.

Borges, Pedro, O.F.M. "Un reformador de Indias y de la orden franciscana bajo Felipe II, Alonso Maldonado de Buendía, O.F.M.," *Archivo Ibero-Americano*, 21 (1961) 53-97.

Bossche, Louis van den. *Anne de Jésus, coadjutrice de Ste. Thérèse d'Avila*. Bruges, 1958.

Bruno de Jésus Marie, O.C.D. *Saint John of the Cross*. London, 1932.

Bullarium carmelitanum; ed. Eliseo Monsignano et Josepho Alberto Ximenez, O. Carm. Roma, 1715-1768. 4v.

Caput unicum, Venetiiis, 1524. See: *Constitutiones*, 1524.

Carini, Francesco. *Monsignore Niccoló Ormaneto, Veronese, vescovo di Padova, nunzio apostolico alla corte di Filippo II, re di Spagna*, 1573-1577. Roma, 1894.

Carmelo de la Cruz, O.C.D. "Gracián y Sega frente a frente," *El Monte Carmelo*, 72 (1964) 365-422.

Catena, Claudio, O. Carm. *Traspontina, guida storica e artistica*. Roma, 1954.

Constitutiones.

1524: Aureaetsaluberrima ordinis Fratrum Deiparae V.M. de Monte Carmelo statuta in capitulo generali... ordinata; Isagogicon ... ad reformationem vitae regularis; Constitutiones ordinatae per R. Magistrum Joannem Soret. Venetiis, 1524.

1540: *Constitutiones fratrum et sororum ordinis et observantiae Beatissimae Genitricis Mariae de Monte Carmelo*. Bononiae, 1540.

1566: *Institutiones et ordinationes observandae a R. Magistris, patribus et fratibus Carmelitis provinciae Bathicae*. Hispali, 1566.

1567: *Has constitutiones, haec instituta a rev. provinciali, prioribus, magistris, vicariis, patribus et fratribus Carmelitis huius provinciae Aragoniae ... executioni demandandas ... confecit Jon. Bapt. ex Rubeis*. Valentiae, 1567.

1568: *Singulis Italiae citra et ultra Pharum rev. mag. provincialibus ... J.B. Rubeus transmittit ... harum constitutionum compendium et summam*. Venetiis, 1568.

1582: *Decreta Rev. Mag. Jo. Bapt. Caffardi quae Mantuanae Congregationis charissimis regularibus in sua solemni visitatione reliquit*. Florentiae, 1582. *Ordinazioni per le monache carmelitane*. Firenze, 1582.

1586: *Constitutiones fratrum ordinis Beatissimae Dei Genitricis Mariae de Monte Carmeli*. Romae, 1586.

1593: *Constitutiones et decreta tam pro reformandis bonarum litterarum studiis quam pro reparanda vitae regularis observantia*. Cremona, 1593.

Crisógono de Jesus Sacramentado, O.C.D. *The Life of St. John of the Cross*. New York, 1958.

Documenta primigenia ab Instituto Historico Teresiano edita. Romae, 1973. 2 v. (Documents numbered continuously through the 2 v.)

Efrén de la Madre de Dios, O.C.D. "El ideal de Santa Teresa en la fundación de San José" *Carmelus*, 10 (1963) 206-230.

Efrén de la Madre de Dios, O.C.D. *Tiempo y vida de Santa Teresa*, por Efrén de la Madre de Dios, O.C.D., Otger Steggink, O. Carm. Madrid, 1968.

Fortes Rodriguez, Antonio, O.C.D. *Bibliografía del P. Jerónimo Gracián de la Madre de Dios; in Archivum bibliographicum carmelitanum*, 15 (1975) 173-203.

Fortunato de Jesús Sacramentado, O.C.D. See: Antolín, Fortunato, O.C.D.

Francisco de Santa María, O.C.D. *Reforma de los Descalzos*. Madrid, 1644-1655. 2 v. Continued by other authors in 7 v. The ms. v. 8 is found at Madrid, Biblioteca Nacional, Ms. 2251.

Gabriel de Ia Cruz, O.C.D. "Elecciones hechos en los primeros capítulos de la reforma teresiana (1581-1622 y 1634)," *El Monte Carmelo*, 74 (1966) 241-279.

Goodier, Alban, S.J. "Saint Teresa and the Dominicans," *The Month*, 168 (1936) 247-256.

Gracián, Jerónimo, O. Carm. *Obras*; ed. Silverio de Santa Teresa. Burgos, 1932-1933. 3 v.

Graziano di Santa Teresa, O.C.D. "Il codice di Avila," *Ephemerides carmeliticae*, 9 (1958) 442-452.

Grégoire de Saint Joseph, O.C.D. *Le Père Jèrôme Gratien de la Mère de Dieu*, Carme Dechauss et ses juges. Rome, 1904.

Hipólito de la Sagrada Familia, O.C.D. "La 'elección machucada' de Santa Teresa," *Ephemerides carmeliticae*, 20 (1969) 168-193.

Huerga, Alvaro, O.P. "I Domenicani nella vita e nella riforma di S. Teresa," *Rivista di vita spirituale*, 17 (1963) 458-74.

Huerga, Alfaro, O.P. "Pedro Fernández, O.P., teólogo en Trento, artifice en la reforma teresiana, hombre espiritual," in *Il Concilio di Trento*, II, 647-65.

List of Sources Cited

Humor y espiritualidad en la escuela teresiana primitiva. Burgos, 1966.

Instituta, Valencia, 1567. See: *Constitutiones*, 1567.

Institutiones et ordinationes, Hispali, 1566. See: *Constitutiones*, 1566.

Isagogicon, Venetiis, 1524. See: *Constitutiones*, 1524.

Jiménez Salas, María. *Santa Teresa de Jesús, bibliografía fundamental.* Madrid, 1962.

Lepée, Marcel. *Bañez et Sainte Thérèse.* Paris, 1947.

Lepée, Marcel. *Sainte Thérèse d'Avila.* Bruges, 1947.

Leroy, Olivier. *Sainte Thérèse d'Avila, biographie spirituelle.* Paris, 1962.

Llamas Martinez, Enrique, O.C.D. S*anta Teresa de Jesús y la Inquisición española.* Madrid, 1972.

Marcellinus a Sancta Theresia, O.C.D. "Cronotaxis illustrata Emin. rum Protectorum ordinis Carmelitarum utriusque Observantiae," AOCD, 4 (1929-1930) 228-232, etc.

Marcora, Carlo. "Nicolò Ormaneto, vicario di S. Carlo (giugno 1564-giugno 1566)," *Memorie della diocesi di Milano*, 8 (1961) 209-590.

María de San José, O.C.D. *Libro de recreaciones*; ed. Simeón de la Sagrada Familia, O.C.D., in *Humor*, 153-351.

Martín, Felipe, O.P. *Santa Teresa de Jesús y la orden de Predicadores.* Avila, 1909.

Martino, Alberto, O. Carm. "Monasteri femminili del Carmelo attraverso i secoli," *Carmelus*, 10 (1963) 263-312.

Montalvo, Efrén, O.C.D. See: Efrén de la Madre de Dios, O.C.D.

Montañés, Jaime, O. Carm. *Espejo de bien vivir y para ayudar a bien morir*; ed. Pablo Garrido, O. Carm. Madrid, 1976.

Monticone, Alberto. "L'applicazione a Roma del concilio di Trento, le visite del 1564-1566," *Rivista di storia della chiesa in Italia*, 7 (1953), 225-250, esp. 242-250.

Moriones, Ildefonso, O.C.D. *Ana de Jesús y la herencia teresiana. ¿Humanismo cristiano o rigor primitivo?* Roma, 1968.

Ottonello, Pier Paolo. *Bibliografía di S. Juan de la Cruz.* Roma, 1967.

Peers, E. Allison. *Handbook to the Life and Times of St. Teresa and St. John of the Cross.* Westminster, Md., 1954.

Peers, E. Allison. *Mother of Carmel.* New York, 1946.

Petersson, Robert T. *The Art of Ecstasy: Teresa, Bernini and Crashaw.* London, 1970.

Procesos de beatificación y canonización de Sta. Teresa de Jesús; ed. Silverio de Sta. Teresa. Burgos, 1934-1935. 3 v.

René de Nantes, O.F.M. Cap. "Saint Pierre d'Alcantara et Sainte Thérèse," *Etudes franciscaines*, 10 (1903), 162-168, 384-394.

Ribera, Francisco de. *Vida de Santa Teresa de Jesús;* ed. Jaime Pons, S.J. Barcelona, 1908.

Robinson, Cuthbert. *Nicolò Ormaneto, A Papal Envoy in the 16th Century.* London, 1920.

Rodriguez, Otilio, O.C.D. "El testamento teresiano," *El Monte Carmelo*, 78 (1970) 11-83.

Rodríguez Carretero, Miguel, O. Carm. *Epytome historial de los Carmelitas Calzados de Andalusia (1804-1807).* Madrid, Biblioteca nacional, Ms. 18.118.

Rossi, Giovanni Battista, O. Carm. *Regesta*; ed. Benedict Zimmerman. Roma, 1936.

Sá, Manuel de, O. Carm. *Memorias históricas dos illustrissimos arcebispos, bispos e escritores portuguezes da ordem de Nossa Senhora do Carmo.* Lisboa, 1724.

Saggi, Ludovico, O. Carm. "Questioni connesse con la riforma teresiana," *Carmelus*, 11 (1964) 161-184.

Saggi, Ludovico, O. Carm. "Santa Teresa, il prior generale Rossi e le 'cattive informazioni,'" *Carmelus*, 12 (1965) 173-222.

Savignol, M.J. *Sainte Thérèse de Jésus et l'ordre de St. Dominique.* Toulouse, 1930.

Silverio de Santa Teresa, O.C.D. *Historia del Carmen Descalzo en España, Portugal y América*. Burgos, 1935-1952. 15 v.

Silverio de Santa Teresa, O.C.D. *Vida de Santa Teresa de Jesús*. Burgos, 1935-1937. 5 v.

Simeón de la Sagrada Familia, O.C.D., "Bibliografia de los impresos oficiales O.C.D.," *El Monte Carmelo*, 73 (1965) 395-430, etc. Co-authors: Bede Edwards, O.C.D., Miguel Angel Diez, O.C.D.

Simeón de la Sagrada Familia, O.C.D. *Bibliographia operum S. Teresiae a Jesu typis editorum (1583-1967)*. Roma, 1969.

Smet, Joachim, O. Carm. *An Outline of Carmelite History*. Washington, D.C., 1966. (Lithographed edition.)

Smet, Joachim, O. Carm. "Some Unpublished Documents Concerning Fray Antonio Vázquez de Espinosa," *Carmelus*, 1 (1954) 151-158.

Spiazzi, Raimondo, O.P. "Riforma domenicana e riforma teresiana nel secolo 16," *Memorie domenicane*, 80 (1963) 152-170, 212-225.

Steggink, Otger, O. Carm. "Beaterios y monasterios carmelitas españoles en los siglos 15 y 16," *Carmelus*, 10 (1963) 149-205.

Steggink, Otger, O. Carm. *La reforma del Carmelo español, la visita canónica del general Rubeo y su encuentro con Santa Teresa (1566-1567)*. Roma, 1965.

Steggink, Otger, O. Carm. *Tiempo y vida de Santa Teresa*. Madrid, 1969.

Teresa, Saint. *Cartas*; notes by Bp. Juan de Palafox y Mendoza (v. 1) and Antonio de San José (v. 2-4). Madrid, 1793. 4 v.

Teresa, Saint. *Complete Works*; tr. and ed. E. Allison Peers. London, 1946. 3 v.

Teresa, Saint. *Letters*; tr. and ed. E. Allison Peers. London, 1951. 2 v. (continuous pagination).

Teresa, Saint. *Obras*; ed. Silverio de Santa Teresa, O.C.D. Burgos, 1915-1924. 9 v.

Teresa, Saint. *Obras completas*; ed. Efrén de la Madre de Dios, O.C.D., Otger Steggink, O. Carm. Madrid, 1951-1959. 3 v.

Teresa, Saint. *Obras completas*; ed. Efrén de la Madre de Dios, O.C.D., Otger Steggink, O. Carm. 4a. ed. Madrid, 1974.

Tomás de la Cruz, O.C.D. See: Alvarez, Tomás, O.C.D.

Victor de Jesús María, O.C.D. "Un conflicto de jurisdicción," *Sanjuanistica*, 413-528.

Victoria Moreno, Dionisio, O.C.D. *Los Carmelitas Descalzos y la conquista espiritual de México, 1585-1612*. México, 1966.

Villiers, Cosmas de, O. Carm. *Bibliotheca carmelitana*. Aurelianis, 1752. Photostatic ed. by Gabriel Wessels, O. Carm. Romae, 1927. 2 v. in 1.

Walsh, William Thomas. *Saint Teresa of Avila*. Milwaukee, 1948.

Wermers, Manuel, O. Carm. *A ordem carmelita e o Carmo em Portugal*. Lisboa, 1963.

Wessels, Gabriel, O. Carm. "De patribus Discalceatis in fine capituli generalis Placentiae 1575," AOC, 3 (1914-1915) 454-463.

Wessels, Gabriel, O. Carm. "Sancta Teresia et capitulum generale Placentiae 1575," AOC, 4 (1917-1922) 176-220.

Wilderink, Vital, O. Carm., *Les Constitutions des premiéres Carmélites en France*. Rome, 1966.

Yepes, Diego de. *Vida de Santa Teresa de Jesús*. Barcelona, 1887. 2 v. (Currently attributed to Tomás de Jesús, O.C.D., 1554-1627).

Index

A

Acosta, Diego, sj 88
Africa, under discalced provincial 106
Agnes of Jesus, ocd 46, 54, 64
Aguila, Juana del, elected prioress of Incarnation 82
Ahumada, Beatrix de, mother of St. Teresa 21
Ahumada, Joanna de, sister of St. Teresa (Joanne) 29-30
Ahumada, Teresa de *see* Teresa of Jesus
Alba de Tormes (monastery founded in 1571) 47, convent of 55
Alba, Duchess of 55-56, 85
Albert, cardinal archduke 110, 114, 117, 124
Albi, congregation of 6
Alcalá Altomira, discalced house 76, 89
Alcalá, college foundation 52, chapter of (1581) 96, constitutions of 98, Teresa's reflections on 98, additions to constitutions regarding the nuns 111, approved 119
Alcalá de Henares, La Imagen (monastery) 10, foundation of college at 20, monastery 32, foundation opened 52
Almodóvar, discalced house 76, chapter of 86, chapter of (1578), 91, chapter of (1583) 98, 103
Almodovar del Campo (foundation) 49, discalced foundation in 1574 52, chapter of 76,
Alonzo of the Mother of God, ocd 17
Altomira (discalced foundation in 1571) 52
Alumbrados 81
Alumbradas 87
Alvarez, Balthasar, sj 25, 28, 46
Alvarez, Catalina, mother of John of the Cross 48
Alvarez, Garcia 87-88
Alvarez Pereira, Nuno, saint 117
Ambrose of St. Benedict, ocd *see* Azaro, Mariano
Ambrose of St. Peter, ocd 58, 103
Andalusia, province Rossi visitation of 10-16, reform of Audet 10, chapter of 1566 12-13, 61, Institutiones et ordinationes, 13-15, statistics in 1566 10-11, monasteries 10, moral condition of monasteries 71-72, 78-79; visit of Gracián 69-74, 78-79
Anna of St. Albert, ocd 80
Anna of the Angels, ocd 46
Anne Mary of Jesus, ocarm 56
Anne of Jesus, ocd 114, on Doria's government 115, 119, 121, punishment of 122, 126, on Carranza 128
Anne of St. Bartholomew, blessed 121-122
Anne of the Incarnation, ocd 46
Antequera (monastery) 10, visitation of 10, 49
Anthony of Jesus (Heredia), ocd prior at Medina del Campo 46-47, draws up constitutions 48-49, open hermitage of St. Peter 51, 54, 68, 76, 85-86, 89, 92, 96, 105, discalced definitor 108, definitor of discalced congregation and member of consulta 112, discalced provincial 122, 127
Antonio, Fray, prior of Toledo 57
Apostasy 73, 76
Apology for Charity Against Some Who Under Color of Observance of the Law Cause Charity to

Grow Cold and Disturb Religious Orders, tract 107
Aracena (monastery) 10, Rossi record of visitation of 10
Aragon, province reform of Audet 10, statistics in 1566 10-11, monasteries 10, visit of Rossi 40-41, chapter of 1567 40-41, Instituta (1567) 41, visit of Hebrera 44-45, 57; visit of Tostado 84
Aranda, Gonzalo de, friend of Teresa 30, represents Teresa legally 31
Arganda, Francis de 74
Audet, Nicholas, ocarm recommends Rossi 1, reform in Spain 10
Augustine of the Kings, ocd 103, discalced definitor 108, 109, definitor of discalced congregation 112, elected discalced provincial of Andalusia 112, 120, 125
Avila, Incarnation beaterio 10, visitation by Rossi 17-18, St. Teresa as prioress, 55
Avila, Julian de, friend of Teresa 30, 35, 86
Avila, Maria de *see* Mary of St. Joseph
Avila (discalced monastery established 1562) 47, 53
Avila, municipal council of, foundation of San José 31
Avila, male novitiate instituted 20
Azaro, Mariano (Ambrose of St. Benedict, ocd) hermitage in El Tardón 50-51, 58, 58-59, 60, 62-65, Teresa's comments on 65, comments on Pinuela 65, 67, 85, placed under arrest 87, 92, 96, 102-103, 105, member of the consulta 112

B

Balthasar of Jesus, *see* Nieto, Balthasar
Bañez, Dominic, op, encourages Teresa to write Way of Perfection 34, comparison between Teresa and Anne of Jesus 115
Báñez, Thomas, in favor of San José 31
Barajas, Count de 121
Barrón, Vincent, op confessor to Teresa's father 23
Bartholomew Baptist, ocd 105
Bartholomew of Jesus, ocd member of the consulta 112
Bartholomew of St. Basil, ocd consultor 122
Beas (monastery founded in 1575) 47
Beatrix of the Mother of God, ocd 87, accusations made by 88
Becerra, Anthony, om 75
Beja (beaterio) 15
Berardi, Timothy, ocarm, procurator general 93
Bernini, sculptor 25
Bérulle, Pierre de, cardinal 122
Blaise of St. Albert, ocd, consultor 122
Bonelli, Michael (Alessandino), cardinal 44
Book of Foundations, by Teresa of Jesus 45
Borromeo, Charles, cardinal, 3 6, letter from Rossi 10, 16, letter from Rossi (March 22, 1567) 19, 61, 71
Bourdaisière, Philbert de la, cardinal 8
Bracamonte, Mary of the Incarnation *see* Mary of the Incarnation 126
Braganza, Teutonio de, archbishop 113-114, 119
Briceño, Bernardine, osb, abbot 93, 95
Briceño, Frances de, ocarm, prioress at Avila 17
Brizuela, Licentiate 31
Bruno of Jesus, remarks on Teresa's painting 50
Brussels 124
Bullón, John *see* John of Jesus
Buoncompagni, Philip, cardinal protector 89, 92-93, appealed to 94

Burgos (monastery founded in 1582) 47

C

Caffardi, John Baptist, ocarm 92 93, confirms discalced provincial 97, 101, 102
Calderón, Antonio, ocarm 117
Callixtus III, pope 43-44
Calvo de Padilla, John 85
Carafa, Diomedes, cardinal 2
Caravaca (monastery founded in 1576) 47
Cardenas, Diego de, ocarm 52, 87-88, 114
Carmelites and *Superioribus mensibus* 20
Carmelites, papal reception of report of visitation of 44
Carmen (Madrid) 87, 101
Carmine (Naples), visitation of Rossi 2
Carmo (Lisbon) 117, 123
Carmona, king's visitation 43, prior reinstated 43
Carranza, Bartholomew de, archbishop of Toledo 26
Carranza, Michael de recommends reform to Philip II 6-7, reformer of Aragon 40, 116-117, at general chapter of Cremona 128
Casset, Jerónimo, ocarm 41
Castagna, John Baptist, nuncio 39, 44, 57
Castel Sant'Angelo 7
Castile, province reform of Audet 10, statistices in 1566 10-11, monasteries in 1566 11, visit of Rossi 16-17, 20; chapter of 1567 20-21, Fernández' decrees 20, visit by Fernández 52-54, chapter of 1571 52-53, of 1576 74-76, of 1579 93
Castillo, Hernando, op 88
Castro, Ambrose de, ocarm 51
Castro, Diego de, ocarm punishment of 13, 24
Catalina, queen of Portugal 16
Catalonia, record of Rossi visitation of 10, visitation of 40, provincial chapter of 1567 41
Catherine of Austria 50
Cepeda y Ocampo, Mary *see* Mary Baptist
Cerda, Louisa de la 29, 87
Cerezo, Pedro 109, 121
Cervini, Marcellus, cardinal 1
Chaplain to Discalced nuns, qualities of 55
Chapter, general of Rome in 1564 3-5, Philip II and 6, of Piacenza in 1575 54, 66, 67, 69, 74, 75, of Rome in 1580 95-96, of Cremona in 1593, establishes discalced Carmelite order 128-129
Charles, prince of Spain 19
Chizzola, John Stephen, ocarm 128
Cimbrón, Maria, ocarm prioress of Incarnation 30
Cistercians 82
Clement VII, pope 5, 112
Clement VIII, pope erects Discalced Carmelite Order 128, proposes Doria continue in office 128
Cloister, Rossi's policy for 17, 68-69; Pius V imposes cloister on nuns 17, Theresa's observance of 21, ordinances of Fernández 52-53, Gracián's visit of Seville monastery 71-72, Gracian's visit of convent 72-74, discalced constitutions of 1581 97
Coello, Claude, painter 50
Columna, Michael de la 80
Complutenses, theological summa from Alcalá 52

Confessions by St. Augustine, role in St. Teresa's 'conversion' 23
Congo, mission from Lisbon 103, mission discontinued 108
Constitutions (discalced men), Duruelo 49, 97; Alcalá 1581 97-98, Madrid 1588 116, Madrid 1590 120, Madrid 1592 122
Constitutions (discalced nuns) Teresa's 33, Fernández' 54-55, Gracián's 98, Alcalá 1581 97-98, 111, 119-120; Madrid 1592 122
Consulta 106, 107, requirements of Gracián 110, in the discalced congregation 111, assigns members for Mexico 111, papal confirmation for 112, membership in discalced congregation 112, 113, decision about Gracián 113, Anne of Jesus's opinion of 115, in Dorian's circular letter (1588) 115, appeal to pope against 119, 120, 121
Corro, Mary del 87
Cota, Peter, ocarm 61-62, 71, 74
Counter-Reformation within the Order 3
Covarrubias, Diego de, bishop 80, 85
Cremona, general chapter of (1593) 128
Crivelli, Alexander, papal nuncio 31
Cuevas, John de las, op 96, 105, 117
Cum de statu (Sixtus V - 1587), raised the discalced reform to the status of a congregation 111-112
Cum gravissimis de causis (Pius V - 1566) 19
Curiel, Roderick, ocarm arrested by police 61

D

Dali, Salvador, artist 56
Dantisco, Juana (Joan), mother of Jerome 59, 118
Dario, John Anthony 4
Dark Night by John of the Cross 84
Dávila, Anne, ocarm 31
Daza, Gaspar, 24, chaplain at San José 30, receives vows 30, 31
Decet Romanum pontificem (Sixtus V - 1587) 112
Depositum 72
Dictamen, by Peter Ibáñez, op 28
Diego Evangelista, ocd consultor 122, 127
Diego of St. Mary, ocd 58
Diego of the Trinity, ocd 91-92
Discalced Congregation institution of 111-112, chapter of Madrid 1588 112-113, 116, extraordinary chapter of Madrid 1590 120-121, chapter of Marid 1591 122, 125-126
Discalced Order erected (1593) 128
Discalced Province Gracián creates a province 76-77, chapter of Almodóvar 1576 76-77, chapter of Almodóvar 1578 86, 91, erected by Gregory XIII 96, chapter of Alcalá 1581 96, 111, statistics 1587 106, divided into four vicariates 106, consulta instituted 106, definitory meeting 1586 107, confirmed by Sixtus V 107, adopts Roman rite 107, granted Roman procurator 107, chapter of Vallodolid 1587 108, 115-116.
Discalced Franciscan nuns 27
Dominicans, visitation by 44
Dominic of St. Albert, ocarm 74
Dominic of the Presentation, ocd 122
Doria, Nicholas (of Jesus and Mary) ocd 96, 101, opinion of Gracián 102, Teresa's opinion of 102, 103, 104, elected provincial 104, as provincial 106, exhortation on observance 106-107, letter to Gracián 111, 112, elected first vicar general of discalced congregation 112, makes Gracián his socius 114, reaction to Gracián's complaints to king 116, letter to king (1589) 117, letter to the king 118, reaction to nun's papal brief 120, 122, on threat

Index

of Gracián 124, represents discalced at Cremona chapter 128
Du Puy, James, cardinal 2
Duruelo, first foundation of discalced friars 47, life in 49

E

Ecija 10, visitation of Rossi 10, 11, novitite instituted in 14, king's visitation 43
Elias of Saint Martin, ocd, rector 89, discalced definitor 108, 109, definitor of discalced congregation 112, elected provincial for New Castile 112, 120
El Tardón, hermitage 50
Escrivá, Nicholas, ocarm 40
Espinel, Francis (of the Conception), ocarm, founder and rector of Alcalá college 52
Espinosa, Diego de, cardinal 39
Estimulo de la propagación de la fe, treatise of Jerome Gracián 108-109
Eugene IV, pope 32, 73, 94
Evora, convent 113, 114, 115

F

Facini, John Stephen, ocarm 1, recommended as prior general 6
Farias, Albert, ocarm provincial 57
Ferdinand of the Mother of God, ocd on Diego Evangelista 127
Fernández, Peter, op 20, visitator for Castile 44, in Castile 52, decrees from chapter of 1571 52, and St. Teresa 54, 55-56, 73, 77, 83, 89, 98
Florence (Italy), Rossi at for provincial chapter 2
Fontiveros, beaterio 10, 20
Forlí, Rossi at provincial chapter 2
Foundations by Teresa of Jesus 87
Francis of St. Mary, ocd historian 37, 58, 74, 76, 82, 86, 104, observations on Doria as provincial 107, details balloting at Madrid chapter 112, 120
Fresneda, Bernard de, ofm, bishop 19
Fuente, Matthew de la, hermit 50

G

Gabriel de la Peñuela 64
Gabriel of the Assumption, ocd placed under arrest 87, 93, 96
Gabriel of the Conception, ocd 59
Galli, Ptolemy, papal secretary 61-63, 69-70 on the reception of Adalusian Carmelites in Rome 71, 72, 74, 77, summary of complaints against Gracián 78, calls for suspension of Gracián's authority 78, instructions to Sega 81, 85
García de Toledo, Diego, op 29
Garcías, Martin, ocarm 67
Genoa, visitation of Rossi 8, under discalced provincial 106
Germain of St. Matthias, ocd removed as confessor of Incarnation 84
Giberti, John Matthew, bishop 61
Goes, Manuel de, ocarm visitator of Order 15
Gómez, Anne, ocarm 31 *see also* Anna of the Angels, ocd
Gómez de Silva, Ruy 50-51, prince of Eboli 52
González, Alonso, ocarm 20, commissary for the nuns 46, gives permission for foundation in Duruelo 48, 51, 54, prior general's vicar 56, rapport with Teresa 56, delegate of nuns 67,
Gracián, Anthony, brother of Jerome 59, 85
Gracián, Diego, father of Jerome 59

Gracián, Jerome, ocd 36, leader of Discalced reform 59, 59-60, relation to Rossi 61, 62-64, relation to Teresa 63, 65, 69, named commissary and reformer 69, 70, patents rejected 70, visitation of Seville 70-72, 71, visitation of the Incarnation of Seville 71, requirements of novitiate in Seville 73, difference between mitagated and primitives 73, plans for separate province 76, establishing separate province 77, 79, summary of Andalusia visitation report 79, accusations against during visitation 80, status after Ormaneto's death 80, 82, 84, 85, 86, imprisoned 87, invesitgation of by Sega 88, accusation against 87-88, elected prior of Seville 89, 92, elected provincial 96, as apostolic commissary 97, constitutions 97, and discalced nuns 98, 102, chooses Doria as *socius* 102, as provincial (1581-1585) 103, elected definitor 104, missionary efforts 104, evaluation as provincial 105, responsibility as definitor 106, attitude towards Doria 107, letter to monasteries 108, treatise on missions 108, vicar of Mexico 108, 109, accusations again 109, response to accusations 109-110, receives admonition 110, response to consulta's admonition 111, reponse of consulta 113, requirements of papal nuncio 113, actions with Mary of St. Joseph 114, appealed to king against Doria 115, reaction to Dorian's government 115, complains to king about Doria 116, in Lisbon 116-117, letter to king's secretary (1589) 118, subject of Doria letter to king (1589) 118, appeals to pope against consulta 119, 120, considered at extraordinary Madrid chapter (1590) 120, trial and punishment 123, on threat of Doria 124, returns to the Carmelites 124, later life 124

Gracián, Thomas, brother of Jerome 59, 85

Granada, 10-12, novitiate instituted in 14, discalced house in 47, 59, 60, abandonment of Discalced house in 67, 76

Graviora et atrociora, requires confirmation by prior general 111, its interpretation 112

Gregory of Nazianzen, ocd, 73, placed under arrest 87, elected definitor 104, 105, elected discalced provincial for Portugal 112, 120

Gregory of the Holy Angel, ocd consultor 122, 123, elected to consulta 126

Gregory XIII, pope 50, 61, *motu proprio* 63, brief of 1575 69, 73, confirm Tostado as visitator and reformer of Spain 75, 81, 93, approved discalced province 96,

Gregory XIV, pope 121

Guarda, Michael, ocarm 40

Gutiérrez de la Magdalena, John, ocarm provincial 74, 82, at election at Incarnation 83, 87

Guzmán, Aldonza de, Teresa's first autobiogrphy addressed to 29

Guzmán, Blanca de, boarder at Incarnation (Seville) 71

H

Habit, discalced 49, 53

Hebrera, Michael, op, visitator for Aragon and Catalonia 44, 45, 57

Henao, Antonia de (of the Holy Spirit), ocd 30

Henry, cardinal infante of Portugal 15-16

Heredia, Anthony de, ocarm *see also* Anthony of Jesus, ocd

Heredia, Diego de *see* Diego of the Trinity 91

Heredia, John de, ocarm 59

Hoyas, Caspar, sj 88

Huerta, Roque de 85

Hugo, cardinal of Santa Sabina 32

Hurtado de Mendoza, Louis, count of Tendilla 86

I

Ibáñez, Peter, op 28-29, assistance with foundation of San José 28, 31, governance of Incarnation in Avila 83

Incarnation (Avila), 18, 21-22, Teresa appointed prioress of 55, election of prioress 82-83,

Index

removal of discalced confessors 84,
Incarnation (Seville), visitation by Gracián 71
Innocent IV, pope mitigation of Rule 32
Inquisition of Toledo 85
Instituta, document of Chapter of Valencia 1567 41
Institutiones et ordinationes, document from 1566 provincial chapter of Andalusia 13-15
Institution of the First Monks (*Institutio primorum monachorum*) 27
Interior Castle by Teresa of Jesus 32, 34
Isabelle of St. Francis, ocd 79
Isabelle of St. Jerome, ocd 79
Isabelle of the Angels, ocd 54
Isabelle of the Cross, ocd 46
Isabelle, queen of Spain 6, 19

J

Jaén, convent Rossi visitation of 10, 109, 111
Jerome of Castile, ocarm punishment of 16
Jerome of St. Joseph, ocd 126
Jimena *see* Anne of Jesus
John Baptist "*el Andaluz*," ocd member of consulta 112
John Baptist "*el de Ronda*," ocd discalced provincial 122
John Baptist "*el Remendado*," ocd discalced definitor 108, elected discalced provincial for Old Castile 112
John Baptist "*el Rondeño*," ocd 104
John Evangelist, ocd 74, 125, 126
John I, king of Portugal 16
John of Avila 50
John of Jesus, ocd *see* Roca, John of Jesus, ocd
John of St. Albert, ocd discalced provincial 122
John of St. Anne, ocd 126, 127
John of St. Diego, ocd 91
John of St. Matthias (John of the Cross), at Salamanca 16, introduced to Teresa 16, 47, 48 (*see also* John of the Cross)
John of the Cross (de Yepes) biographical information 48, draws up constitutions 49, accompanies Teresa to Valladolid 48, Teresa's comments on 56, influence at Incarnation (Avila) 56, 76, removed as confessor of Incarnation (Avila) 84, writings while in prison 84, 89, 96, 101, elected definitor 104, responsibility as definitor 106, definitor of discalced congregation 112, member of consulta 112, dedicated *Spiritual Canticle* to Anne of Jesus 115, 120, proposed as commisary 120, role of in reformation 124-125, later life 124-126, 125, assigned to Mexico 126, final months and death of 127 (*see also* John of St. Matthias)
John of the Mother of God, ocd 104
Jordán, Jerome, ocarm 40
Joseph of Christ, ocd 49
Juan Evangelista, ocarm 74
Julian de Avila, 18, confessor at St. Joseph's 36

L

Lagos (monastery) 15
La Peñuela, discalced house foundation in 59, 60, abandonment of Discalced house in 67, 76, 127

La Roda (discalced foundation in 1571) 52, 76, 105
Las Cuevas, wrote letter to Gracián's mother 118-119
Lasso, Pedro, printer 98
León, Diego de, ocarm 11, 57
León, Louis de, osa 115, 119, 120, 121, 122
Leone, Mariano di, ocarm vistator of Toledo 17, procurator at Spanish court 40
Lérida (convent) 43
Limpo, John, ocarm provincial of Portugal 15
Lisbon 16, discalced foundation made 103, 116
Loaysa, García de 113, 116
Los Mártires, Granada 59
Los Remedios, Seville 60, 62, 101
Louis of St. Gregory, ocd member of consulta 112
Louis of St. Jerome, ocd 73, discalced provincial 122
Luz, Louis da, ocarm visitator of Order 15, elected provincial 16

M

Madrid, chapter of (1588) implements *Cum de statu* 112, 116
Madrid, congregation chapter at (1591) 122
Madrid, extraordinary chapter of (1590) 120
Maffei, Mark Anthony, cardinal 96
Magdalena de la Cruz, mystic 54
Magdalena, John de la, ocarm punishment of 13
Malagón (monastery founded in 1568) 47
Maldonado, Alonso, ofm encouragement to Teresa 36
Maldonado, Ferdinand, ocarm 83
Mancera de Abajo (discalced foundation) 50, 76
Manrique, Louis, royal chaplain 88
Mantuan Congregation 6, 47
Marcellino, Graziano, ocarm 2
Margarita of the Conception, ocd 79, 87-88
Mármol, Barnaby del 118-121
Martin Ignatius de Loyola, ofm 104
Mary Baptist (Ocampo), ocd niece of Teresa of Jesus 27, 46, 63
Mary of Jesus (Yepes), ocarm 10, 29, 32-33
Mary of St. Jerome, ocd 122
Mary of St. Joseph (Salazar), ocd 30, 52, accusation against 87-88, restored as prioress 90, 101, 103-104, opinion on consulta 108, under investigation 114, 117-118, 121, punishment of 122,
Mary of the Incarnation (Mary Bracamonte), ocd 126
Mary of the Incarnation (Yolante de Salazar), ocd 119-120, 126
Mary of the Nativity, ocd punishment of 122
Mascareñas, Leonor de 85
Maxime cuperemus (Pius V - 1566), entrusts reform of religious orders to bishops 19
Mazzapica, Desiderio, ocarm 7, procurator to Spanish court 7, 11, attacked by Melchior Nieto 11, 17
Medina del Campo (monastery founded in 1567) 20, 46-47, letter from Rossi 47, 49, 54, 64
Medina, Ferdinand de 80
Mejia, Rafael, offers house in Duruelo 48
Mendoza, Alvaro de, bishop of Avila 21, 30-31, 36, 80, 83
Mendoza, Luis Hurtado de 85
Mendoza, Maria de 56

Mercado y Peñalosa, Anne del 127
Mercedarians and *Superioribus mensibus* 20
Mercedarians, visitation report of 44
Mexico mission under discalced provincial 106 , 108, Gracián vicar of Mexico 108, John of the Cross assigned to Mexico 126
Montañaés, James, named prior 8, letter on reform to Rossi 40, 40-41
Monte Oliveto 9
Montoni, Valerius, ocarm busar of curia 8
Montoya, Diego de 85, 91
Mora, John de, ocarm prior of Seville 12, prior of Utrera 12, 19, 39, 41, expelled from the Order 42, vicar provincial 42-43, imprisoned, absolved from excommunication 43, 51, 69
Muñoz, Francis, op 123

N

Nadal, John, ocarm provincial of Valencia 40
Narducci, John (John de la Miseria), ocd 50
Navarrete, Louis de, ocarm 71
New Mexico, plans for abandoned 108
Nicholas of Jesus and Mary *see* Doria, Nicholas
Nieto, Balthazar (of Jesus), 3, attack on prior 11, actions to free Melchior 11, 12, 19, 40, imprisoned and expelled from the Order 42, absolved from excommunication 43, 51-52, vicar provincial 57, 59, Teresa's comments on 65, 67, 80-81, 109, 110.
Nieto, Caspar 11, actions in Melchior's attack on Mazzapica 11, prior of Castro del Rio 12, as provincial 12, 19, 39, 41, expelled from Order 42, absolved from excommunication 43, 51, 69
Nieto, Melchior 11, attack on Mazzapica 11, 12, 19, stabs two friars 42, 51
Nunneries in Andalucia, in report of visitation 79
Nuns, provision for in Alcalá chapter 98

O

Ocampo, Maria de *see* Maria Baptist, ocd
Occhino, Bernardine, ofm 1
Olivares, Count de, royal ambassador 121
Onda, convent 8, reform of 40, 41
Ordóñez, Mary, ocarm 31
Ormaneto, Nicholas, nuncio 61-63, on Teresa's travels 68, 69-70, renovation of monastery grill 71, on conditions of Andalusian nunneries 72, 74-75, 77, response to papal secretary 78, death of 79, 81-82, 84-85, 89
Ortiz, Diego 56
Osuna (college), no visit by Rossi 11
Osuna (monastery) 10
Osuna, Francisco de, ofm 22
Ovalle, John de, brother-in-law of Teresa of Jesus 29-30

P

Pacheco, Peter, cardinal 7
Palencia, monastery founded in 1580 47
Pardo de Saavedra, Arias 29
Pastoralis officii (Clement VIII - 1593) papal constitution, erects Discalced Carmelite Order 128
Pastrana monastery founded in 1569 47, second foundation of discalced friars 50, 51, novitiate established in 53, 59, discalced house 76, chapter of 1585 98, 106,

Paterna del Campo, monastery 10, scandal in nunnery of 79
Paul III, pope 2
Paul IV, pope 2, 25
Paz, Maria de la (of the Cross) 30
Pazos y Figueros, Anthony Maurice 84, president of royal council 89
Peers, E. Allison 65
Peña, Isabel de la 31
Peñuela, Gabriel de la, prior of Granada 12, punishment of 13, 59
Peter of Alcantara, saint, encounter with Teresa 25, advice on San José 28, 29, appearance to Teresa 31,
Peter of the Angels, ocd 91, 105
Peter of the Mother of God, ocd 105
Peter of the Purification, ocd 119
Philip II, king of Spain 6, 7, 19, 73, 81, 84, 89, 93, 95, Doria advised 101, sponsors request for discalced congregation 112, 113
Philip of Jesus, ocd consultor 122
Piacenza, general chapter 1575 54, 66, 67, 69, 74, 75
Pia consideratione (Gregory XIII - 1580), letter approving discalced province 96
Piedad, John de, ocarm 2
Piedrahita, beaterio 10, visitation by Rossi 17
Pilgrimage of Anastasius by Jerome Gracián 71
Pinuela 65
Pius IV, pope 1, 3, 6, grants new site for Traspontina 7, grants faculties for Rossi's visit 8, 71
Pius V, saint and pope authorizes new Traspontina 7, creates apostolic commission 8, 19, entrusts visitation to Dominicans 44, Superioribus mensibus revoked 44, 61, 68, 75, 95, 112
Ponce de León, Lope 43
Portugal, Rossi visitation of 8, 15-17, statistics 16, chapter of 1566 16, visit of Tostado 75, visit of Gracián 116-117
Prádanos, John de, sj confessor to St. Teresa 24

Q

Quadra, John de la 12, 19, 39, 41-44
Quesada, Teresa de, ocarm 54
Quiroga, Caspar de, archbishop 81, 82, 85, 91
Quiroga, Joseph of Jesus and Mary, ocd 126
Quoniam non ignoramus (Gregory XIV - 1591), papal brief 121

R

Ragusio, Bartholomew, ocarm 8
Ramírez, Hernan king's visitator 43, 98
Requeséns, Louis de 6-7, 19
Revilla, Ursula de (of the Saints), ocd put in charge of San José by Teresa 30
Ribera, Francis de, sj biographer of St. Teresa 26
Ridolfi, Nicholas, cardinal 1
Ripera, Lawrence, ocarm, prior 43
Ristori, Julian, ocarm 1
Roca, John of Jesus, ocd 59, 77, 91-92, 96, 102-103, discalced procurator 107, elected discalced provincial for Aragon 112
Rojas y Sandoval, Christopher, archbishop 74, 101
Romeu, Antique, ocarm 15

Index

Rossi, John Baptist, ocarm, prior general 3, re-location of Transpontina 7, dispute of San Martino 8, method of visitation 8, contact with Monte Oliveto 9, on visit to Spain 10, provincial chapter at Andalusia 12, directives from Andalucia provincial chapter 13, visitation of Portugal 13-14, 16, visitation of Castille 16, revocation of dispensations from cloister 17, visitation of Avila (Incarnation) 17, visitation of Piedrahita (monastery) 17, visit to Avila 35, patent for expanding the reform 37, credentials challenged 39, requests audience with King Philip 40, aftermath of the visitation to Iberian peninsula 42, report of visitation to Holy See 43, actions against king's reformers 44, renews faculties of Teresa 47, letter to nuns at Medina del Campo 47, appoints 20 commissaries in Spain 45, decisions regarding the nuns 55, 60, 61, relation to Gracián 61, 62, 64, 67, on Piacenza decrees 68, 72, death of 90

Rouhier, Nicholas, ocarm secretary to Rossi 8, 10

Rule (1247), Teresa's "primitive Rule" 32

Rusticucci, Jerome, papal secretary 57

S

Saint Joseph, *see* San José

Salamanca, friary 16, monastery founded in 1570 47, studium 48, novitiate established in 53, 54

Salazar, Angel de, ocarm 15, provincial 28, rebukes Teresa 30, 37, gives permission to Teresa for Duruelo foundation 48, 51, 54, 55, 57, 59, provincial of Castile 67, 68, 89, 90, 93

Salazar, Gaspar de, sj 28, 55

Salazar, Yolante, *see* Mary of the Incarnation, ocd

Salcedo, Francis de, friend of Teresa 24, 30

Salmanticenses, theological summa from Salamanca 52

Salvatoris (Sixtus V - 1590) 119

Sánchez de Cepeda, Alonso, father of St. Teresa 21, death of 23

Sánchez, Juan, paternal grandfather of St. Teresa 21

San Giuliano, church 3

San José, monastery 21, foundation 27, life in 32, 80

San Juan del Puerto, house 58, 60

San Martino ai Martino, priory 2-3, dispute over 8

San Pablo de la Moraleja 20, 52-53, 74, 84

Santiago, Gabriel de, ocarm 15

Santoya, Bartholomew, majordomo to King Philip 40

Sanz, Juan, ocarm 41

Sapienza, Rossi lecturing at the 2

Sarmiento, Francisco, bishop 109

Sayal 97

Sebastian, king of Portugal 16

Sega, Philip, nuncio 46, 81, 82, recounts fall of Padilla 85, 86, response to chapter of Almodovar 86, investigation of Gracián 88, 89, verdict on Gracián 89, urges separate province 92, 93, 126

Segovia (monastery founded in 1574) 47, 126

Segovia, Francis de 123

Seville visitation of Rossi 10, site of provincial chapter of 1566 12, novitiate instituted in 14, 47, 61, 62, 64, discalced house 60, abandonment of discalced house in 67, results of visitation of 72-74, 76

Silverio de Santa Teresa, ocd 91

Sixtus V, pope confirms independence of discalced province 107, raises discalced to congregation 111, on the discalced nuns 119, death of 121

Soria, monastery founded in 1581 47
Spain, Rossi visitation of 8-42, statistics in 1566 10; nunneries 10-11, king's reform 42-44, reform by Dominicans 44-46; discalced reform 45-129
Speroni, Sperone 1
Speziano, Caesar, nuncio 112, orders to Graziano 113, 115
Spiritual Canticle by John of the Cross 84, dedicated to Anne of Jesus 115, 125
St. Joseph *see* San José
Suarez, Augustine, ocarm 62, 67, 69
Suarez de Figueroa, Gómez, lord of Zafara supporter of Nietos 11, 39
Superioribus mensibus (Pius V - 1567) 19-20, 40-42, revoked 44
Suriano, John Baptist, ocarm procurator of Carmelites 74

T

Tapia, Anna de, cousin of Teresa of Jesus 30
Tapia, Inés de, cousin of Teresa of Jesus 30
Tentugal, monastery 15
Teresa of Jesus (de Ahumada) 1, opinion of Rossi, 1, comment on John of the Cross 17, life at Incarnation 21ff, foundress of San José, "conversion" of 23ff, first vision 25, encounter with St. Peter of Alcantara 25, vision of hell 26, desire to live a stricter life 26, writes first version of autobiography 29, ideal of Carmelite life 32, encouraged to continue the reform by Rossi 35, on Rossi's visit to Avila 35, expansion of the reform 36, keeps prior general informed 46, meets John of the Cross 47, draws up constitutions 49, 54, prioress of Incarnation (Avila) 54-55, on confessors 56, attains mystical marriage 56, in Andalusia 63, 63, 64, status of Seville house 65, relation with Rossi 65, restrictions on after Piacenza 68, 69, vision during prayer of Rossi 70, reaction to chapter of Almodovar 77, reaction to charges against Gracián 81, role of 83, 84, receives Sega letter 86, accusation against 87-88, on Beatrix 88, urges separate province 91, thoughts on Chapter of Alcala 98, death of 99, on Nicholas Doria 101-102, 113
Teresa del Pilar, ocd 46
Third Spiritual Alphabet, by Francisco de Osuna 22
Thomas of Aquinas, ocd consultor 122
Toledo, visitation of 17, friary 43, novitiate instituted 20, monastery founded in 1569 47, novitiate established 53, imprisonment of John of the Cross 84
Tostado, Jerome, ocarm 8, named reformer general 41, 57, 75, role in visitation 78, 79, 81, 82, 83, 84
Traspontina, Santa Maria in 3, re-location of 7, general chapter 1580 95
Trent, Council of, 2, election rules 83
Trinitarians and *Superioribus mensibus* 20, visitation report of 44

U

Ubeda, discalced convent 109
Ugento, Mazzapica made bishop of 11
Ulloa, Ferdinand de, ocarm 57
Ulloa, Guiomar de 24-25, 27-29, Teresa's first manuscript addressed to 29
Ulloa, Michael de, ocarm attacked by Balthasar Nieto 11, prior of Seville 12, 57, 64, 70
Urban VII, pope 121
Ursula of the Saints, ocd *see* Revilla, Ursula
Utrera, convent 12, 19

V

Valdemoro, Alonso, ocarm 84

Valderas, friary 43
Valderrabano, Aldonza de, ocarm. 18
Valencia, monastery 10, visitation of Rossi 40
Valladolid 20, monastery 47, 48, 59, 63, 85, 103, chaper of 1587 rejects the consulta 112, 108, 114, 115
Vargas, Christopher de, ocarm, sub-prior comment on Melchior Nieto 11, 19
Vargas, Francis, op, visitator for Andalusia 44, 45, reports on chapter 57, 58-60, 62, mandates Andalusia houses 66, apostolic visitator 88
Vázquez de Mármol, John 118
Velasco, John Lopez de 118
Vestiarium 72
Villanueva de la Jara, monastery founded in 1580 47
Villavicencio, Laurence, osa 88
Vincent de la Trinidad, ocarm vicar provincial 39, 69
Vinculo de hermandad misionera, document of agreement between Jesuits and Discalced 104
Visitatio hispanica, Rossi account of visitation of Spain 10
Visitator of nuns, requirements of 55
Vitelli, Vitelozzo, cardinal 2

W

Way of Perfection by Teresa of Jesus 32, 34, regarding foundation of St. Joseph's 34

X

Xerga 35, 97

Y

Yepes, Gonzalo, father of John of the Cross 48

Z

Zapata, Francis 74
Zapata del Mármol, Peter 123
Zayas, Gabriel de, king's secretary 118
Zelator, overseer of observance 76-77

Recommended Carmelite Websites

For more information about the Carmelites today,
our spirituality and our ministries worldwide, visit:
carmelites.net
ocarm.org
carmelites.info

For a listing of Carmelite provinces worldwide, visit:
carmelites.info/provinces

For a listing of Monasteries of Carmelite nuns, visit:
carmelites.info/nuns

For a listing of Carmelite Hermitages, please visit:
carmelites.info/hermits

For a listing of sites about Lay Carmelites:
carmelites.info/lay carmel

For a listing of Affiliated Congregations and Institutes:
carmelites.info/congregations

For more information about our work
with the United Nations, visit:
carmelitengo.org

For more information about other publications
available from the Carmelites, visit:
carmelites.info/publications

www.ingramcontent.com/pod-product-compliance
Lightning Source LLC
Chambersburg PA
CBHW032048150426
43194CB00006B/454